accidentally

ON PURPOSE

ACKNOWLEDGMENTS

This book is the result of years of work; a labor of love and determination. It could never have been written without the aid of many people—friends, students, and enemies. I have them all to thank for their help in giving me the strength to continue working over the years, in between directing projects, when I could teach and had the time necessary for reflection and writing. I can't mention everyone, but the most important are: my wife, Anne, whose spirit, beauty, and love of life makes life worth living, as well as the one who makes home a work of art and a place one wants to be; my editor and publisher, Glenn Young, whose knowledge, dedication, love, and friendship has made the task possible; and my sister, Susan, who gave me help, support, and advice that I don't expect to get from any family member. I also want to mention Jeffrey Geist, friend and master astrologer; Patty Bosworth; Rawn Harding; Julian Bach; and Steffi Sidney, who lent a hand in an important moment; and Ros Ribas, for the wonderfully alive photos that the always takes.

accidentally
ON PURPOSE

REFLECTIONS ON LIFE, ACTING, AND THE NINE NATURAL LAWS OF CREATIVITY

JOHN STRASBERG

APPLAUSE
NEW YORK • LONDON

An Applause Original

ACCIDENTALLY ON PURPOSE: REFLECTIONS ON LIFE, ACTING, AND THE NINE NATURAL LAWS OF CREATIVITY
By John Strasberg

Library of Congress Cataloging-In-Publication Data
Strasberg, John
    Accidentally on purpose : reflections on life, acting, and the
nine natural laws of creativity / John Strasberg.
      p. cm.
    ISBN 1-55783-196-3
    1. Strasberg, John. 2. Theatrical producers and directors--United
States--Biography. 3. Strasberg, Lee.   I. Title.
PN2287.S768A3   1996
792'.0233'092--dc20
[B]   96-28376
                                                          CIP

British Library Catalogue in Publication Data
A catalogue record for this book is avaible from the British Library

APPLAUSE BOOKS   A&C BLACK

211 West 71st Street   Howard Road, Eaton Socon
New York, NY 10023   Huntington, Cambs PE19 3EZ
Phone (212) 496-7511   Phone 0171-242 0946
Fax: (212) 721-2856   Fax 0171-831 8478

Distributed in the U.K. and European Union by A&C Black

TABLE OF CONTENTS

Long Day's Journey Into Night directed by John Strasberg with the
Compania Julieta Serrano at Festival de Oroño (Madrid) 1991

INTRODUCTION

When *Strasberg at The Actors Studio* was published in 1965, Lee Strasberg, my father and the artistic director of that organization, was at the height of his artistic prominence. So was the Studio. "The Method" was a word known to the public and widely used. It was the first time, to my knowledge, that an artistic process had become national news. I was twenty-four at the time. My father gave me a copy of the book with the inscription, "To my son John, who will I hope, one day go further. Lee Strasberg." Signing it, "Love, Dad" would have had no apparant value. Love was for people who were special and talented. I was unaccustomed to being considered in that light.

Deep within us, we never forget. I have seen memory assert itself in human behavior, thousands of times, in a dozen countries. I have seen people whose talent, perception, and sense of life have been damaged, if not broken. I recognize it, because it happened to me, and I haven't forgotten. Talent is part of human nature. We are born with it. We can learn to recognize and use it, but to do this we must never ignore, forget, or hide who we are. This process of discovering ourselves and our own capacities and perceptions is what half of most people's personal training work is about.

It's difficult for anyone to grow up with a real sense of values in a world obsessed with material success and power. My parents were too busy with their own dreams of success, fame, and happiness to reflect over ambitions for me. In some ways, my sister Susan and I weren't raised. We just grew up. I watched my mother choose to sacrifice herself and her acting career in order to make my father famous. Without the world that she created for him, bringing people to him because he would never reach out to them, Lee Strasberg probably would have remained an insulated, relatively obscure figure.

Being sensitive, Susan and I felt that we existed only to serve my parents' hopes and dreams. My mother wanted Susan to become what she had denied herself. She lived through Susan's career for as long as she could, diminishing Susan's pleasure in it. When Susan began working, and with startling rapidity became more famous than my father, he used her money for his own needs and never said "Thank you." My mother was always borrowing money from wealthy friends to pay for the books and records he bought, which arrived daily from all over the world whether or not he could afford them. My parents justified this behavior as part of their dream to become a great theater family.

I lived outside of this orbit, and never expressed any interest in the theater. I played sports, went to school, and wanted to become a doctor. At home, only theater was really important. Only in relation to theater was love, truth, and any of the simple and profound spiritual values which are the foundation of real and natural life, ever expressed.

My mother loved everything in the world but herself. My father was obsessed with his work and terrified of leaving his own world. It was difficult for me to believe that my father valued me as a person in my own right. Everything that I wished for or had achieved seemed to me to be unimportant to them.

I love to work. While in the thick of it, I know who I am. Looking at what we do, how well we do it, and whether we enjoy what we do is tremendously satisfying and reveals our true nature to ourselves and others. When I was fifteen, I had an opportunity to work on a summer construction project. My parents objected, saying that they worked hard and done unpleasant things so that I wouldn't have to. And, of course, being a construction worker did not fit into their heavily guarded image of me as their sensitive and fragile son. I fought against, and suffered from, my mother's relentless, neurotic anxiety about me. She made me feel that I was weak.

That summer, surreptitiously, I went to work at a water-ski school on Fire Island, where they rented a house every summer from the time I was ten or eleven. (Feeling that I had to hide who I really was and what I really felt became a part of my behavior for many years to come.) No cars were allowed on the island, other than police, fire, and emergency vehicles, though there was a Jeep taxi service that went up and down the beach in the evenings. It was an ideal vacation place, only an hour from New York. My mother hated sunshine and the beach, but she martyred herself for us, dressing in huge hats, sunglasses, and black smocks to avoid the glare, the heat, and the possibility of sunburn.

In spite of the fact that my father loved the ocean, he never went in the water. One day I asked him why, and he told me that he had, in fact, once decided to bathe. He put on his trunks and, with a firm resolve, walked down to the water's edge, "to make friends with the sea," as he put it. There he stopped, watching as the waves broke onto the clean, sandy beaches that cover the length of the Island. He stayed there, in contemplation of the ocean, before finally, tentatively, putting the toes of one foot into the water, standing in silent conversation with the swirling surf for a very long time. In his humorous, Talmudic way of making the point, he said, "I looked at the ocean, and the ocean looked at me, and we stood there, together." He spoke to the sea, and the sea was speaking to him in its magnificent rolling booms and ssisses. With the slight shrug of his shoulders with which he would punctuate the end of his stories, he said, "Finally, I decided not to get involved."

In a sense, my book is about involvement. It's a book about a continuous bathing in the sea of life; floating in the cosmic ocean and living spontaneously, moment to moment. To me, his story revealed his own fear of losing control and becoming involved, a fear that I inherited—"by osmosis," as Susan would say. Eliminating this fear of life and losing control, and rediscovering myself, took many years of pain, hard work, and truth. "The Method" made it seem as though acting was a controllable manner of creating and expressing emotion, and that a creative process could be reduced to a clear, rational, mechanical system. This was one of the functions of the sense memory exercises which my father taught in his private classes. His work at the Actors Studio was not the same as "the Method" that he taught outside its walls. At the Studio, he shared his own passion, talent, dreams, and knowledge, and left the technique up to the actor's own personal discipline.

My father, Stella Adler, Harold Clurman, Sandy Meisner, and Bobby Lewis all came out of The Group Theater of the late twenties, a dedicated effort to create a theater with the same depth of reality that was expressed in the ensemble work of The Moscow Art Theater. It was also born of a reaction to what they felt to be the overly commercial concerns of the New York theater.

The Group and its descendants profoundly influenced the American actor, and created what the world thinks of as American acting. I feel profound sadness at the fact that, after the Group disintegrated, they all ended up with various degrees of contempt for one another. With the exception of Harold, who forever remained a working idealist, each one of these teachers developed a technique that they claimed was far better than anyone else's. The competitive jealousy between my father and Stella spawned the notion that there exists an ultimate technique for becoming an artist. This misapprehension has mistakenly led us to believe that an artist is the result of his technique, rather than that technique is the means by which the artist articulates his talent; what he perceives and dreams. It has made teachers lay claim to being responsible for creating artists.

My father is credited with turning Marlon Brando, Robert DeNiro, James Dean, Montgomery Clift, and anyone else who was a member of The Actors Studio into what and who they are. This just isn't true. Marlon didn't study with, or even like, my father. James Dean worked there once, and when my father criticized him, he never came back. However, the myth has led us to think that it is the system one studied, rather than the way in which the artist develops himself from that study, that is important. Some teachers are better than others, but the inspirational, heart-and-soul relationship between teacher and student is as important as some abstract "method" that is responsible for any artist's development of a personal form of expression. My own evolution required fifteen years of work, eight of which were spent undoing some of the habits of thought and expression I had acquired from my training.

My question during my own search for self-expression was not, "How do all these teachers differ," but "What do they have in common?" My father's "Method" is based on an organized, workable technique for creating and expressing sensation and emotion; Stella's work is based on one's ability to become involved as the result of an analysis of the play. He lacked imagination and spontaneity; she lacked the organization to consciously impart to others what she was really doing. My father only spoke of Stella to the extent that, "There are some teachers whom I won't mention." He saw her as overemotional, and lacking in discipline; her talent was fantastic if it could be controlled and channeled. He said that the best work she ever did was when he threatened her and forced her to be simple; she said that he ruined her pleasure. She hated his work, and accused him of not understanding Stanislavski. He only dealt with Sense Memory and exercises on emotion, ignoring imagination; and he did not do work on the play. He countered that Stanislavski, in *Creating a Role*, went back on his own principles at the end of his life. I think they're both wrong: Stanislavski's work evolved, and his earlier sense memory work was synthesized into his expanding knowledge as he continued to search and change. Anyway, in the end he exists as the standard by which we measure ourselves.

My father focused his work on helping people to express what they felt but couldn't articulate, which is how he was as a person. I once asked him why he didn't go into therapy. He looked at me and said, in that joking manner that he used when he revealed something about himself, "Because I'm afraid of what I might find out." He also said that his work was complete, but I think everyone knows that it isn't. What we need to do is recognize what we can use, take it, and move on. Stella was an imaginative, brilliant actress, capable of being inspired, and she loved to act. Her contact with and understanding of a play, her analysis, was brilliant. To be able to use what she taught depended on your ability to understand her point of view. She shared the organic process of how she perceived what she did in a play by acting the part for you. If she liked you enough to teach you how to do for yourself what she did, you might learn what she knew. She did not deal with the need to organize talent, awareness, or expression. To do this she would have to have been consciously disciplined.

Sandy is especially known for developing a technique that trained the actor's presence, contact, and sense of truth. The Mirror exercise was based on this aspect of an actor's work. Sandy and Bobby developed very organized means for breaking down a scene. They both used forms of improvisation, a technique that, when well used, develops an actor's habit of truthful behavior and expression.

All of them were, or are, charismatic teachers who approached learning as an artist's need and passion, involving one's heart and soul. The atmosphere they created, their contemplation of the artistic process, and the spirit of love and committment to acting as an art form, are the most important parts of what they taught. In retrospect, I think these are often confused with the actual systems and techniques they taught. I was always bothered by the idea that they taught their systems in exercises outside of actual scenework. It seemed indirect and confusing, because everyone always wondered how to apply what you were learning to a play. I don't think that Sandy or Bobby's teachings reach the depth of emotional expression that Stella's and my father's did, but they all had, or have, a deep respect for the humanity and truthfulness of an artistic process.

New York City is a fantastic school, where an actor can design his own program: voice and speech, acting, dance, singing, all forms of movement. There is an extraordinary concentration of interesting and independent teachers there. Anyone who studies with me will have to study with other teachers. I can't teach an actor everything. I think I can, however, help actors to understand what each system may or may not help them do.

I define acting as the art of transformation. Of course, all art is transformational, but an actor, when he is inspired, becomes a living work of art. He lives another life. Good actors transform where and when they live by creating the imaginary world of the play and living in it. Great actors not only transform the circumstances of life: they transform who they are, and become someone else. We remember great actors, not by the plays and films that they were in, but by the characters that they created. Acting as an art form illuminates human behavior, and this includes our ability to change ourselves. An artist's vision of life, developed in what I call their Personal Dream Space, is personal, intimate, and original.

Exactly why some great artists, scientists, and leaders perceive and express more, and can do what others of us can't, has been hidden behind the secret veil we call talent.

Talent, the basis and raw material for everything we do, is the exceptional, natural capacity to sense and perceive life, and then to consciously and intuitively express that sensation and perception in an artistic form. Being sensitive is only a part of talent. I know many sensitive people who can't articulate what they feel in a form; they can't make it conscious, or adequately direct it. Art involves a conscious process. Consciousness is based on perception. Great artists use their intelligence and intuition to "choose between" options when they apply what they know and what they perceive to be true to a particular work of art. A good teacher's approach is based on knowing how to stimulate the desire of each individual to be able to do what they believe the play's life requires.

If only talented people became successful, most actors wouldn't exist. What most people define as talent, talented people know is really an enormous amount of hard work and discipline. My father never made talent a prerequisite for studying, and neither do I. Desire and committment are the criteria. There are talented people who didn't make it, and vice versa. Aristotle said about the virtue of happiness: "An activity, on the other hand, must produce a result: an active person will necessarily act and act well. Just as the crown in the Olympic Games is not awarded to the most beautiful and the strongest but to the participants in the contests—for it is among them that the victors are found." Success goes to those who commit themselves, get involved, and try, because they are in movement.

The chief beauty of theater is that it is a living work of art. And yet, some theater artists think that they are not supposed to become personally involved. If one said, "Do not get involved," to a painter, writer, or dancer, or even to an athlete, architect, or scientist, they would look at you as if you were crazy. How can anyone create anything without becoming involved? Don't confuse the capacity to perceive with being distanced and uninvolved.

One of the basic qualities of talent and the creative process is the capacity of the artist to dream and imagine life in relation to a specific reality, directing one's talent to intentionally dream about a specific world, to become involved and make this world so real that observers are transported into it and feel it as real life, happening here and now. There is no separation between subject and object; one becomes what one is creating. An artist lives in his art. When I felt estranged by using exercises as the basis for my work, my father informed me that I was thinking too much.

The idea that art is only inspiration makes the artist afraid to use intelligence and consciousness in the creative process. The impediment to any serious investigation of the creative process is compounded by our ignorance, fear of life, fear of being conscious, and resistance to change. This is part of people's fear of self-knowledge. The attitude makes creativity seem otherworldly, rather than a topographical part of the maps that chart life. It is part of the world that people have been taught to fear and ignore. They deny its existence, treat it as being mystical, or label it as crazy. There are people who may still think artists are deranged.

The taboo is as old as the Bible. It is part of the world of the Serpent, whose crime was that of giving us consciousness, which in turn made us aware of who, what, where, and why we are. We are living in an age that history will designate as a time of the transformation of consciousness. However, there remains the fact that many artists and scientists are afraid that this consciousness will stifle their creative capacity and imagination. If consciousness is indeed a detrimental attribute, the human race is biologically doomed.

In the twentieth century, with the cartography of Freud and Einstein, our maps of life and consciousness are changing. They are no longer two-dimensional, defined by linear Cartesian thinking and mechanical logic. We have discovered quantum life, a perception of the constant movement and change that governs all life as we know it. Science is no longer fixed by a materialistic orientation; it is a meditation and contemplation of probabilities and random encounters between fields of energy. People no longer ignore the feeling of being in more than one place at the same time, or living with the past and future occurring in the present moment. Perception is subjective, and relative. What was once considered irrational to Occidental thought now has a scientific rationale. What and how we think radically alters when we think of intelligence as life energy and consciousness. Truly intelligent beings perceive, feel, and know more. The only limits to intelligence or consciousness are those we impose ourselves.

Artists, scientists, and philosophers from Aristotle to Einstein have mused on the nature of creativity. It commingles with the wonder of discovery. Psychiatrists and psychologists are "discovering" what actors have known for a long time, and are using these transformational techniques as tools for the reeducation of human behavior. Psychodrama, sense memory, and the emotional reliving of traumatic experiences are prime examples. But the overall creative process has been ignored, or relegated (on our old consciousness maps) to the territory of talent. It is stranded on the far shore of the mystical ocean, in the Robinson Crusoe-world of a talented, creative person. I live in, and explore, this irrational dream world.

The best way for me to communicate the innately personal nature of the creative process is to describe my own discovery of its natural laws from my own life and professional experience. To say personal and professional seems to admit that there is a disparity between these two elements; in fact, when one loves one's work there is no separation. We are possessed by the need to create something that expresses who we are. When I create another life, I learn how to live my own. It is difficult to say where the frontier between myself-the-actor and myself-the-character lies. When I was beginning as an actor, I was irritated by the fact that I was freer and more expressive when I acted than in life. I called myself a coward and wanted to be able to do in life what I did in my work. Acting transformed my life. Wilhelm Reich, whose orgonomy (a form of psychoanalysis) I underwent said, "Art is either self-cure, or a celebration of life."

Over the years my work has evolved into what I call Organic Script Analysis, so called because the creative process for an actor begins when he reads the play. His creation depends upon the dreams and imaginings of life that the play's essence evokes, and that his talent and knowledge develops into a composition of life.

What is the "Realistic" school of acting? It can be confusing if we all have our own criteria for defining reality. When I was a teenager, I went to see the Kabuki Theater when it came to New York. The actors wore masks and performed precise movements in a very stylized theater form, but even within the confines of that relatively rigid form, one in particular was alive. He exhibited the fact one can be real within any form. Being real means expressing one's knowledge and humanity in the form of human behavior, which goes deeper than any mechanical skill. Actors tend to define their art either by their technical skill, or their capacity to express their humanity. I define it as the synthesis of both.

When I was a young actor, I was a prince of the theater, which seems quite Shakespearean to me. My mother often said, "Remember who you are." I, knowing that signalled her disapproval of something I was doing, always responded, "Who am I?" I'm fifty-four at the moment, and still seek the answer to that question. For most of my life, whenever someone asked me how I am, I've said, "Changing." That's not just an evasive answer, it's also true. Life moves all the time; it doesn't have batteries or cords. It's already plugged in to some cosmic energy. Call it whatever you want.

Art is a healing process, for both the artist and the culture. The artist expresses his perception and knowledge in his work, and our observation of it causes our perceptions to change. To deny the reality of its therapeutic nature is a foolish reaction based in the fear of knowledge. Questions about one's person, or illness, are hard enough to answer; when they are about yourself, or a character, they can be downright painful. An actor has to meditate on how to become involved in the process of creating life, and ask penetrating questions about what prevents this from happening. This contemplation can also be emotionally healing. Some pains are symptomatic; they announce that you are using yourself in a novel way, to grow and change.

While I'm on the subject of pain, one of the strangest things about acting is that actors love to suffer. This is not because actors are neurotic, but because an actor chooses to transform and live another reality. Perversely, when we're consciously creating life, it feels good. One thinks, "Oh my God. I really feel as though the woman I love is dead, that my mother has betrayed me, that I killed my uncle, that I'm really dying. This is great!" In fact, at that moment, I'd be in pain if I weren't suffering.

Any book on acting must choose between portraying the actor as an artist and as a technician. In the classroom, this line becomes very ephemeral: a technician needs to discover the artist, and the artist has to learn to be a technician. In the theater, both types are necessary. But in the end, a theater that has no artists is cold and stagnant. I certainly have no desire to make anyone feel that I have a secret recipe for acting. This book traces my discovery of the natural laws of creativity that lead to our own true natures, the nature of acting and a creative process in harmony with nature.

> John Strasberg, Paris,
> May 1996

> There are more things in heaven and earth, Horatio,
> Than are dreamt of in your philosophy.

> *Hamlet*, Act I, Scene v

> Imagination is more important than knowledge, because with imagination you can change reality.

> Albert Einstein

Maria Rosa by Angel Guimbra directed by John Strasberg
at Centro Dramatic de Catalunta (Barcelona) 1983

CHAPTER ONE

SENSE MEMORY AND EMOTIONAL TIME

"Forgive and forget" is a fine philosophy for those who never want to learn or change anything, including themselves. I can forgive, but don't ever want to forget.

It was about half past four when I rang the bell of our apartment at 320 West 76th Street, between Riverside Drive and West End Avenue. We had moved back to New York the previous year, during the incredible winter of 1947, when I was six. I had wanted to jump out of the fifth floor window into the enormous snow piles that were higher than the cars. I'd fervently believed that the snow was so deep that I would not have been hurt.

When my mother answered the door that afternoon, her large blue eyes sent me messages that signaled some important happening. Her anxious look was accompanied by a clenched jaw whose tension ground her teeth into nothing while she slept. She was in pain for the twenty-five years I knew her, which were my first and her last. As I stood in the foyer, I saw a group of men in the living room, two of whom were kneeling on the floor. One of them was almost naked; he was crying, and his arms were handcuffed behind his back. The other was also handcuffed, but he was dressed, and his dark eyes had a piercing intensity. My father stood near them, talking to several men dressed in police uniforms. Two of them had drawn guns.

I felt my mother hovering over me with that attitude she had when God—my father—was at work. I thought for a while that that's why my initials were J.C.! I knew they were supposed to stand for John Carl, the middle name after my mother's father, but if I believed in the divinity of this family it might have held another message. I went quietly down the hallway and went into my room. I didn't say hello because I knew better than to disturb them when they were rehearsing. Besides, my father never said hello to anybody; he was proud of being tight-lipped.

That evening, as we were sitting at the dinner table, my parents looked at me curiously and asked what I had thought about the scene that I had observed that afternoon. I said, "Not much." I figured they had been rehearsing a play that my father was directing, *Skipper Next to God*. It featured John Garfield, a movie star, and one of the few friends my father had. Most of my father's friendships dated back to the Group Theater. Aside from my godfather, Franchot Tone, who came from a wealthy French Canadian family, and Elia Kazan, who was born in Turkey of Greek parents, they all came from Jewish immigrant families and had grown up on the Lower East Side of New York. Garfield was one of the few people who made real contact with me. We often visited him in his duplex apartment at 88 Central Park West, which had a wonderful, winding staircase, with a banister that was great for sliding down on because it had a wide, almost flat surface. John would always kneel down so that he could really look at me and talk. He had wonderfully alive, dark eyes that seemed to be tough and good-natured at the same time. He had great teeth and a genuine smile, which sparkled with humor and gentleness. I liked him better in life than in the movies.

My parents explained what had really happened in that way that some adults talk to children: as though they are stupid and fragile, or as though the truth may cause permanent damage, which made me angry. What I had witnessed was not a rehearsal. The two handcuffed men were brothers who had come to the house to kill my father. Although they had never studied with my father, they held him responsible for the fact that they were not famous actors. While the naked one had cried at my father's feet, the other had sat on the windowsill, cradling a loaded gun in his hand. My father had a paper cutter that he used to cut the pages of the rare theater books that he collected, and he had hidden it behind his back. (Books came from all over the world, and were stored in kitchen cabinets, hallways, bathrooms, and any available floor or closet space in any of the apartments that we lived in. We moved to have more room for the books and records.)

He'd been terrified that the deranged brothers might try to harm my sister Susan, three years my senior, who for some reason had not gone to school that day. My mother convinced them that when I came home from school, a little after four o'clock, I might bring some of my friends with me. If that happened, she argued, their parents would soon come looking for them. For some reason they agreed to let my mother leave, and she promptly called the police, who returned with her, entering the apartment with guns drawn. I arrived about ten minutes later. I was very upset when I realized that they hadn't told me these were real policemen, with real guns.

My father had left Hollywood to return to the theater. He hadn't liked Los Angeles, preferring climates that had four seasons. He disliked the commercial orientation of the movie industry, particularly the way in which the power brokers decided what he thought were artistic questions. He was not a man who enjoyed infighting. Harry Cohn had offered him a blank check to create a training program at Twentieth Century-Fox, which he turned down. Whether he did this because he was still intent on a directing career, which was why he had gone to Hollywood in the first place, or out of a sense of maintaining artistic independence, I don't know. I do know that he was a man who lived by his own artistic standard, a standard which had a demanding purity and which gave his work, and himself, a quality that people either loved or hated. He didn't return until his reappearance as an actor thirty years later. Al Pacino, who was the son to him that I never was, convinced him to play a part in *The Godfather, Part II*. My father was a natural teacher; his position as artistic director of the Actors Studio was his natural place. This was the job that he had just begun at the time of my story.

The theater was as real to me as life. If anything, it often seemed more real than life. My parents lived for it, and later, when I began to work in the theater, it became the place where I could tell the truth and be believed. I found the opposite in life, where even my sister was afraid to believe what I perceived; as she said in the introduction to her second book, *Marilyn and Me*: "...and my brother Johnny, who told the truth even when I didn't want to hear it."

My parents were artistic, non-physical, and involved entirely in their own little world. My mother had been a member of the Group Theater's Communist Party cell when she was young. Many of them were blacklisted during the McCarthy era, though most of them were not hard-line Communists. They were young, and during the depression people aspired to an alternative to the system they saw as greedy and inhumane.

Several members of the Group had their lives ruined. My mother's acting career was ended. Garfield, who hadn't been a Communist, but in whose house the meetings took place, died of a heart attack, and perhaps a broken heart, in 1951, when he was only fifty. Phil Loeb was another victim. A wonderful and kind human being, actor, and stage manager, he gave my father his first theater job. Phil threw himself in front of a subway train because he couldn't work to pay for the special home in which his retarded son lived. I remember my own confusion when I'd seen him crying in our kitchen a few days before his suicide. My parents never explained any of this to me. My family simply never talked personally about life. My mother was called before the House Un-American Activities Committee, but she never discussed it with me. She once casually mentioned that several uncles and cousins were mayors, policemen, and firemen, but I never met any of them, not even the cop, whom she seemed to have really adored.

What an artist has to say about life begins with what he imagines he knows. Laurette Taylor, the American actress who created the role of Amanda in *The Glass Menagerie*, was the first person to confirm what I already felt. She said, "How often does an actress play a part so as to leave you with the feeling that you have so intimate a knowledge of the character that you could imagine its conduct in any position, aside from the situations involved in the action of the play? Unless this happens...you realize that...there was something missing."

When I was a very young boy I believed that my broom handle, to which I had attached a wooden clothespin, a nail, and a rubber band, was my Kentucky rifle as I ran through the woods in my room, fleeing from imaginary Hurons. Sometimes I woke up at night in a panic, believing that I would be crushed by the elephants who surrounded my bed. Most adults have forgotten how to experience this sense of wonder. Much of what I do revolves around my capacity to concretely construct the emotional world that I am imagining. I can then direct my perceptions into the living form that is any good play. Theater is alive; it isn't a museum piece. It is where classics are brought to life in relation to our emotional time. Emotional time is the feeling that past, present, and future exist in the same moment. If we were to visualize emotional time, we would see it not as a rigid string of points connected together in two-dimensional space but as a string of points whose shape and relationship is constantly moving and changing in a holographic space. This shape is also affected by the perspective from which we view it. Change the perspective, and the shape and relationship of the points change too.

Webster's New World Dictionary defines intelligence as "the capacity to choose between," so it can be felt, like consciousness, which is defined as "the state of being conscious: awareness." I link them together as consciousness-intelligence, meaning knowing how to choose. We can feel this reality, and may someday be able to measure it. After the Second World War, I was in accelerated classes in grade school. A group of us were used as guinea pigs, and would be herded into the cafeteria each week to take some kind of intelligence test. I remember thinking, "But it's not any of these answers. The truth isn't any one of these three or four multiple choices." There are so many truths, each one dependent on your point of view. We are finally beginning to sense that this cosmic energy we define in so many ways not only exists in everything, it is everything.

There are those who seem to be more aware; they express it readily in their work, if not always in their private lives. Their perception of reality is so exquisitely personal that it becomes simple and clear to us when we see it; though each of us enjoys a different experience, we touch their truth through our own personal sense of life. Who would call art a technique in which all artists paint apples alike? Who would separate art and technique? The Greeks didn't; to them *techne* meant art.

My original lack of commitment to acting was rooted in my fear of finding out if I was as good as I desperately needed to be. Considering my family background, I realized why I was holding myself back: if I failed, I could always say I hadn't really tried. This was a purely personal reflection; other people thought I was a talented actor.

I wondered whether I would ever be able to recognize when someone was telling me the truth. It's no wonder I was insecure. Would I even recognize my own sense of truth? Ultimately, I realized that doubt, confusion, and chaos are the beginnings of the creative process.

When I was young, I was angry and jealous of the theater; I blamed it for my parent's emotional neglect. I retaliated by saying that actors had to be either stupid or neurotic. My sister and I had hundreds of rivals: George Peppard, Anthony Franciosa, Shelley Winters, Ben Gazzara, Steve McQueen, Anne Bancroft, Jane Fonda, Marilyn Monroe, and Al Pacino, to name just a few. For each one who succeeded, there were many who didn't. The night Jack Garfein (a director and teacher who married Carol Baker in our house) called to say that James Dean had died, my parents seemed more genuinely upset than they had ever been about anything that happened to me. Of course, I hadn't died. I never really contemplated suicide as a means of getting attention. I knew too many people who had committed suicide; it held no appeal or glamour for me. Even the family cat, Sweetie Pie, got more attention. He had been abused as a kitten, and my father gave him love in order to study his behavior and cure him. (I lost my sister to the theater when I was eleven and she went away to play the part of a young prostitute in *Maya*, with Jo Van Fleet. The role of Juliet came a year later and I didn't really get my sister back, as opposed to Susan Strasberg, the actress, until I was forty-four. She's written about her perceptions of life in her two books, *Bittersweet* and *Me and Marilyn*.)

My mother used to say, with fervent conviction, that Austrian actresses were allowed by law to legally change their ages on their passports by up to seven years. I don't know if that's true; my mother lied to an extent which exceeded the limits of an active imagination. She made so many promises that never materialized that I can't begin to list them. They were mostly about time we would spend together—the moments on which love depends. Her lack of time for me meant that there was always time for someone else.

Now that I'm an adult I can see that her lies compensated for her need to have her own life. This in turn leads to the question of why my parents ever had my sister and me. The other day, Susan told me that she had learned from a close friend of our parents that my mother had wanted to abort her. I doubt that my mother's obsession with taking care of everyone else really made her feel better; she probably hoped that someone would do the same for her. My father, on the other hand, enjoyed living in his private world. He had what he needed, and revealed little of whatever dissatisfactions he endured; he lived the intellectual life that he wanted. My mother's dream had been different; she hoped that my father would direct her as an actress. As life went on, she continued to make the compromises, submitting her own desires to those of her mate.

My mother never stopped lamenting her lot in life. From the time I was eight or nine, I remember sitting by her bedside in a rocking chair. (Her bed was her office. She did a lot of business lying down.) She would express her life's regrets and speak of her desire to validate herself. She blamed my father for being selfish.

These sessions were torture for me, and they made me feel responsible for my parents' situation. I would squirm in the chair, feeling very grown up. In my love and trust I remember thinking, "What should I do? What can I do to help?" To my mother I would say, "But why don't you tell him?" "He wouldn't understand. He doesn't care. Your father's a very special person." "But so are you." "I will. I'll do something. I can't live like this forever." "What do you want to do?" "I love to produce. That's what I'd really like to do." "Do it. You must. I'll help you. I love you."

So it was that I grew up feeling that I was supposed to protect and serve her. As I got older, and nothing changed, I began to rebel against my servitude. No matter how angry I was, though, I did not escape the effects of years of indoctrination. Love and loyalty had caused a submission of my will to their needs. This feeling haunted me well into my adult life; I hadn't yet learned to have any respect for my own value or to take care of my own needs. Whenever I did, I felt I was turning into my father. Success meant becoming cold, distant, selfish. It meant sacrificing love and family to one's career and personal interests.

My anger burst out in adolescence, with a fury that led to direct confrontation with my father, who rarely got angry. When he did (I saw it happen in class when someone didn't do what he wanted them to do, and when someone like my mother would try to convince him to do something that he was afraid of, or didn't want to do), he would explode with an almost uncontrollable rage. One day, while I was peacefully watching a baseball game on television, he came in and began hollering at me, "I've told you to be careful how you touch people. You're too rough with them. You've got to stop." He then pushed me hard enough to knock me off the chair I was sitting in. I came up off the floor with my fists clenched, livid with anger. He backed away as I moved towards him, screaming, "I didn't do anything. Don't treat me like that." He backed up against the wall, furious but terrified; I was now bigger than he. In point of fact, I had never been physically intimidated by him, only emotionally. The punishment I had suffered came from brainwashing, guilt, and being ignored. When I was younger, I made him wrestle with me; I loved physical contact. He underestimated his own strength, and once threw me so that I fell against the edge of a table and cut my head open. The wound looked worse than it was, but it signaled an end to our physical contact.

His arms were pinned to his sides as I backed him up against the wall. He looked helpless, and his eyes betrayed anger and terror at the same time. I don't know if he was only afraid of me, or of his own feelings as well. It would fit with his passionate, but totally repressed, personality. I realize now that he must have been in constant conflict with himself. He had been raised in an orthodox Jewish home. I imagine the relationship he had with his father was exemplified by the fact that my grandfather never visited our home, because we were neither practicing Jews nor did my parents keep a kosher home.

From his pinned position, my father looked at me and screamed, "Who do you think I am? Your mother?" It was such a strange thing to say that I burst out laughing. What on earth did he mean? That I couldn't scream at him the way I did at her? That it was acceptable to mistreat her but not him? My mother appeared at that moment, separated us, and sent me to my room. Later, she told me to apologize but I refused, saying that my father had started it. I wasn't going to take the blame as everybody else always did. We didn't speak a word for a month. The silence ended when Dane Clark, an actor who also came from the Lower East Side, took us to a Giants baseball doubleheader against the Pirates at the old Polo Grounds on 159th Street and Morningside Heights. He had great box seats on the third base side just behind the Pirates dugout. My father and I talked as we always had, avoiding anything deeply personal. We never discussed the argument. Several years later, I asked him what he had meant when he had said, "Who do you think I am. Your mother?" He claimed that he didn't remember, but that's what he always said to avoid facing the facts.

I don't remember feeling any peace or harmony from the moment we moved back to New York in 1947 until I began spending summers in Canada with Franchot Tone when I was twelve. We hunted and fished, camping in Quebec's wilderness country.

Franchot's wealthy industrialist family owned three houses that sat on a ridge of land between two lakes that were part of the Gatineau Fish and Game Club, near Gracefield, Quebec. We portaged deep into land that he owned, smearing honey under the canoes of poachers so that the bears would destroy them. Franchot became one of my heroes, once I realized that heroes could be human. He was married four times to quite volatile women, Joan Crawford among them. Normally quiet and reflective, he could be very temperamental. He was a movie star, but above all, to me, he was a Renaissance man. He thought about more than just the theater. He gave me books he loved, like the writings of the Comte de Roche-chouart and Walt Whitman's Leaves of Grass, and a Marlin .22 lever action rifle, the gift of which startled my parents and endeared Franchot to me even more. He exposed me to a world that I loved and felt at home in, and that my parents knew nothing about. He loved women, smoked two packs of unfiltered Camel cigarettes a day, and drank double vodkas. So did I, but some years later. He was definitely more of what I wanted to be than was my father, and I often wonder what kind of a father he was to his own children. Franchot's humanity touched me deeply. It was due in part to his influence that I learned to define success on my own terms. Above all, he taught me that work is part of one's natural respect and love of human life, but it is not a way to ignore or dominate it.

It's hard to remember my parents paying attention to me though I know that they must have. My mother, for example, read to me when I was little, and invented a series of stories starring Dora the Cow, who gave different flavors of milk and ice cream from each udder. I have accepted the pain of needing to be loved by them when they just weren't there. I was alone too often but it's no good blaming them now; they were just trying to live their lives as best as they could. I began to numb myself when I was two or three. I have almost no recollection of anything between the ages of three to six, when we lived in California. When I was thirty-five, I made a deliberate effort to remember this painful time.

I remember beating up a kid who peed on my sister, and a girl's hair catching on fire as we carried pumpkins with candles in them from house to house on Halloween. We lived in a big house in Brentwood, with a huge lawn and an old tree that I used to climb. People often thought I was a little girl because I had blond, curly hair that my mother wouldn't cut; I kicked a lot of shins to prove I was a boy. We had a greenhouse behind the house where I hid in the hopes that someone would come looking for me. Nobody ever did. I recall Charlie Chaplin giving me a piggyback ride, and Gregory Ratoff taking me for a ride on his motorcycle. I remember two dogs called Ranger and Ryder, after the Lone Ranger and Red Ryder. I remember them as Irish setters, but my mother, who should know, said they were Belgian sheepdogs.

One of my happiest memories is of playing in the Santa Monica Mountains. We then lived on East Rustic Canyon Road, a small canyon at the bottom of winding Chattaqua Boulevard, which runs from San Vicente Boulevard and Seventh Street in the Pacific Palisades down to the Pacific Coast Highway. I still treasure the peaceful and healing smell of eucalyptus, the golden glow of the high dry grass, and the California scrub oaks that give the land its particular look. The Pacific Ocean was a five minute walk from the mouth of the little canyon: turn right, walk to the corner, and cross the Pacific Coast Highway. It was like living in a Maxfield Parrish painting.

I also remember swallowing a penny and being given a spray that made me vomit green. I contracted poison oak, and my dog Taffy, a tan cocker spaniel, died there, but these unpleasant memories cannot diminish those encounters with nature. There are still blanks that shroud some very deep, old pains, but I remember running barefoot in the sun, giving myself up to the multitude of sensations I felt by touching paradise on earth.

I would love to own the two-story, fairy-tale house my parents had bought. It felt like a fairy-tale because it seemed small and protected as it sat at the bottom of the canyon (it still seemed so when I passed by it several years ago) beside a dry creek bed whose bottom and sides had been covered by cement. This was done to create an aqueduct to help prevent flooding; the rainy season in L.A. causes mud slides which demolish houses in the canyons and wreak havoc everywhere. We had to park on the road and cross over a little wooden bridge to get to the house. Susan and I slept on a screened-in porch on the second floor, which had swinging doors, like those in western movie bars. It was intimate, tucked in a corner between hills on two sides and the creek on the other.

We had a two-door car with a rumbleseat, which my mother drove. My father told me he had once tried to learn to drive but the very first time he was behind the wheel he barely avoided a collision with a taxicab in the middle of Columbus Circle. He got out of the car, moved to the passenger's side, and never attempted to drive again. It was one of the few stories I know about his life. Is it my fault if I like my mother better?

It was here that I fell in love for the first time, though I can't remember the girl's name. We had a mysterious relationship. She lived in a house at the top of the canyon, and our parents never met each other. She had long blond hair, blue eyes, and a nurse that accompanied her almost all of the time. I remember her waiting for me when I came home from the hospital after a tonsillectomy, and the pounding of my heart when we were together. I have a vague memory of being punished by her nurse when she caught us playing "doctor," exploring each other's bodies in the bushes. What were we doing wrong? We were in love.

I remember wanting my parents to admire my physical ability at sports. When I was about twenty they came to see me play on the Actors Studio softball team. Their appearance surprised me and made me wonder who they had really come to see. My teammates were Al Pacino, Bruce Dern, Arthur Penn, Ron Leibman, Pete Masterson, Bob Macbeth, Dick Bradford (one of my closest friends), Allen Miller, Bill Smithers, and a host of other actors, teachers, and directors. We all felt unsuccessful, unnoticed, and unimportant, though most of us were too young to feel forgotten.

During the nervous breakdown I had when I was seventeen, I had actually forgotten that I had been athletic as a child. When I was eight and nine, I had been a pitcher and batted fourth on a baseball team, and was a quarterback in football. I remember once breaking away from several tackles and running for a touchdown, but just before I reached the goal line, I suddenly stopped, thinking that I had run out of bounds. No whistle had blown. My coach couldn't believe I had done it. This was not atypical of my life. On another occasion I took myself out of a game I was pitching because I thought the umpire, who worked for the other club, was cheating. I turned my anger on myself. My coach wasn't there that day. These strange manifestations of my depressing myself seem almost unreal to me.

I may always have a love/hate relationship with the theater, because of my Sense and Emotional Memories. Neurologists now know that we remember everything, but our problem is whether we want to be able to recall it. Stanislavski, when he was searching to develop his own capacity, discovered that actors had been doing this for hundreds of years. The first recorded instance I know of actors using their own pain is recounted by a Greek actor named Polus, playing in Sophocles' *Electra*, who embraces the urn that was supposed to contain the ashes of Orestes. In fact, it held the real ashes of his own dead son. As he carried the urn onto the stage, he "filled the place, not with the appearance and imitation of sorrow, but with genuine grief and unfeigned lamentation." The search for truth and reality is not a new invention; it's the organic (inherent, inborn) need for any creative artist.

We try to distance ourselves from our true emotions, and in the process we lose touch with the best part of ourselves. We learn to ignore or forget who we really are, but art makes us recognize that life is a gift to be fully used; otherwise it is wasted. There are those who prefer to seek peace and harmony by intellectualizing their feelings. They long to become perfect. To them I say, "Close the book now; buy a computer, and begin practicing to become one." I've never wanted to be a machine. I have wanted to be perfect. For years, I have longed for peace, but not at the expense of not knowing or feeling. Giving up the desire for this machine- or cow-like existence has taken a long time.

My earliest, verifiable memory is of a room in which I lived during the first year of my life. The walls are white; to my left is a window that has a grill of bars on the outside. To my right is a square pillar. In front of me, to my left, is an entrance to the room; behind me and to my right is another door in the center of the wall. I see this room as though I am lying on my back. My parents seemed surprised by my capacity to remember these details. They said I was describing a room I had lived in on East 78th Street. We had a ground floor apartment in a brownstone building, where they brought me after I was born in Lenox Hill Hospital on East 76th street.

I have an earlier recollection which first presented itself during a therapy session; eventually I began to be conscious of it on my own. In this memory I can't breathe; an oozing liquid is clogging my nose and throat. It tastes salty sweet and has a sticky mucous quality. I feel stuck, afraid that I will suffocate. I want to scream, a scream that bubbles in my throat, even today. It is part of the asthma that used to choke me, before I learned to let this old, confusing fear of abandonment flow out of me. I believe the sensations are memories of my birth, though I can't swear that they're real. Maybe I was only imagining them, but, as Dr. Baker (my analyst) said, what matters is that what I felt was real to me.

There was another experience of which I became conscious during Orgone Therapy (the name for Wilhelm Reich's therapy). It came to me in another terrifying dream. I am surrounded by people in a large white room. In front of me is a man dressed in black; he has a long, white beard, and I see something shiny and flashing in his hand. I hear people talking and laughing, and though I do not understand the words, I can feel how excited and anxious everyone is. Suddenly, the bearded man reaches down, and I feel a horrible pain between my legs. I do not know what has happened. I scream and cry, struggling to push him away, with arms that are too small to do anything but flail at the air. I feel helpless. I do not see my parents, or any recognizable faces among those that are peering down and smiling, all of whom seem to be laughing at my pain. Dr. Baker said nothing about whether he thought this was a dream or an actual memory. But then, Dr. Baker once said to me, "I think that whatever human beings imagine is real, or else we wouldn't be able to imagine it."

Stranger still is that several months later on in therapy, the tip of my penis, which hurt and throbbed from the moment that I had the "dream," began to have greater sensation than ever. Was this a real or imaginary memory of my "briss," or circumcision?

Because I believe these experiences to be real, they greatly influence my work. Both my parents ignored this non-rational side of themselves, my father out of fear, and my mother out of resignation. I, however, know that we have the senses to perceive much more than our maps of human experience indicate. There are many fascinating books being published about mind/body research, spearheaded by Wilhelm Reich's Orgone therapy. In its simplistic form, Reich recognized that a lot of illness results from blocking the natural flow of energy, and that it is possible to eliminate neuroses by freeing this blocked energy. I undertook this analysis with Dr. Baker in 1975, the late Dr. Albert Duvall, and Dr. Barbara Koopman. I wanted to experience the full strength of my feelings without fear and to free myself from my characteristic habit of depressing myself. I also knew that I needed help if I was going to change. I don't know if reading Reich's books, *The Function of the Orgasm* and *Character Analysis*, or Dr. Baker's book, *Man in the Trap*, will help you understand more about character, but reading Shakespeare will.

All doctors should be obliged to study Shakespeare, not just as a great dramatic poet, but as someone who so patently understands character. Conversely, if you want to read Stanislavski's books on acting because you want to know how to act, I wish you all the luck in the world. After you know how to act they are very simple and clear, but knowledge without experience makes people dangerous. Novices think they understand something just because they saw it on television, but an actor never really knows anything unless he can feel it in his heart, body, and soul.

In 1958, I was seventeen, and in the worst depression of my life. I was diagnosed with a nervous breakdown, which had been coming on for three years. My adolescence was a process of falling apart. I no longer knew who I was, or what I wanted. I felt that I couldn't talk to anyone, and that no one would listen anyway. I felt like a volcano waiting to erupt. Adolescence is painful for parents, too, who often seem more helpless than their children. With no goal to focus on, and no outlet for expression, I felt the oldest I have ever felt at any time before or since.

I attended the University of Wisconsin for one year, partly because it was a good school, and partly because it was the farthest away I could get from my family. I had graduated from the Bronx High School of Science with good enough grades to receive a New York State scholarship, and was accepted into several universities. Franchot had sponsored me for Cornell, which his family endowed, but for unstated reasons I wasn't accepted. When I was interviewed by an alumnus, a doctor on East 79th Street, he asked me what my religion was. I told him it was none of his business. Although they denied it, Ivy league schools had a 6 percent Jewish quota in those days.

I had thought about going to college in California until my mother reminded me that Aunt Bea lived there. Even in Wisconsin, people thought I should be proud to be a Strasberg; they were shocked to discover I was not. No one understood the frustration I felt in needing to be my own person.

The only course I attended regularly was the medieval history class given by Professor George Mosse, a German Jew whose family had fled Germany in the early Thirties, leaving behind a publishing empire. Mosse was brilliant, an expert in medieval and Renaissance history. The rest of the courses I was supposed to take were dry and boring, but for the first time boredom became an important feeling in my life. Most people think that we should never get bored: we should always be filling up our time with projects and hobbies. But sometimes, thinking about why you're bored may make you discover what you really want to be doing. Boredom can be a valuable state, if one knows how to learn from it.

History was, and still is, one of my passions. The memorization of dates is pointless, but learning about movements of consciousness and discovery constitutes the real history of humanity as organically alive and free. Out of the need for socialization and protection, most people willingly renounce their freedom in order to belong to a society, a nation, or a religion. A conflict arises between an individual's need to evolve consciousness through an exchange of ideas with others and society's demand that we become dependent. Most people end up living in submission, constantly at war with Nature. There is a deep internal conflict between the longing to be free and the fear of being alone.

After the first week, I never went to any classes. Out of anger, I began drinking. I would start at 8:00 A.M. after my roommate, who was a law student, left for his morning classes. Because I was only seventeen, I had to find people over twenty-one to buy me bottles. I was expelled about a month into the spring term. A month later, in mid-April, I finally told my parents I had been expelled and wanted to come home for my birthday, which is the 20th of May. Despite the fact that I was unhappy and no longer in school, my parents wanted me to stay in Wisconsin. When I finally did come home, I surprised them again by asking to go into analysis. I knew I needed someone to listen to me. Until then, I had been so proud of hiding my feelings from the world. Perhaps it was the only ego I could muster.

I was terrified that I would be discovered as the liar I was. The memory is particularly painful because lying runs counter to my character. I was so insecure that I felt compelled to lie to cover my true feelings, but it only made me feel worse. It was unimaginable that I might have talent or any value as a person. My self-hatred was worse than anything I did to anyone else, including my mother, who was a prime target for my anger during my adolescent years. I even hung a sign on the door to my room saying, "Everyone allowed in, except Mother." I was angry at her for continually interfering with me. Every time I began to feel private, she would appear and ask me what I was doing. This had a strange, almost sexual, feeling to it, compounded by her giving me a copy of *Fanny Hill* when I was thirteen. I felt spied upon, pinned down, and held back.

My father, in the total absence of any emotional contact, was left somewhere in limbo. All we shared was a love of spectator sports and food, interests which I had encouraged in him. But his abiding obsession was his art; he loved it more than any living creature. In its exercise, he was a man among men. My mother, on the one hand, complained bitterly about him to me, seeking out my support and love; on the other, she protected him and made our home into one of the most fantastic theatrical salons in the world.

Sundays were open house, where we entertained the likes of Bill Daniels and Bonnie Bartlett, Marta and Jerry Orbach, Marilyn, Franchot, Jane Fonda, Andreas Voutsinas, Mark Rydell, Shelley Winters, Frank Corsaro, Elia Kazan (especially when his first wife, Molly Day Thatcher, was still alive), Arthur and Peggy Penn, Rip Torn and Geraldine Page, Dick Bradford (one of my true friends at the time; strangely, we hardly ever see each other now), George Gaines and Allyn Ann McLeary, and Mary and Arthur Schwartz. English actors appearing in New York, like Albert Finney, were always invited in a bid to allay their homesickness. It was bagels and lox from Barney Greengrass, or cold cuts from Fine and Shapiro; there would be sports on television, music in my father's study, casual conversations in the kitchen, and more intimate ones with mother in her office bed. It was easy to imagine that it was a dream come true, especially if you didn't live there. My blasé reaction, however, was to admit that the only actor whose autograph I might ask for was John Wayne. Wayne was neither a member of the Actors Studio, nor an admirer of my father, and he never came to the house. But my father did respect his work in a film, *The Quiet Man*, recognizing the aura of truth that all movie stars have. People mistakenly believe such simplicity is easy to achieve.

Dr. Finger, our family doctor, recommended a classic Freudian analyst. This meant lying on a couch and presenting dream material for interpretation, with no direct contact between me and the analyst. Dr. Finger had always taken a personal interest in me; he invested more time in helping me than did my father. During my senior year of high school, I again came close to physically attacking my father. I was in total confusion as to what I wanted to do. I was no longer sure I wanted to be a doctor. The only thing I felt I did want to do was not go to college and to begin to work instead—at any kind of job, until I knew what I really wanted. I tried to talk to him about this, and he refused to give me the desperately needed opinion and advice I was asking for, insisting that he didn't want to unduly influence me. I told him that I sought only his opinion and that I would then make up my own mind. Underneath, I just needed him to say that he loved me and that he wanted me to do whatever made me happy. My promise not to blindly agree with him threatened his sense of security. My father always needed to feel that he was in control, and couldn't tolerate the idea that his opinion might be challenged or rejected. Seeing him as I do today, it is easy to imagine that he felt more abandoned and insecure than I.

My analyst (whom I call Dr. M.) owned a brownstone house on 82nd Street between Madison and Park Avenues. I went to see him for three years, four times a week. His waiting room was a small alcove at the foot of a narrow winding staircase that spiraled up to his large office. I would lie on the couch and stare at the brown, cork covered walls, either prevaricating or saying nothing. He sat behind me in a large leather chair, where he often snored away. I don't think that his snoring was a therapeutic device, but who knows? If I mentioned a real dream or thought, he might make a sound of acknowledgment, and ask what I thought it meant. I never felt that he gave me any of the contact that therapy should give. I felt utterly incapable of making a move in any direction.

Feeling alone and ignored was what I expected. I had become afraid of being criticized, and terrified I would explode. During three years of therapy, the only important dialogue I remember was when he discouraged me from leaving home; he said that it would be running away from the problem, namely my relationship with my family. It made me furious, but since I desperately needed permission to be myself, I continued to see him. Finally, I asked myself what a successful analysis would be. I concluded that if I were healthy I would trust myself; I would do what I wanted to, unafraid of not pleasing everybody. The first thing I did was leave therapy. I don't know how many years of life I've lost or wasted by not trusting myself. I confused natural aggression with the need to prove myself a man, getting into fights or driving too fast. I accepted any dare. I only wish someone had dared me to learn to love myself and live with the same simple courage as the pioneer I so desperately wanted to believe I was.

My need to understand success has been another major influence in my life. When I was younger, I subscribed to my father's definition that greatness was the measure of a man's worth. He was obsessed with defining art and artists in those terms. He thought Rembrandt was the greatest painter, followed closely by Leonardo; Beethoven was the greatest composer, then Bach. Shakespeare was the greatest writer, with Chekhov, Euripides, and Moliere in his wake. (Language differences made him waver.) Music and painting should be universal forms, but I always felt that since I preferred Bach there was something wrong with me. I didn't appreciate that feeling of inferiority and I hated going to museums or concerts because I felt stupid for liking what my father did not consider to be the greatest. I argued with him about this during my adolescence. He always responded that one could like whatever they liked, but whenever he spoke of Bruegel or Goya or El Greco, I never really believed that he meant it; I always felt as though he were talking to me with a tinge of condescension.

I always felt the need to prove that I was the best, which put me under enormous pressure. I never seriously committed myself to anything, and derived no pleasure from the many things I did well. There always seemed to be someone smarter, faster, stronger, more sensitive. My all-around talent as a human seemed to be a handicap. To be great, one apparently had to be more than human; one had to control and dominate one's fundamental weakness. This obsession with perfection and control affected my acting. I was always surprised when I was complimented on my work, because I never expected any praise. The moments that I thought were special, after having worked hard on their design, were not the ones that moved people.

I remember a scene I did at the Actors Studio when I was in my early twenties. Walter Beakel, then a director, asked me to work on *Cheri*, the Anita Loos play based on Colette's novel. Mary Sinclair, a beautiful, pale-skinned, dark-haired actress, whom I secretly adored, was playing Nana. (I was not yet a Studio member, but I could participate because it was a director's project.) We were to present two scenes: the one before and the one after Cheri and Nana make love. The scenes were linked by a blackout, during which we made a transition in time. I was anxious that my real desire for Mary would cause me a very real erection. We rehearsed in

Mary's studio apartment in Carnegie Hall. Mary and I were both embarrassed at first, but Walter's sensitive presence made us feel freer. He was a good director who never pushed us, but directed us in the exploration of the relationship. Mary was not only beautiful, she was simple and kind. She had been a movie star for ten seconds, and I don't know what happened. It's not talent that makes one remain a star; she just wasn't tough enough. Walter never said much to me about the character, recognizing that I already understood a lot about Cheri. Walter always cared about me. He hired me to teach at Columbia Pictures in their talent program, and later represented me as an actor when he became an agent.

I wanted to create something that no one else could think of doing—to be great. I worked on Cheri's physical behavior, particularly through the use of my hands, which I was discovering were very important to me. I often wonder about what a character's hands feel and do. I was wearing a dress shirt with lace cuffs, as part of the demimonde, Parisian world that Colette knew so well. I instinctively knew how alone and abandoned Cheri felt growing up in that world; in a sense, he had never been a child.

In the first scene, Cheri and Nana come home after a party, and undress to go to bed. The day we did the scene, the Studio was packed. In the front row were my father and mother, and Shelley Winters, whom I've always thought of as my second mother. She has been a member of my extended theater family ever since I can remember. After my mother died and I was living in California, she helped and fed me when I was broke, and years later, after I tore my Achilles tendon, she bought me a pair of bright red, Italian shoes with very high heels. It wasn't exactly what the doctor had recommended, but it was Shelley's loving and personal interpretation of his prescription. Shelley has been a substitute mother for a lot of young actors.

Among the others present were Anne Bancroft, Arthur Penn, Mark Rydell, and Viveca Lindfors. It was the heyday of the Studio, past, present, and future. Who was there depended on who was in town from California, and who was next in line to go. The scene was going well. I had good concentration, and was unperturbed by the starry ambiance. I could see them, as we set up the scene, but once I had created my own world the audience no longer mattered.

Towards the end of the first part, I was in my underwear. (There was never total nudity in those pre-Beatles days.) I remember moving to the bed, and lying down with Mary-Nana. As we began to make love I wondered if an actor should put his tongue into an actress' mouth. Making love on stage is never a matter of literal behavior; it is about believing and expressing the feeling of love with one's heart and soul. Our bodies touched. I was excited, but I got no erection, though I felt as though I were making love. I felt more in love than I ever dared to let myself feel in life. As we embraced, the lights went out. I lay there for a few seconds, floating through emotional time, calming myself. I imagined having made love, and lay there feeling alone again as people often do at such times.

The lights came up for the second part of the scene. I felt restless and uncomfortable, so I got up and walked over to an imaginary window. I stood there and looked out of it for a long moment before the dialogue began. Nana asks Cheri what's wrong, but he can't, or won't, answer. At the end of the play, Cheri kills himself. The moment that excited my father, and everybody else, was the moment at the window. People talked about seeing the character's sadness and loneliness, the emptiness of his unfulfilled life. The comments surprised me; I hadn't planned anything in that moment. Shelley asked me, "HOW could you undress and do THAT in front of your parents?" Everybody laughed. I didn't understand why she thought it would be difficult; I was acting. Whenever I did my best work, I never felt self-conscious the way I did in life. When I worked, my energy filled whatever theater or room I was in, embracing the audience; I never felt inhibited.

My inner life raced along with such a nervous, explosive force that I always feared I would burst out in some new self-destructive direction. I spent fifteen years of my life trying to rip aside the veil of defenses with which I surrounded my feelings and controlled my life before I began to consciously become myself.

The therapy I began with Dr. Baker in 1975 affirmed so many unexpressed perceptions and feelings which I had barely been conscious of all of my life. I was coming home to discover that I had been there all the time. What I had always felt was real, and I was not crazy.

My internal conflict stems from the confusion of not knowing whether to trust my own perceptions or to believe the opinions of others. Laying to rest the ghosts of old insecurities and the severe damage to my ego finally enabled me to define success for myself. I have always been ruled by how I feel, and that determines what I want and need. I admire people who, while being emotional wrecks, can continue to be ambitious and obtain the world's version of success. I was never like that. The materialism by which most people define success only seems to be a pleasure to me if things come as the result of living in the way I choose to live, because to me success is

being in harmony with myself and the universe. My life may be more fulfilled on a deep level now, but the first forty-odd years were hell on earth.
I have since discovered that paradise can also be here on earth.

More. Bigger. The Best. The Greatest. When I consider the movie
icons of the past several decades, I see vast changes in these reflections of
ourselves, whom we worship, and how we define a successful human being. How do we compare the great names of the screen with the host of
puppets, machines, and special effects which now clutter our vision? Some
of these inventions are more human than we are. I think Yoda should have
won an Academy Award for Best Supporting Actor. What do we now perceive as being expressive of our inner life? Is America a Shakespearean
tragedy?

At the end of the 1950s, I only knew what I didn't want. I drank, went
to nightclubs and listened to the great jazz that flourished in New York at
the time—Gerry Mulligan, Charley Mingus, Bill Evans, Art Blakey, Stan
Getz, Oscar Peterson, Ornette Coleman, Miles Davis, and Dizzy
Gillespie. There was Latin music, like Perez Prado, and the Palladium on
Wednesday nights, known as White Night. I lied to everyone, including
my friends and family. I misinterpreted my contempt as a demonstration
of my strength; I didn't realize how deep the contempt for myself was, or
the extent of my feelings of weakness.

I didn't want to emulate the rich, famous, and powerful people I knew.
Everybody else thought they lived such admirable lives, dedicated to
knowledge, art, and creation; all I needed was simple love, respect, and
truth. It was confusing to see how their private lives failed to reflect their
public images. No wonder I thought I was crazy.

I told everyone that I was enrolled in Columbia University's General
Studies program, but in fact I didn't even register. I thought that I would
be rejected, so I never even asked for an application form. I would drive
up to the Columbia campus at 116th Street and Broadway. There I would
sit on the campus green, watching the passing students, whose lives
seemed to be lived in a bubble. I would get back into my car and drive up
the Henry Hudson Parkway to the Sawmill River Parkway and continue
up the Taconic State. That drive takes on a naive, enchanted look in au-
tumn. It may seem that life is dying, but it's only going into hibernation,
to sleep, perchance to dream. As I drove, I did some of my best thinking.
Having a car probably saved my life, because driving brought me some

rare moments of peace. After my drive back, I would finish the morning by running around the famous reservoir at 90th Street which in 1958 was a deserted part of Central Park.

The car was a black, 1956, Ford Thunderbird, 1956 being one of the three years that Ford made the two-seater. The spare tire was encased in a metal cover attached to the rear of the car; a handle released its position for access to the trunk. The car was a classic, but I don't own it anymore: I traded it in several years later on an MG Midget, because I wanted a sports car.

Marilyn Monroe gave me the T-bird for my eighteenth birthday, just after I returned from Wisconsin in the midst of my nightmare depression. This was the spontaneous kind of love and generosity of which she was capable. Maybe she saw how much I was suffering or maybe she just wanted me to like her. At any rate, I looked gratefully at her, and she smiled warmly back; we could touch with our eyes. She was smart enough and vulnerable enough to have recognized another victim.

I was always too shy to approach Marilyn, and my parents were always hovering protectively over her. I remember feeling that everybody used Marilyn; they said that they only wanted to help, but they devoured her energy. Damaged and desperate as she was, she mistook this attention for love. As a needy child grasps for affection, Marilyn shyly tried to reach out for help. The two of us were rarely alone together, though occasionally she lived with us and was considered part of the family. She stayed with us whenever she was suffering through some emotional crisis. Conveniently, her psychiatrist lived in our building. We had an enormous apartment in one of those pre-war buildings that characterize New York, at 135 Central Park West. We were on the seventh floor: nine rooms, three bedrooms, kitchen and alcove, foyer, three-and-a-half baths. There were windows in every room, three of which directly overlooked the park.

When Marilyn stayed over, I slept in the living room. I was long used to sharing my parents with other "talented" children. I often imagined myself as an orphan being adopted and loved by Roy Rogers and Dale Evans; they seemed more like real, loving parents to me. I think that if I had not been their son, my parents would have recognized my talent more readily, and loved me more. They might have found the time and love for me that they reserved for all the other starving, gifted children who made up our extended family.

Marilyn once came half-crawling into the living room where I was asleep in the early hours of the morning. She groped along the wall in an effort to stand up. She wore a wrinkled white slip of a nightgown. I was seventeen. "Johnny, I can't sleep," she whispered, in her unique woman-child's voice. She floated over to where I was now sitting up, and slumped down next to me. Her body odor was heavy with the drugs that she was taking, though I don't think that she had been drinking. Whenever she did drink, she constantly used Binaca mouth spray to mask the odor. "I think it's probably too late to wake them up. Don't you?" There was an awkward pause. "Do you mind if we just sit here a while?" We looked at each other. I didn't know what to do. The situation that millions of men fantasized about terrified me. Marilyn never struck me as particularly sexy; she seemed more like a child. At that moment, she was so doped up that I wasn't sure she knew where she was. She was semi-lucid, but she faded in and out without even moving.

I anxiously debated what I should do. Would my parents be more angry if I didn't wake them than if I did? They were on twenty-four hour call with Marilyn. Sitting with her in that state, I was painfully aware that anything could happen. Drugs and anxiety make one's energy field loose; ours intermingled, like smoke filtering into the atmosphere. We talked; or rather she rambled on senselessly while I half-listened, wondering when she would calm down or tire out. She finally did go back to sleep. I often pondered, later on in life, what might have happened if either of us had reached out in that thick, smoky air. Would we have held one another in the embrace of a man and a woman, or would it have been the desperate embrace of longing to love and be loved that is known to children of all ages who cannot bear to be alone?

To some men, it would have been a dream come true: to have a beautiful, drugged, and helpless woman who will do anything for love in a position where she doesn't know what she's doing. To me, it seemed nightmarish and incredibly sad that a human being who gave so much pleasure to so many people felt utterly alone and unloved. As broken and ill as she was, her death, whether deliberate or accidental, could only have been a relief. Fools who dispute Marilyn's demise for their own personal or political interests are too blind to understand the real tragedy of her life.

How could I have any illusions about fame and fortune, when this was what I knew the truth to be? My parents were shocked and jealous that Marilyn cared about me and took so much notice of me. Not that it cost her anything. The car she gave me, for instance, had been presented to her as a publicity ploy by the Ford Motor Co. She had recently married

Arthur Miller, and they had a magnificent, racing-green Jaguar. The T-Bird lay abandoned for two years, covered by a plastic cloth in the barn of their Connecticut home. I got stung by a wasp on the middle finger of my right hand as I removed that cover. I still remember how my swollen hand felt as I drove back to New York, despite the mud I packed on it to reduce the inflammation.

I lived through a year of increasing depression. So, apparently, did many of the famous people I knew: I often picked them up off the floor of our apartment during my parents' New Year's Eve parties. These were a major cultural event in New York, at which visiting British actors got drunker than anyone else; maybe they had more reason to. Peter O'Toole, Richard Burton, and Kenneth Tynan numbered among the more memorable drunks of my life. Tennessee Williams was an American who could party with any of them. He once came to the house to talk to my parents about something and wanted a drink. My parents drank only an occasional glass of champagne, though my mother, if she had let herself be who she really was, would have smoked and drunk a scotch now and then. Tennessee, with all his natural elegance, asked me if I would accompany him in a drink because it wasn't polite to let a guest drink alone; I felt bold enough to say yes, as my parents would never refuse anything to such illustrious company. Tennessee went to the bar and mixed two perfectly-layered drinks using ten or twelve liquors, delicately pouring one on top of the other into the highball glasses. It was a work of art, as intoxicating to the eye as it was to the rest of me.

I went nightclubbing with my friends, Cambiz and Kamron Baher. Cambiz was my best friend when we were kids. His parents, who were Iranian, had left what was then Persia because their inter-faith marriage was forbidden. We would often date girls who lived at the Grace Downs Airline Hostess School on East 26th and First Avenue. Most of them came from outside of New York. Even when I liked one of them, I didn't know how to develop a relationship; I couldn't imagine any of them being really interested in me. I never made love, even with the girls who seemed willing. I would get excited, and then scared, often having premature ejaculations which made me feel even more inadequate. I discussed none of this in therapy. I can't explain why I continued to go, or why I didn't try to change doctors. Feeling helpless rage and numbing stupidity was simply my state of being: I was stuck, and no one around me behaved as though life was anything but normal.

Perhaps as a cry for help, I asked my father if I could observe his private classes. I don't know if I had been thinking of doing this; I just did it. I told him that I didn't want to continue my (imaginary) classes at Columbia. There was a cold, blank silence. It seemed as if the room was holding its breath in anticipation of a hard, uninviting moment of truth. When I was eight or nine, I used to enjoy going to the theater because it was a magical place to explore; this was the first time since then that I had manifested any further interest. My father remained silent, giving me a long look, during which his eyes slid away to his private world. He then smiled slightly and said, "OK. If you want to." It was more contact than we'd had in over a year. There was one other fleeting moment of intimacy, a couple of years later, during a period when we were alone. Susan had become a star and was living in Rome, and my mother was away with Marilyn, when he came in to the television room where I was collapsed in my Barcalounger. As he stood behind me, out of sight, he mumbled, "Johnny, if you ever want to talk to me, I want you to know that I'm here." I remember saying, "Thanks." He said, "Really. I mean it. I would like to." I thought, "Why now? It's too damn late," but I said, "I'd like that, too."

So I began to audit my father's classes. I took my commitment seriously, without understanding how zealous a person I actually was. I attended both classes almost every day, and sometimes went to the Actors Studio where he led the Tuesday and Friday morning Acting sessions, as well as the Monday afternoon Director's unit. After a year of observing the exercise and scene work that he taught, I asked if I could work with him. He was totally non-committal, and without asking why, he just said yes. It was as though two strangers had agreed to do business together. Whenever we worked together our relationship was always very professional and impersonal. After I had done my first scene, which went very well, he finally admitted that he had been terrified about what he would say to me if I wasn't any good. By that he meant that he thought I had talent.

I think he was more afraid than he let on, perhaps even to himself, that he would be judged by my ability. It was as though my presence interfered with his world. I always remember him as being under constant pressure. He used to tell his students stories about himself, to share with them the fact that he had the same difficulty they had in expressing themselves. He said that he had dreaded picking up Susan and me when we were babies because he was terrified of dropping or hurting us. I can feel his fear in me and used to believe it to be mine. I learned to behave like him, "by osmosis," as Susan loved to say. There are still things I do, attitudes of my body, or a way of thinking, that I recognize as being unconsciously acquired habits of his.

In the mid '60's, during the period of the Actors Studio Theater, my father once casually recalled that he and my mother had always felt that I was the child who would go into the theater, rather than Susan. They had been surprised when I hadn't seemed to want to. Why had he never told me before? I wondered why he was giving me this compliment, and why we never had simple and real conversations as I always imagined families did. He was trying to express his love for me; he wanted to make contact with me on a more personal level than when we discussed sports, food, or the theater. I reacted with a child's understandable anger and vengeance. I had gone from being "the sunshine of his life," as he described me as a child, to someone insecure, suspicious, and angry. Building a wall to defend myself was the only way someone who felt as worthless as I did could survive and function.

With all of this going on under the surface, at the end of 1959 I began to study acting. While I wanted his love and approval, in a deep sense I wasn't afraid of him. The only fear I have is of myself, and not knowing what I am capable of doing.

If I hadn't become an actor, I would have been happy doing the undersea research work of Jacques Cousteau. I love nature and the outdoors. The ocean itself lends another dimension of reality; it keeps us reaching out to touch, discover, and understand. Living with the constantly mutable ocean makes life a meaningful adventure. I also think my love of analyzing and understanding life would have made me a good doctor. My work shares much with brain surgery and psychiatry. From another perspective, art can be viewed as a means of sharing and healing human suffering. I do feel, sometimes, that I am rewiring actors. My explorations have led me to believe that all problems and solutions in the creative process begin and end with knowing what real, organic thinking is.

I can remember almost every Sense Memory exercise I did in my father's classes. I'm always shocked when students don't remember what they did last week, since my memories are now over thirty years old. They are often clearer, and more detailed, than memories from my private life. Sense Memory is a structured learning process, like athletics or dance: what one learns, one never forgets. Doing the exercises I felt more in contact with reality than I did in life. Acting taught me a lot about living, and made me change myself: I wanted to be able to express myself as directly in life as I did when I acted. If I concentrate, as the exercise work taught me to do, any reality can be made present. That immediacy of life, imaginary or real, is one of the main properties of Sense Memory training. The experience makes you consciously aware of moment-to-moment sensations that often pass unnoticed, as if we are unconscious of just how fantastically our sensory gifts function. Most of the time, we only notice when something is different from normal, at which time we become irritated at having been awakened.

Sense and memory are natural to human beings. So why do people not understand how they function? Are they less talented, or do they not want to know? This can only be judged by time and experience. Certainly, we have all imagined loving someone that we don't really know: a co-worker, a movie star. We feel more strongly when we dream about them than we do when a real person is present. We all remember how our favorite food tastes, and readily salivate when we imagine tasting or smelling it. We've all imagined that we see someone we know on the street, only to feel foolish when we discover that we have mistaken them for somebody else. These are all simple examples. Sense Memory trains, and retrains, the natural function of our senses, our memories, and our imaginations.

My Sense Memory work began with "What I Drink for Breakfast." I had moments of believing I actually felt what only existed in my imagination: the steam heat on my face; the color of the liquid; the feel of its weight as it moves out of rhythm with the cup; the warmth that my hand feels; the slightly bitter aftertaste in my mouth. We never used the real object in the basic exercises. We recalled sensations that we felt every day, but hardly noticed until we had to consciously recreate them. Many years later my father explained that Sense Memory was a training of imagination, not a training of emotion. Many people, including myself, mistakenly assumed them to be the same.

Beginning work was based on using your senses and imagination to recall real memories of objects and sensations from your own life. Because the memories are real, you learn to recognize what you have recreated. Learning to become present in the here and now and knowing how you have created the reality of your choices are two of the most important aspects of the Method. Even though I'd observed people doing the exercises every day for over a year, I didn't realize how powerful the technique was until I used it myself.

My first experiences of this altered transformation of reality happened during a Sharp Pain exercise, then in an Overall Sensation exercise, and then in an exercise called Personal Object. A Personal Object is something for which you have such strong feelings that if your house were burning down, you would risk your life to save it. After several months of practicing the relaxation and concentration which form a fundamental part of the technique, I had completed the basic exercises of: "What you drink for breakfast," "Looking in the mirror and shaving (or putting on makeup)," "Sunshine." I was now assigned to do Sharp Pain.

I had chosen a memory of a time I was rushed to Dr. Finger: I was about ten and had an infected thumb. Dr. Finger was normally very gentle and always told me beforehand what he was going to do. On this occasion, he took me into his office, selected a scalpel, and lanced the thumb. He rubbed the infected wound clean of blood and pus with cloth and cotton. I yelled lustily, as much from surprise as from the pain. In the midst of my exploration and sensory recall, I passed my finger over the area where the infection had been. Moving my thumb in a manner that would have been unbearable had the wound actually been there, I began to recall how strongly I had felt the pulsing of the blood. I affectively remembered how hot my thumb felt, how swollen and red was the skin; it was stretched so taut from being full of pus and infected blood that my fingerprints were almost nonexistent.

After several minutes of the exercise I burst into tears; my thumb began to behave as though the infection was really there. It became rigid, and there was an irritated tingling feeling exactly like the one I had actually felt, but had never remembered with such affective force. As I sobbed and writhed from the remembered pain I had recreated, that was, and wasn't, there, I opened my eyes and looked at my thumb, and then at the class and my father. The reality of the pain neither stopped nor diminished. It was the first time that I experienced being and remaining conscious of several simultaneous levels of reality. I knew where I was and what I was doing; I also knew that my concentration on and recall of a real memory in this imaginary world was the cause of my reaction. From the moment the exercise worked, I maintained my concentration on the sensory elements of the reality that I had created. My father even had me suspend my concentration, calm down for a minute, and then begin again. The exercise worked again. I was astounded at my ability to create this reality at will.

I am always amused to read opinions such as those by Diderot, the French playwright-philosopher, who postulated that it is impossible for an actor to be truly inspired and yet remain sufficiently conscious to move a chair that he realizes has been misplaced on stage. To someone who has never done it, being emotionally involved in an imaginary situation and remaining conscious of several simultaneous levels of reality may seem impossible. But it isn't. I've done it, and seen it done, many times. Actually, when we are inspired, whether we achieve this consciously through practice or by accident through the gift of nature, we experience a complete involvement with our reality, however imaginary. We are more aware of the many levels of conscious and unconscious experience than at any other time. The magnified detail of thought and sense perception is abundant in artists, athletes, lovers, warriors, and religious adepts. When the goal is to live and be totally present in the moment, the reward is success.

In the normal sequence of my father's Method came exercises in Sharp Taste, Sharp Smell, Shower or Bath, Putting on Shoes and Stockings or Undergarments, and then Overall Sensations (heat, cold, fever, illnesses, rain, snow, lying in hay). I had a powerful reaction in one of the Overall Sensations I did; an exercise that was so powerful that my father said afterwards that it was an Emotional Memory for me. Emotional Memory Exercises were normally not done until the actor had studied for at least a year, because the actor had to have developed sufficient technique to be able to control his concentration in an exercise that would bring him into contact with old, and deep, emotional experiences that would be released during the Emotional (sometimes called Affective) Memory Exercise. I picked the smell of ether as an Overall Sensation, and had no idea that the Emotional Memory would occur. I vaguely remembered the ether from when we lived in California and I had my tonsils out.

When I practiced at home by myself, my senses were always vague; in class I could concentrate better and become more involved. There was always a dramatic change in this respect whenever I was onstage. After I had relaxed, I worked on the memory by creating an imaginary bottle that I could open and close, which helped me to be specific in my exploration. Soon the smell of ether began to overwhelm me; the cold, thick, sharp and sweet smelling vapors started to infiltrate my sinuses and flow up towards my brain. I began to feel nauseated, and that triggered an experience that I hadn't realized was connected to the ether. I imagined, or remembered, lying on a cold table with clean-smelling sheets, and being wheeled along a light green corridor. I heard the sound of the clicking wheels, like a small train passing by. We rolled through swinging doors and came to a stop. I looked up into a large lamp, seeing the thick gray-white glass that covered the front of it. A doctor, wearing a mask and large, dark-rimmed glasses, bent over me to turn on the light, which hurt my eyes and made me unable to see people clearly unless they bent down and put themselves between the light and me. He told me to relax, and not to be afraid, but I was afraid I was going to die. (The only other time I had been near a hospital was when my mother's father died. I loved him very much. He came from Vienna, smoked cigars, ate bonbons, and was a carpenter. I remember his eyes, which twinkled and smiled, and his hands. Both I and, surprisingly, my father bear a physical resemblance to him.)

As my memory continues, I turn my head, straining to move my nose away from the cotton or cloth that the doctor is holding over it; trying to avoid an alcoholic smell that rushes up my sinuses. In a voice that tries to be sweet, but is hard and authoritative, he tells me to hold still. He assures me that it won't hurt, that I am going to sleep for a while and that when I wake up everything will be over. The coldness of the ether is numbing my nose, and the bright alcoholic odor runs up through my nose and rushes into the top and back of my head in a wave so thick that I can feel it. My nose feels very cold. I try not to breathe, but the doctor forces the cotton over my nose, and I can't resist for very long. The smell makes me want to vomit. I fight not to lose consciousness and see three other persons in white, their faces covered, converging on me from all sides. Then everything starts to become vague, and I go black. The smell, however, remained completely present in my consciousness, and in the exercise I was recalling it. The doctor keeps telling me not to fight. I struggle in vain and after several unmeasurable moments of emotional time I can feel myself becoming still, my eyelids unable to resist closing, everything becoming soft-focused; I float, or fall, into what appears to be outer space. Even my nose felt cold, as it did originally. I opened my eyes, and continued to work on the smell, this time without the emotional difficulty I had had in the Sharp Pain exercise. It is one of the strongest sense memories I have, and one that I discovered early on; I often used it in my acting work. It is the connection to the event, which I did not remember until I did the exercise, that classifies it as an Emotional Memory.

I was finally assigned the Personal Object exercise. In the emotional state I was in at the time, I couldn't think of one. My father smiled his knowing smile and casually said that I would. He went on to explain that people who had difficulty remembering were often the most sensitive; they had so many powerful feelings in their memories that remembering them became too traumatic. It was a backhanded compliment, which I was very glad to receive. My parents always made me feel that a good actor had emotional problems: consciousness, rationality, and intelligence seemed like a kiss of death. I, therefore, equated talent with neurosis. My father would say that it bothered him when people didn't want to be

healthy because they were afraid they would lose their creative capacity;
what more might Beethoven have achieved had he been healthy? But both
my parents would say that if someone was talented enough it justified any
neurotic behavior, making it seem that neurosis was part of talent. My
mother wanted my father to see Nat Ackerman, a famous therapist in
New York in the 1950s, to solve some of their marital problems. He went
once, got furious, and refused to go again. My sister hated Ackerman, and
said that he had tried to seduce her when she went to him.

After unsuccessfully struggling with the personal object for a week or
so, I unearthed a vague memory of a pair of baseball spikes. Gifford Reid,
who was one of my first older brother figures, had given them to me when
I was about six. Our family had moved back to the East Coast, and we were
living in the caretaker's cottage on the Eitingon estate in Stamford,
Connecticut. Bess and Motte Eitingon had been benefactors of the Group
Theater, and we lived on the estate for a time in 1946 because my parents
were broke; we had made the cross country journey three times between
1941 and 1947. The estate covered several acres and had three houses, an
artificial lake, gardens, and some forest land. The small house we lived in
was attached to the barn. The kitchen door—a Dutch door—opened into
the barn, where I saw cows milked, and drank fresh, warm milk, for the first
time in my life. I had thought, until then, that milk was naturally cold.

Harold Clurman talks about the Eitingons in his book *The Fervent
Years*, which captures the passion and devotion that they all had for the
American theater. I never got really close to Harold when I was a child and
remember that he made infrequent visits to our house; I think that my father couldn't have friends who treated him as an equal artistically, as both
Harold and Elia Kazan did. The older I get, however, the more I love
Harold for his knowledgeable contribution to the American theater. To di-
gress for a second, my sharpest impression of him is a memory of accidentally running into him in Paris, his favorite city. He was wearing a large,
floppy-brimmed, black hat and a flowing cape, and was carrying a walking
stick. He was the quintessential artist, a man whose passion was so overwhelming that he could, with all the best intentions, scream at an actor,
"RELAX." Harold's love and knowledge were inspirational. He had been
married to Stella Adler, but neither received the recognition they deserved.

Harold shared Stella's incredible love for play analysis. He came to see
a play called *Slugger* that I co-produced with my second wife, Sabra Jones.
(We later created The Mirror Repertory Company.) We produced it a
second time with a young man starting out in the business, Rick

Nathanson. Sabra and I acted in both productions under the direction of Marshall Mason, whom I knew when I worked at the Circle Repertory Company in 1975. Harold's comment on the play went something like, "I'm not going to review it, because I haven't got enough good to say. The production and the acting are good, but basically, you've got a one act play. Take the wonderful scene at the end of the first act and start from there." That was a seduction scene between the wife of the protagonist, Slugger, and his best friend, a pitcher. Slugger has been sent down to the minor leagues in Midland, Texas, because of a drinking problem; the pitcher has a great fastball, but he's wild. Sabra played the wife, I played the friend, and Alan Feinstein played Slugger. Harold's "review" was an act of kindness and love, but Harold was a critic who loved the theater.

Harold's reviews and critiques made you think about what theater was. You learned something other than what he thought should be a hit. He didn't turn criticism into an exercise of power, as Frank Rich did during his years at *The New York Times*. Rich took more pleasure in closing plays than in improving the lot of theater. But Harold was a director, a theater man, and he defined for me the true roots of theater. A critic should know and love his subject and should criticize it with the aim of making it better.

Returning to my Personal Object, I remember having to stuff those baseball shoes with newspapers to keep from falling out of them. Giff made me feel he had given me some of the power and manliness that I admired in him. The shoes said that I, too, was strong, rather then the overly sensitive, nervous person that my parents were teaching me to be. I was in open conflict with my mother, who was impregnating me with her fear. She saw danger everywhere and thought that I would hurt myself climbing trees in the forest or swimming. A friend of the family, Polly Rose, the sister of the entrepreneur millionaire, Billy Rose, took me to the Beverly Hills Hotel where the lifeguard taught me how to swim. I can still smell and feel the suntan lotion he had on his back; a pungent mixture of iodine and Johnson's Baby Lotion. My parents never realized that they weren't teaching me to be careful, they were teaching me to mistrust myself.

I looked through my belongings, and was very surprised to discover the shoes buried in a dresser drawer; I had kept them for over twelve years. I studied them but felt nothing in particular, other than that they looked old and worn. I practiced my exercise at home to see if anything would happen, trying to react, but nothing did. (Very little ever happened to me when I rehearsed, so I thought that I would never become an actor.) On this occasion I felt desperate and panicky, fully expecting the exercise to be a failure. However, I was stuck; I could think of nothing else.

In class, I was more anxious and nervous than ever. I relaxed in the chair, as we always did in preparation, and then began. I imagined that I was holding one of the shoes in my right hand, re-creating its shape, weight, and texture. I tried to use the technique of concentrating on actualizing the imaginary realities that I was learning. I directed my senses towards the worn lines on the old leather, the dirt that I had noticed on the shoe bottoms, the particularity of the worn, metal cleats whose detailed wear I had tried to memorize. I did not do this just in my head, as do many actors who think that exploring sensation is a cerebral process. Sense Memory technique is not cerebral; it is sensual, using the body, the nervous system, and the soul. It trains the mind (what the Greeks called the psyche), one's intelligence, consciousness, heart and soul, to interact with the environment. It teaches that the details of observation and sensation pave the path to developing a consistent habit of recall. The process activates the nervous system, stimulates and recalls the memories, and brings them affectively into the present. Sense Memory can also be called Affective Memory.

I felt a kind of white light energy in the top and back of my head, and a blankness in my forehead. I began to sigh as I anxiously sensed the images growing dim in my mind's eye. I seemed to be losing concentration. I felt empty and worried that nothing was going to happen, an anticipation of failure I always experience just before I give in to whatever I am feeling. At that moment, I was hit with a sudden charge of emotion that felt like a powerful electric shock. My body began to tingle and stiffen; and the force nearly knocked me out of my chair. I began to sob uncontrollably in shock and surprise as the spontaneous organic process jolted my senses into doing the thinking for me.

I was stunned to discover the depth of my feeling for someone whom I didn't consciously remember loving so much. My chest began to heave as I began to breathe more deeply than I had in years. (Controlling emotions with shallow breathing is a common habit.) My head tingled and I was afraid that I was going to faint. Then I heard my father's voice. I opened my eyes, bringing me into contact with the other world, and looked out into the darkened theater. I saw him and the blurred faces of the students through the stage lights that form the frontier of an actor's world. I looked at my hand, still cupped as though I was holding the shoe, and I was again amazed by the sensation of knowing I was in several places at the same moment, a sensation common to the world of emotional time. I perceived this consciously even as I continued to hold this imaginary personal object that had suddenly become totally real. At my father's command, I suspended my belief for a moment, showing me that I was directly in control of my feelings. After a minute or so, I began to explore anew the object that was, and was not, really there: the emotion again poured out effortlessly.

Since then, I have never questioned the principle of Sense Memory exercises, or their validity as part of an actor's technique. Human beings do have the capacity to create imaginary reality by transforming and altering real life experience. I don't see how anyone who has practiced these exercises properly could ignore or deny this fundamental truth. I can only conclude that most human beings don't like to be conscious of the forces in their lives: the profound simplicity and directness of reality is just too terrifying.

My father and I never talked about personal feelings, either at work or in private. It was not uncomfortable to be impersonal at work, and when I began studying we had more contact than ever before. Did he wonder why Giff's shoe was such a powerful memory for me? I didn't. I had lost my curiosity about why I felt a certain way. What I knew of the world was only expressed personally when I worked; I cut myself off from my painful feelings in real life. So the curtain came down between my father and myself. We slipped back into our daily selves, hiding away the human parts at the remote borders of consciousness. This deep, human reality is part of the unexplored or forgotten territory not found on most conscious maps that guide people through existence. It is the world of mystery, the world where religions relieve our fear and anxiety of the unknown, the world where science and art search and discover. It is identified by the artist as part of his talent and imagination, and it is the basis of what I call the artist's personal dream space. The dream space is what I call our capacity to create an internal area where realities that we are studying can be isolated, in order to be concentrated on, imagined, explored, developed, and transformed. It is how we discover and create. Many discoveries and developments of our art, science, and philosophy is first developed in the dream space.

Man, Beast, and Virtue by Luigi Pirandello
directed by John Strasberg at Centre Dramatic de Valencia 1988

CHAPTER TWO

DEATH, RELAXATION, AND A PREPARATION FOR THE SONG AND DANCE OF LIFE

Do the boundaries in the cartography of life we are taught to believe in actually exist? Or are they temporary illusions that explain what we don't know so that we don't have to think about things that frighten us? We compartmentalize our lives depending on which illusions make us feel most comfortable. What my father feared and ran from in life was what he devoted his lifetime of instruction to: helping people to channel emotion into their work. He was a better father as a teacher. I still wonder if I didn't choose to become an actor because it was the only way in which I could receive his, and my mother's, love and approval. I went into the theater in order to belong to my family.

Our paradigms of reality are slow to change, as the reactions to the discoveries of Galileo, Copernicus, and William Harvey (discoverer of the circulation of the blood) attest. There are few natural thinkers. Most people's thoughts are not expressions of what they really sense and perceive about life; rather they are intellectualized concepts without empirical knowledge; they are based on nothing.

During a rehearsal one day, Geraldine Page looked at me in the way that she did when she didn't know what the hell I was talking about, and asked me, "What do you mean, organic life? What's the difference?" It's very simple: inorganic life has a battery or a cord. You have to plug it in. Organic life doesn't have to be plugged in. It has its own cosmic energy source. And when something is dead, you can tell. It stops moving. It's not plugged in anymore. Some people seem to be plugged in, but they're not connected to anything.

Organic, functional thought is always revolutionary. One of its qualities is that it perceives the fundamental property of life as being movement and change. The truth we discover today will reveal another, deeper perception of life to our consciousness tomorrow. Our inherent, inborn thoughts, because they are a direct expression of what we sense life to be, are not afraid to know that there may be no end to this process; it knows that life moves in a spiral, not a circle.

The man walked onto the stage and, bending over slightly, he reached down and picked up the entire hillside. I was seven or eight at the time and was stunned by his strength. I squealed and ran up to him. He smiled, and asked me if I wanted to help. I nodded my head with amazement. He pointed to another hill, told me to pick it up and follow him. I said that I wasn't strong enough. He laughed, turned his hill upside down, and showed me that it was made out of papier-mâché and wood. The shock I felt still resonates in my memory.

It dissolved my belief that everything was real. Three years earlier, in 1946, when my parents left Susan and me with our Aunt Bea in California, another reality had been shattered. Coming after they had promised they would never leave us again, that breach left a permanent scar. It was the decisive moment in which my character was formed. I finally believed, once and forever, that my parents didn't really love me. My life's strategy became to find a way to behave so that I would get them to love me in the way that I wanted to be loved. I became eager to please everyone except myself. I had no value in and for myself. I needed validation from elsewhere, and needed permission to live.

In the final analysis, my parents were lying to themselves about how they felt. They probably felt as badly as we did, but they accomplished exactly the opposite of what they wanted by thoughtlessly teaching their habits to me. My father's own father was very severe, an orthodox Jew from Galicia, in what is now Poland. My father was an immigrant who came to this country without being able to speak a word of English. His obsessive rationalism led him to mock any efforts to explore what was beyond the world of his accepted perceptions. My anxiety to please and take responsibility for everyone made me feel that I had to ignore myself. It's no surprise that I was so angry for so many years, feeling constrained by this "reality."

If my mother had lived out her true nature, she would have been a feminist or a hippie; she was born out of her time. It made me so angry that she wouldn't live her own life. I was fighting against the feelings of submission and cowardice which she passed on to me and Susan. I felt oddly liberated when she died. Any change in my life was accompanied by the knowledge that something had to die so that I could live more truly as myself. The natural pain and guilt is beautifully explained in Reich's *The Murder of Christ* and Alice Miller's *The Drama of the Gifted Child*.

I was about two when I began to ignore my own feelings, and consciously lied for the first time, to hide what my parents didn't love. It is what most people do in order to be loved. Their needs became more important than mine. It made life between us easier. If I confronted them, I was punished for wanting to know what the truth was. They just shut me off, or shut me out. I began to depress myself because I didn't want to feel the pain of being abandoned. While things were easier on the surface, my parents lost my trust and confidence. I also lost, because I began to mistrust myself.

DEATH

Susan had been living and working in California for several years after leaving New York in 1964. She installed herself in Los Angeles with the same doubts that every actor I know has when they go West. New York and California are almost three thousand miles apart, but that seems a much shorter distance than the one between many actors' desires to work in both theater and film. This ongoing split is the real disease of the American actor's art. Some of us look longingly to London, where actors can work more easily in both. London is what New York used to be; it was always where they returned to nourish and improve their hearts and souls. If theater ever dies, it will be because theater artists think they don't need it anymore.

Susan was sharing her life with Christopher Jones, an actor unknown at the time. He had seen her on television, fallen in love with her, and proceeded to pursue her all over the world. Her career was going full steam; it didn't shut down until she deferred her needs for those of the man that she loved, as she had been raised to do. Christopher was as jealous and selfish as our father. He was charismatic and agreed with those who thought he was the next James Dean. What positive qualities he had, among them a kind of intuitive sensuality that is very attractive, did not in the long run, make up for his selfish and manipulative manner. She fought with Christopher constantly during their passionate relationship, and at times even came to my father for help. Those were the only times I saw him try to be a father. He supported her when she went to Europe in 1960 and promised that my mother wouldn't interfere. Susan went to Rome in order to make *Kapo*, a film in which she was fantastic. The film was nominated for an Academy Award for Best Foreign Film in 1960. It was directed by Gillo Pontecorvo, and co-starred Susan and Laurent Terzieff. She played a young Jewish girl who goes to a concentration camp and becomes a Kapo or camp commandant. She falls in love with a Russian soldier (Terzieff) and eventually dies in order to free him. When I saw the film in a private screening, I, who was proud of hiding my feelings, burst into almost uncontrollable tears. The film was so real to me it was as if I was seeing Susan die.

Her relationship with Chris was volatile, to say the least, and involved physical abuse and drugs. On another of the occasions on which Susan enlisted my father's help, she had come to the house in tears with tales of Christopher beating her. She wanted to leave him, but was afraid of what he might do. My father arranged to have Christopher come to the Morosco theater, where we were rehearsing the Actors Studio Theater production of *The Three Sisters*. Everyone was afraid of Christopher's temper and violence, so Marty Fried (a student of my father's, family friend, and Production Stage Manager of the play) and I hid in the wings in case he attacked my father. They had a screaming argument during which my father called him a son of a bitch and threatened to have him put in jail. Christopher maintained that he loved Susan, that he was sorry that he'd hit her, but that it was none of my father's business. My father tried everything he could to make Christopher stay away from Susan.

Susan had such tremendous and early success. While I was going through my nervous breakdown, she had already created the role of Anne Frank, been in several films including *Picnic*, and was co-starring on Broadway in *Time Remembered* with Helen Hayes and Richard Burton. Despite her apparent success, she suffered at heart from the family habit of suppressing her needs to those of whomever she loved. Everyone in our family did, except for my father. Despite everyone's help and her own real feelings, she went back to live with Christopher. They were married in Las Vegas in 1965.

My mother's illness didn't make an impression on me, nor did the fact that she was bedridden. I was too accustomed to sitting in the rocking chair that lived beside her bed while she complained, in need of my love and attention. I had been doing this since I was eight. I had sworn off crying at nine, and aside from my reaction when I saw Susan work in *The Diary of Anne Frank* and *Kapo*, I didn't start crying again until I studied acting: I would lock myself in the bathroom and practice. I cried when I listened to some classical music behind closed doors: *La Boheme, La Traviata, Madame Butterfly, Swan Lake,* Bach.

My mother's illness didn't make me cry. Her bedroom substituted for her office; she telephoned, received visits, and did business from bed. The only difference now was that she was in bed more, rather than just lying on it. She just seemed to be more comfortable lying down. She had a weight problem, which she sometimes complained was the result of my birth (thanks, Mom). She complained all her life that her feet hurt, blaming this on the bad shoes that her mother had bought her. She was constantly searching for comfortable shoes. Bally slippers were her favorites. Of course, Pisces rules the feet, and I'm sure that a lot of psychiatrists would have a lot to say about a complaint that one's feet hurt. She had many pairs in her closet, as they wore out quickly.

Mother lived in the bedroom, and my father lived in his study, reading and listening to music. We ate together, though we didn't talk a hell of a lot. We even read at the table, when there were no guests. My parents slept together, meaning in the same bed, but they had no intimate relations after my birth. I didn't take the blame for that one.

When I knew that she had cancer it was hard for me to react; I couldn't be sure of what was real or what she really felt. The doctors had originally told her that nothing was wrong, but now that she was proven to have been right she seemed almost pleased. I felt as confused and angry as I had for all those years when I sat in that chair, squirming with discomfort. I felt I had to do something, but I didn't know what. All my talk and encouragement changed nothing. My life was being eaten up by her needs, and one day I screamed at her to do something about what she dreamed of doing instead of just lying there and complaining. But she never really wanted to change. Certainly she was much loved by the many people whose careers and lives she influenced. Maybe she was afraid to live for herself. I will never know. The anger that covered the sorrow dissolves in the old tears that I once swallowed, but have now allowed to flow out. It has made me sad, but not sadder, and certainly wiser.

At any rate, I wanted to leave, whether by car or by plane. California and Susan's pregnancy in 1966 gave me the opportunity; I wanted to go, neither for Susan nor my mother, but for myself. I felt as though I was waiting for a wave to sweep me into living my own life. I was, at the time, involved in the first serious love relationship of my adult life. I lived part-time in another house with Shirley, a divorcée several years my senior. Shirley had two children and didn't want her ex-husband to know that we were together because she was afraid she'd lose the alimony. The first time we made love was in her ex-husband's apartment. It was the first time I really experienced pleasure in lovemaking rather than just worrying about premature ejaculation or whether I would be good enough. What I remember about his East 66th Street apartment are the fur rugs scattered across the parquet floors that always had some loose pieces. His two Persian cats had been de-clawed so that they wouldn't ruin the plush furniture.

Our relationship lasted for over two years. She finally began to promise that after we were married she would do unimaginable sexual things with me. She was fond of telling me about the men with whom she had had relationships, such as Frank Sinatra. This didn't really excite me to new heights of desire or commitment as I suffered unspoken thoughts of comparison. I was in a constant state of emotional flux. This concern about pleasing the other and serving them before I could take care of my own needs dominated all of my love relationships up until the last ten years. When I had fleeting relationships or increasingly frequent sexual encounters I would feel extremely free, but incapable of commitment. As a matter of fact, the only women to whom I wanted to commit to were ones who weren't interested in me.

I loved Shirley as much as I was capable of loving, considering that I was someone who couldn't express feelings of love for himself. I thought I was being bribed. I could not endure the mental torture of these other men in my head. I would hide under the covers in the morning when her daughters woke up, so that they wouldn't know I was there. I would even get up, get dressed, and sneak out to ring the doorbell as though I was just arriving, in order to play the charade to the end.

Susan's daughter, Jennifer Robin, has the same hair and skin color as my mother. She was born on March 14, a Pisces like my mother, though mother celebrated her birthday on Valentine's Day.

Mother bought herself a wedding ring on my parents' twenty-fifth anniversary, saying that my father had promised to buy her a real ring when they had the money. Broken promises to loved ones were accepted as normal. Nothing personal. As the surrogate man in my mother's life, I went with her to Le Vieille Russe on Fifth Avenue and 59th Street. I went on many expeditions with my mother: Serendipity, Hammacher Schlemmer for the gadgets, T. Anthony for the red wallets, Mark Cross for the red luggage, the brand new Haagen-Daas, as though a quart of her favorite coffee or strawberry ice cream at midnight would ease the pain.

My father was never so adventurous. He took vitamin drops with an eye dropper every morning and was very careful about his weight. I swallow up to fifteen pills at a time, just to prove to myself that I'm not like him. My parents only went out together to the theater. I would go to book and record shops with him, or to the occasional Giants baseball game. We sat behind home plate with my cousin Sy the first time Willie Mays played in the Polo Grounds. He hit a towering home run over the left field roof, clear out of the triple-tiered stadium.

My father was passionate in his creation of one of the great private theater libraries in the world. He tried to read books that he couldn't understand, and found students who could read and translate Russian, Japanese, Chinese, and French for him. He could read and speak German himself. He was known to book stores and collectors all over the world. Books arrived almost every day, some of which he had been searching for for years. He loved his books and what he learned from them.

My mother's ring had a hundred small diamond chips in a beautiful platinum setting. It was a classic example of Victorian jewelry, and it was the only thing of hers that I wanted when she died. I left it in keeping with a friend in L.A. when I came back to New York in 1969. I never saw it again. Moving, as someone said, is like having your house burn down: It strips you to the essentials. I'd like to have the ring, but I love her without it. I can still feel her in me, and she still appears to me from time to time to tell me that she loves me, or that she is sorry, or to give me a little advice.

A month after Jennifer was born, Susan and I were phoned by the family business manager, David Cogan, who urged us to come to New York immediately. Mother was dying and refused to go to the hospital. My Aunt Bea had arrived to be with her. I had disliked Bea from the time my parents had left us in California to live with her, my Uncle Mickey, and their children Annie and Richard. On the day we moved in, Bea wanted to give me an enema, not because I was ill, but because she thought it was a good thing to do. When I refused, Bea gave an enema to Annie, who was younger than I was, just to show me that it wasn't painful. I submitted, but I am still sorry that I did. I could not have resisted because I was too little, and I knew that Uncle Mickey used to hit Richard with a belt. It was not like home.

Pop got on the phone and said that it wasn't really urgent, but Susan and I believed Cogan. We took the overnight flight to New York and arrived at the house at about 7:30 in the morning. My mother was on intravenous feeding and was dehydrating rapidly. She kept pulling out the needle that was indifferently interfering with her desire to die. Mother was in a stupor. She seemed to recognize Susan, but when she got to me her eyes wandered. They were the blind, drugged eyes of ecstatics, the tortured, the dying; a milky-blue glass. Her skin was gray and hung off her face as though there were no longer any bones inside. She was an almost empty sack of life, like Michelangelo's corpse on the ceiling of the Sistine Chapel.

I sat in the rocking chair next to her bed as I had for so many years. She couldn't sleep, but she was not fully conscious either. She was being kept alive, seemingly against her wishes, by husbands, doctors, family, and friends. She would neither eat nor drink. Delos Smith, a friend who acted as a family biographer, kept a detailed diary of my father's classes, ever since Susan and mother had met him in Hutchinson, Kansas, during the filming of *Picnic*. He said my mother had told him she wanted to die in her own bed. My father couldn't believe that she was dying. He seemed like a frightened little boy.

I sent everyone out of the room and closed the door. There is no tense or direction to describe the emotional time for realities like my love for her, no matter how much she confused me, used me, and lied to me. I sat watching the patient toss and turn in the hospital bed that occupied what had been my parents' bedroom until Susan and I had left home. They had then moved to the suite of rooms in the middle of the apartment that were quieter and more private. My heart began to pound, and the room seemed to be full of an excited, grayish energy. I wished that she had recognized me. She writhed in pain, as though she was being tortured alive, trapped in the body that she had hated ever since I was born. She was once a young and beautiful actress, but her body had fallen apart. She had never done anything other than repeatedly gain and lose the same thirty or forty pounds as she tried every new diet ever invented. I felt pulled towards her.

My eyes became channels that poured energy from me to her. The experience was different from any I had previously encountered and it was easy to think that I was imagining something that was not real.

Without speaking or touching, I projected my energy out to her, enveloping her, as I wordlessly told her that everything was all right; I was there and she could rest now. After several minutes, the atmosphere in the room began to change. The dull gray air calmed, and bluish-white particles sparkled and moved fluidly over her. I was alternately calm and excited; there was the same anxiety in my breathing which preceded an asthma attack. I was not a serious asthmatic, but I could, and do, have difficulty breathing on occasion. I felt as though I were inside a thick cloud, seeing the air move the way a child sees the world behind his eyelids, until he is told that what he is seeing is only his imagination. The room became calm, still, and clear, as the air is after a storm. Mother was asleep, and everything was peaceful. I began to sweat from the enormous concentration of force that I was using.

At this moment, Aunt Bea entered the room, disturbing the calm atmosphere. I looked into her eyes, which were fixed on her sister with a curious glow. I do not know if she enjoyed the feeling of being needed by the sister who had often ignored her, if she felt the same reality that I did, or was excited by the sense of imminent death. I sent a wave of energy towards her which backed her out of the room. This all took place wordlessly. I continued to sit perfectly still, feeling my heart pounding, as mother slept calmly for half an hour.

The arrival of the ambulance to take her to the hospital broke the spell. She died at midnight, on the same day, the 29th of April, calling out for her "Mama." In the nightmares that she had throughout her life she would call out for "Mama." My father would shrug them off and when I met him in the hallway he would say, "It's nothing. She has dreams. It's nothing. Go back to sleep." He was always afraid of whatever he could not logically explain or control. My father, by her side until the end, could only report that she kept mistaking him for her mother. He held her hand, fighting against her desire to pull out the intravenous needle, putting it back whenever she succeeded in removing her last connection to this world. Her autopsy, performed at the insistence of Dr. Finger, revealed that the cancer had spread to the very marrow of her bones.

Mother's gift to me throughout her life was a different perspective. My father dismissed her belief in tarot cars, astrology, and psychiatry. He respected Freud, but any other part of my mother's emotional life that led her to define the world as she saw it was roundly mocked as mystical. I adopted his tone with her, which is probably why she didn't share more of her beliefs with me. She would just nod her head sadly, eyes downcast, and say, "You'll see. You'll see that I'm right. Someday, you'll be sorry. Someday, you'll all be sorry." The only time my father acknowledged the possibility of some other reality was in his momentary reflections on Einstein's thoughts about God and the Universe. He would also casually speculate that if he had to choose a religion he would be a Buddhist, because they accepted all creeds.

The conflict between my parents, their legacy of differing perceptions and beliefs, created an inner pressure that I had to learn to alleviate; I was afraid I would self-destruct. I practiced yoga, vegetarianism, martial arts, and meditation, and underwent therapy. I fought within myself my parents' silent battle about what life is and how to live it. My mother fed lamb to my father for years. She said that he hated the taste and smell of it, but she simply told him it was roast beef and he ate it. He may have known a lot, but she had more common sense. They seemed to be diametrically opposed. He lived by a Cartesian map measured in Newtonian time, and she saw the world as an unbelieving dreamer. I wonder what their life was like as they lay, alone together, in the bed they shared without intimacy. My mother tantalized me with her world, promising to read my cards, but never did so. I can't say that I'd have believed her anyway, because I agreed with my father about that sort of thing, until I discovered that my dreams were real. Death brought their worlds together. Death is indifferent to what we believe.

After mother's death I acted as the head of the family; my father was always treated like a person in need of care. I made the decisions about funeral arrangements, one of which was that her coffin would be closed. I said that if people loved her they would remember how she looked in life. I had expected to feel sad, but was shocked to find I was in a rage. The first funeral I had attended was my father's father, and I remember feeling frightened and seeing a lot of people crying and wailing. This sight made me laugh and I remember trying to stop myself by covering my mouth. My parents and Uncle Arthur looked straight ahead, their eyes glazed over. I couldn't tell what they were feeling, or what I was supposed to feel.

I didn't know my grandfather very well. He had never come to our house because it wasn't kosher. He arrived in the United States when he was almost sixty, and never learned to speak English because he didn't think he'd live long enough to make the effort worthwhile; he lived to be over ninety. The only time he regretted not speaking it was after Susan and I were born because we never learned to speak Yiddish and so he couldn't talk to us. We only saw him when we went to celebrate Passover at my Aunt Becky's home in the Bronx. Aunt Becky was a doll, not at all like my mother's sister, and my Uncle Arthur had the bluest eyes and the most simple loving soul of anyone I've ever met. My grandfather seemed severe, and my cousins were always saying that he was. He obviously disapproved of my father, which must have been very difficult for my father to deal with. My father never spoke to me about himself as a person, the way Franchot did on those evenings we tied fishing lines together, on the porch in Canada.

I was surprised to feel anger at the death of a loved one. I hope that when I die, I will have lived fully enough that death seems like part of life. I intend to say good-bye to those that I love, if they are still on the planet. The strangest thing I felt when my parents died was that I could love them as I had always wanted to: for who they were, their real knowledge, what they loved, their humanity, their pain, their truth—all the things they hid away in private, or saved for work, or felt they wouldn't or couldn't share with me, suddenly became available by their deaths. I could love what had been denied me when they were alive. I find this terribly sad and a horrible waste of life.

Mother's funeral, held at the Westside Funeral Parlor on Amsterdam Avenue and 76th Street, was attended by a large crowd. My mother was loved by many people whose lives had been affected by her generosity. Of the herds of people who came to say good-bye, famous and unknown, I spoke only to Sandy Hacker, the head electrician from the Actors' Studio Theater, and to Marta Curro and Jerry Orbach. "Where were they all when she needed them?" and "Hypocrites" is all I said. Why hadn't they helped her, as she had helped so many of them when she was alive? Most of those who cried, cried for themselves: they had only been using her. I had the same thought when Marilyn died. People confuse love with needing and being needed, using and being used. Most people form bonds because they are incapable of being alone.

I sat across the aisle from Susan and my father. I don't know why; we just did it that way. They sat, tight-lipped, masked, clutching each other. They seemed frozen. I had never noticed how much they looked alike. The look in their eyes and the way they clamped down the emotion in their lips was so close to identical it was hard to believe. Shelley Winters delivered a eulogy followed by a plea for money for the Actors Studio in the memory of Paula Miller, the actress, and what she fought for and cared about. I wanted to scream that a funeral is not a fund-raiser. We drove in silence to the cemetery in Ardsley, NY, up the same Saw Mill River Parkway I had driven so many times. Susan and my father had the same glazed look, staring straight ahead, as though if their eyes moved they would feel something that terrified them.

At the cemetery the rabbi spoke briefly. Before they filled the grave, I placed a bouquet of gardenias on the coffin because gardenia was Mother's favorite perfume. I wanted to hurl myself into the grave. The rabbi announced that we were finished and everyone drifted back to the waiting limousines. I was relieved because I needed to be alone to grieve in private. I felt watched by the others and by myself. I was splitting off from the powerful feelings. The rabbi took me by the arm, but I pulled away. "I'm not through," I said. "But we have to wait for you." "I don't care. I'll leave when I'm ready. I'll find my way back." "Everybody," he called, "wait one moment." Damn him. Everyone stopped, and came back. Why don't people know that there are times when we want to be alone? The workman stopped shoveling earth into the grave where her body lay. I asked for one of the gardenias that I had placed on the coffin to make her feel more at home. I reached down, picked up some earth in my hand and scattered it over the cold, newly varnished wood that would conserve—what? Our memory of her? She was no longer there. "To make it personal for you," I said. Gardenias smell wonderful, but they don't live very long in most parts of the world. I would only have, and bury, one mother in my lifetime. One is enough. Susan asked for a flower, then Aunt Bea, and then someone else. I wasn't paying attention; I was ready to leave then. I had said my good-byes, forever, so I thought.

As we walked down the sloping grass hill to the gravel roadway filled with cars, the rabbi walked beside me. He asked me why I had thrown dirt onto the coffin. "I felt like it. I wanted her to feel that it was personal." "Do you know that is a tradition?" he said. "No." "Yes. In the Jewish religion, each member of the family puts a shovel full of earth onto the coffin." The most pleasurable way to discover traditions is by intuition. "Why didn't you have us stay to do that? Why did you ask everyone to leave before they buried her?" I asked him. "It's upsetting for most people to see." "Not to me. It makes it real." "For most people." "Not for me. Why did you ask the others to stay?" "I didn't want you to be left alone." "I wanted to be alone." I am one of those people, I eventually discovered, who likes and needs solitude. I learned to understand the difference between feeling lonely and being alone.

When we got back to the house I was desperate to escape from the people who hugged me and sobbed about how awful they felt and how sad it was. I needed to be left alone with my own feelings. "Tomorrow," I thought, "they will go about their lives as they always have." It is hard for me, even today, to feel how much I loved my mother. It no longer matters how much I believe that she emotionally abandoned me and used me for what she needed.

I went into the quiet of my parents' bedroom. After a few minutes, Susan, Bea, and I don't know who else, came in and began to go through her jewelry. It felt like my mother was being looted. I claimed her wedding ring before everything was gone. I had murderous thoughts, like the ones I had when I was a child. My feelings of being abandoned led to repetitive dreams in which my parents died in an airplane crash, and I, who felt like an orphan, actually became one. Sometimes Susan lived, and sometimes she died, too.

Someone asked me if I could open my mother's red Mark Cross vanity case; she had loved it as much for the color as for the quality. "It's great for traveling. You can spot it in the airport right away," she would say. It was locked to them, but without any resistance it opened for me. Looking inside, I was surprised to discover a .38 caliber snubnose Colt Cobra revolver and two boxes of ammunition. I felt as though she had been reading my mind. I lifted it out, and said, "There's no jewelry in here." I asked my father why she wanted a gun, but he only shrugged and said that he didn't know. The discovery of this secret world of hers was startling enough that I pursued the question until he finally answered that she was afraid that someone would try to kill her. "Who?" "Someone. She had strange fears." Susan said that Mother had once told her that she was afraid her first husband would come after her, but that kind of undeveloped revelation was as far as personal conversations ever went with either of our parents.

Song and Dance

The juxtaposition of this avoidance of personal contact with the precision in the Method my father developed is exemplified by two exercises he invented that were designed to help the actor make contact with and express the hidden part of himself. The exercises are called the Private Moment and the Song and Dance. In the Private Moment the actor demonstrates a repeated behavior that would change if anyone was watching. The Private Moment must always happen in a particular place, so the actor would bring real objects that helped to create the surroundings in which the activity took place. Some people confuse being alone with being private, but that isn't necessarily true. They might think that brushing their teeth or going to the bathroom is a private moment. However, it is the quality and depth of inner life that qualifies one's behavior as being truly private. Some people may have a private moment when they are in the middle of a crowd, simply because it is there that they feel sufficiently safe and anonymous to allow themselves to be truly personal and intimate in their own thoughts and feelings. One of my Private Moments was listening to music. Sometimes, when listening to *Swan Lake*, I would dance. Feelings of longing, sadness, and love poured out of me in the dark. I would neither dance nor listen when I was with other people.

Another Private Moment for me is how I look at myself in the mirror. I have always wanted my body to look different than it does. I would only see the things in myself that I disliked. I wanted to have straight hair that I could flip back over my head when it was wet, the way some guys did when they got out of the pool; I wanted a slim waist and great muscular definition, not muscles that flopped when I jumped up and down. This didn't change until I saw Mohammed Ali box. I loved to watch the beauty of his naturally powerful body, which had none of the manufactured look of most fighters. My body image is still changing. Therapy filled out a body that I had depressed into being small, expanding my weight from 158 to 175 pounds. It's gone out of proportion lately; I'll get it back when I can feel how I really want it to be.

I think it's safe to say that most human beings have real thoughts and feelings that are extremely private; most of us are different from our public personas, even to people that are the closest to us. What about being exactly who we are? My father never had me do this exercise in class, because he said my work was already deep and personal enough. I think he meant it. He has described how he developed this exercise in his book, *A Dream of Passion*. It was published several years after his death though it was a book he never finished. He worked on it for years, trying to put down perfectly everything that he believed he knew. It was an impossible task. The book is interesting, voluminously edited, and is a shell of the man whose entire life was a private moment.

My father invented the Song and Dance exercise while working with opera singers. They had come to him in the hopes that he could teach them to be better actors and more expressive when they sang. He tried to create a form which would change the singer's habits of rigidity and non-movement, which are considered necessary and correct. The habits of formal training gave them beautiful voices, but they didn't function well if they moved or experienced real feeling. (Feeling is an Old English word, and means "to touch, to be aware.") The spontaneous flow of natural life threatened the vocal techniques that regulated their movement and expression. Control is either based on the capacity to hold back or the capacity to give in. Organic technique has the capacity to consciously direct an impulse into a particular area of expression, while remaining in contact with all the levels of reality that are involved in the creative process. The impulse is specifically directed rather than expressed indirectly in superficial intellectualized thought or impulsive emotional bursts that are not part of a form.

The Song and Dance exercise terrified everyone because its goal was to remove the habits of control that stopped you from expressing how you felt. You were put on the spot in front of everyone, and you felt naked and vulnerable. In the Song part, you stood facing the class, arms hanging loosely at the sides, feet set naturally apart, and adopted a neutral, receptive position, with no tension, anticipation, or defensiveness in the physical attitude. Only small children and animals do this naturally. Watch a child walk into a room full of strangers; its gaze is so direct that it is difficult for most adults not to become extremely uncomfortable.

We were told to make eye contact with the class members, not with the ceiling, floor, walls, chairbacks, the space in between people, or people's foreheads. Body parts were OK, because that generally caused a reaction. My father would often pick up your arm and let it drop to see if there was any tension in the body. As we were relaxing and working on being present, we would sing a song, separating the words into syllables, like HA-PPY-BIRTH-DAY, vibrating each syllable for an entire breath, centering the voice in the chest, and singing on pitch. Sometimes he patted our backs, like burping a baby, to help us center ourselves. We weren't actually singing a song; the exercise trained us to be present and to change our habits of behavior at will. We could do this without forgetting the words and singing on key. If we had emotional impulses, we were supposed to allow that emotion to express itself in the sound. It often felt like torture! Our labyrinths of habits to hide thoughts and feelings were under attack. People would shift weight onto one leg, or the fingers would twitch, or faces and eyes would go dead; we would try any way possible to hide, or to let the emotion express itself through some form of screened behavior. It was often very difficult to discover and eliminate these habits of indirect expression.

I remember one actor (we'll call him Ray) who had a great deal of repressed anger; he was a human pressure cooker. His habitual defenses were so clever that my father could not discover where the emotion was locked in his body. Ray scared us as we all waited for him to explode. The repression of his feelings made his anger appear dangerous. He couldn't get work because of this problem. The emotion never came out until one day when he was in his stocking feet. Ray began the exercise, building up his habitual compressed head of steam; he had always seemed relaxed, however, whenever my father checked his body. On this day, we noticed that his toes were curled. When asked to relax them, he couldn't without the emotion bursting forth almost uncontrollably. His eyes bulged out of their sockets, his voice was strangled somewhere between a scream and a growl, and his face flushed red. As a result of this discovery he began to change the habitual tension that blocked his expression. He began to make great strides in his work; pun intended. His ability to let go in his toes and express this repressed emotion made him truly relax; his work became freer and more interesting. Within several months, Ray had started to work more steadily as an actor, and was much less combative. This sense of terror and holding back was present in almost everyone; a sense that one was forbidden to let go.

In the Dance part, we were told to allow the body to establish a movement. We weren't supposed to think about what we were doing, only to let our bodies do the thinking. Once we were conscious of the movement we were supposed to repeat it so that it became rhythmic. We were then to sing the song, exploding each word, syllable by syllable, from the chest and on key. Melody was less important. My father would periodically say, "Change." We were supposed to change the movement spontaneously, without stopping to plan or think. It rarely happened like that; everyone tried to exert some control. Strangely, the people who had the most problems in this part of the exercise were professional dancers, whose bodies rarely moved spontaneously. Their technical training and rigid discipline inhibited natural expression.

Song and Dance is intended to aid the teacher and student to identify habits that repress impulse and expression, and develop habits that will allow one to consciously come out of hiding. I think it is my father's equivalent of Meisner's Mirror exercise. Examining it also gives some insight into the manner in which my father always needed to establish mental control over his emotions. He needed to feel safe in order to express emotion. It was difficult to remember all the things one had to do and not to do while responding spontaneously. I did the exercise correctly, as I did most of my work, since I am basically very conscientious, disciplined, and thorough. Consciously, I would rarely let go; my emotions were either expressed explosively or intuitively. It was only in Sense Memory and in my scene work that they were expressed honestly. I think that's because I felt freer living another life. When it was just me I was always too concerned with trying to do things the right way. That was part of my defense against open and direct contact and expression.

In Song and Dance, I never made eye contact with my father for very long, for fear of what I might feel and express. I would look just long enough to prove to myself that I wasn't a coward. When our eyes met, he hid behind the tight, slight smile that he often wore. I shared both his defenses against natural, spontaneous feeling and his belief that greatness meant always being perfectly in control. This habit of caution and control needed to be challenged and changed. My father had to help by achieving a level of personal contact that he didn't or couldn't make, particularly with me.

I know now that he was probably more afraid than I was. Sometimes, my anger would begin to surge and he would encourage me, but it never really discharged spontaneously; all the things we had to remember restricted us. Control was an essential part of the exercise. There is a moment in natural expression when one doesn't know what one is going to do: if one stops to think, the impulse is lost. A boxer cannot see a punch or an opening and stop to think about what he is going to do. The complicated instructions for the exercise didn't help to achieve this spontaneity. Either my father did not sufficiently understand how habits of character could be eliminated without so many mental controls, or he was trapped by his fear of spontaneous expression. I believed he didn't really want anyone to express unpremeditated feeling. Real contact, for him, had to be made in a controllable manner; it was impersonal, or otherwise forced upon him by some impulsive, emotional outburst. I learned my habits of holding back from him.

In spite of its complexity, the contact demanded by the exercise caused extensive changes in habits of presence and expression. Intelligent, conscientious, and truthful actors, like Dustin Hoffman, for instance, extol the benefits of the exercise; in the same way that many of Sandy's pupils do the Mirror exercise. Overall, I think that the Mirror exercise is simpler and goes deeper into developing the actors presence and contact without labyrinthine instructions. In spite of that, the second part of my father's exercise was particularly helpful to me because I could let myself go without the mental constraints or the problem of direct eye contact. Physical work has always been therapeutic to me: I love sports, and have studied dance, martial arts, and acrobatics. Martial arts, in particular, relieves the pressure that depression, lack of contact, and holding back aggression causes and directs it into positive and pleasurable channels which relax and calm me.

In musical theater, everybody works hard; dancers, like athletes, are always working hurt (the late Mickey Mantle being an extreme example, though I've rarely known a dancer who wasn't hurting somewhere). The American theater's long musical tradition has contributed enormously to the physicality of American acting. Most American actors, whether or not they are considering working in musicals, study singing and dance. One of the observable realities of a healthy theater is that actors work in several arenas at the same time: theater, film, television, musicals, comedy, tragedy. The forms are different but not separate. Theater traditions which impose barriers between these realms generally become more stilted and intellectualized. Fencing and other disciplines, such as acrobatics and Tai Chi Chuan, are all disciplines I have studied.

My lifelong interest in Tai Chi began when my father and I realized that the Chinese actors of the Peking Opera whom we saw in Montreal in 1959 possessed an extraordinary quality of relaxation and concentration. Kazan had called the house and asked my father if he wanted to go up to Montreal to see the Peking Opera, which was banished from the United States in those days, as we were staunch supporters of the Formosan government. Together with Sol Colin and me, the four of us flew up there in an almost empty Elektra prop jet. What we saw was mind-blowing. The entire troupe stood around on the brightly lit stage as though they were there to watch someone else perform, until suddenly, with unanticipated and effortless grace, agility, spontaneity, relaxation, and centering, they would leap into the air, or tumble, or swordfight, or row an imaginary boat across an imaginary lake with such a humble sense of reality that we believed. Imagine actors who could do this, and play Hamlet. Acting requires a commitment of energy and concentration that most human beings (even though many actors seem to become less human when they work) never even perceive. It is as demanding as that of any athletic discipline, or dancing, or singing. Not only does it require as complete a commitment as do those domains, it also demands that one be able to instantly fall in love or have the desire to kill someone. Most actors will never be able to truly play major roles because they lack the energy and concentration to maintain their involvement in an imaginary world for three hours. Seeing the Peking Opera, my father engaged a teacher, Sophia Delza, who gave free classes in Tai Chi to the Actors Studio membership. About five of us went regularly. The poor attendance was the first of many examples of any student in the theater, beginner or professional, failing to take advantage of the gift of learning that didn't come with a bill.

I studied Afro-Cuban dance with one of the great teachers in New York, Syvilla Fort. Syvilla, who had worked with Kathryn Dunham, ran a studio with her husband Buddy Philips, on 44th Street between Seventh and Sixth. Her large brown eyes wore a clear, innocent expression. She saw each person's body individually, and would make you expand, move, and arch as though you were important. Her classes were a mixture of exercises, bar work, stretching, and dance. There was always at least one conga drummer, and sometimes a whole troupe of musicians. More than once, a group of visiting Brazilians would file into the studio, take a seat, and all erupt into sound.

It was impossible not to dance as the drums made our bodies and the room vibrate. I was shy about moving my body in ways that awoke my pelvis to the fact that men and women are sensual creatures, created to express desire and love for one another. Uptight as I was, I began to loosen up. Syvilla taught me to have pleasure in movement and to conquer the fear that held back my body. I also took a class at her studio in acrobatics. If I had discovered this aspect earlier in my life, I might have become a gymnast. Are you as shocked as I am to know that I danced on Broadway? (I'll come to it.)

My father held back his feelings with an anal compulsion that could give him nose bleeds. I remember one evening when Susan, who was nineteen at the time, was co-starring in Jean Anouilh's *Time Remembered*. Although she lived at home, she was a having a love affair with Richard Burton, during which time my father would open the door to this married man at any hour of day or night. I remember thinking that anything was OK to them as long as someone was famous enough. Maybe they simply believed it was none of their business.

My mother was trying to get my father to listen to Susan and to give her some advice and help about an acting problem, something he gave freely to most of his students and the members of the Actors Studio. But with Susan, he remained distant and uncommunicative. On this particular evening, my mother refused to let him remain uninvolved, and her insistence finally started to get him mad. His battle to control himself was frightening: his lips disappeared into a thin line, and his face changed colors. I had been asleep and came into the kitchen when I heard their voices raised in argument. I said I was hungry, and my father insisted on cooking something for me; it was clear that he was trying to avoid doing what my mother wanted. Susan looked anxious and terrified, and kept saying that it didn't matter. She obviously felt responsible for creating a situation between them although it was not her fault.

My mother kept insisting, "You always help anyone who asks, how can you not want to help your own daughter? You answer the phone at three in the morning and talk to a student if they call [which was true], so what's the problem taking a moment now?" He retorted that Susan didn't need his help, and when my mother asked how he knew that when he wouldn't talk to her, he finally exploded. Throwing the pot of hot cereal that he was cooking for me onto the floor, he screamed at the top of his lungs, "It's none of your business what I do! Stop butting in. If Susan wants help, she can ask for it!" His nose suddenly began to gush blood. He stopped yelling, clutched the cloth handkerchief that he always carried to his nose, and stormed into his study. The sliding doors slammed shut. My mother stood there for a moment, and then said icily, "Someday, he'll get a nosebleed and die." At that moment it sounded as though that was what she really wanted. She fled into their bedroom, sobbing a threat that one day she would throw herself out of the window. Susan came to me as I stood halfway between them in the hallway; she was afraid that our mother meant it. Susan pleaded with me to do something. I said to let her jump if she wanted to. I was angry; I didn't want to feel responsible, but I did. All this commotion was about giving a little advice. Had it been anyone else, he would have listened to reason, but I think that he was hurt and resentful of Susan's success and fame. She didn't study with him, was more famous than he was, and was making more money than he did. Whatever he felt, it wasn't enough to stop him from using the money she made as though it was his own.

From 1954 on, when my mother worked with Marilyn on *Bus Stop*, she had been complaining to me about having to travel too much. She lived with Marilyn more than she did with us during a large part of the rest of her life. By 1959, when I had my nervous breakdown and began studying acting, she was tired, and sick from the cancer that would soon lead to her mastectomy and chemotherapy. I was in a rage, as I often was, and tried to defend her to my father. Of course, I doubt that my efforts would have meant anything; she had compromised too long ago, and was not going to change. She died instead.

I often sensed that my father reacted to life as an emotional child. According to Uncle Arthur he was the one their mother spoiled. The only memory I have of a simple, direct conversation, such as I often had with Franchot, was during this period, when I accused him of living for the moment, never planning for the future. My mother was responsible for all problem solving. I was furious because there was no plan for what would happen if there was an emergency. He just shrugged his shoulders and said that it would work out. By that he meant my mother would do something.

My father, in his defense, proceeded to tell me a more personal story than any I ever remember his telling me. He had decided to live for the moment when his best friend, Ben Slutsky, had died. Ben and he had grown up together, and my father had loved him more than anyone except a brother and my father's first wife, both of whom had died young. When Ben, a baker, was dying of cancer in the hospital, he told my father that his one dream had always been to go back to their homeland of Galicia, Poland. As many Jews had, his family fled the pogroms that erupted in the early 1900s. I remember Ilia Lopert telling me how he watched his best friend being trampled to death by Cossacks who stormed through the ghetto. Ben deeply regretted that he hadn't gone, and now it was too late. He would never do the one thing he had most wanted to do. My father recounted his tale with as much simple feeling as I'd ever seen in him. Whether or not I agreed, I understood how deeply affected he had been and why he now lived his life as he did.

When I was eleven, Ben took me to Abraham and Strauss on 14th Street, near Union Square. He bought me the bicycle that I desperately wanted, and that my parents had refused me. My mother said that they were afraid I would ride it in the streets, and I did. I would have grown up a lot less angry if they hadn't blocked every effort of mine to be myself. I was a pretty healthy kid underneath it all. The freer I am, and the more myself, the less I have had any anger or resentment towards them. I just feel sad at how much of our mutual love was wasted and unexpressed; too much of my life was confused, short-circuited, and misdirected due to a simple lack of contact. I still have my father's money habits, except that I gave mine away to those I loved, rather than taking it from them. And I'm just now learning how to plan and build for the future. It never seemed important before. But I also have never had children.

The atmosphere in his classroom was driven by his charismatic energy. Like any good teacher he charged his students with his own passion, determination, and desire. But I always felt that the expression of feeling was fearsome, forbidden, and dangerous. A sense of repression, and a compulsive obsession with control, made it seem that latent explosive feelings could only be expressed within rigidly controlled boundaries. Spontaneity was treated as unreliable; imagination was incidental. My father's inflexible personality defined his view of acting technique: a systematized way in which an actor expressed his own personal feelings.

RELAXATION, OR PREPARATION

Relaxation always preceded exercises. My father taught relaxation in the way that he understood it. We began by sitting in a chair and systematically checking the body and the brain for areas of tension. It was similar to what many of us might call meditation, especially when preparing to alter one's state of being. Originally, this was done by sitting still and mentally checking the body, from bottom to top or top to bottom. Years later, he added movement and sound. Actors were told to systematically move their arms and legs to check for tension, making controlled, explosive, vibrated sounds. It is still being taught that way, by teachers who don't necessarily understand why it works, or what principles it is based on. This is surprising, especially when we consider the tremendous progress in our understanding of mind/body work, meditation, and altered states. Why in the chair, and not lying down, or standing up? First, he always insisted that control was involved in any form or act of expression; and second, one could always find a place to sit down backstage. After ten or fifteen minutes, we would signal that we thought we were ready to begin. Sometimes he would check our relaxation, and he might instruct people to begin before they felt ready, or tell them to continue to relax because he didn't think they had relaxed enough. Sometimes emotions would spill out, as they normally do when people let down their defenses. My father discouraged this kind of discharge. Feeling needed to be expressed consciously and with control. If we went to sleep, would that be relaxed? Yes, but it was not what we were supposed to do. We weren't just relaxing; we were getting ready to do something.

Relaxation occurs naturally after the release of tension. Many teachers, my father included, use the word relaxation when they really mean preparation. This has led a lot of actors to eliminate the feeling of excitement and tension that is normal when you're preparing for work. What do we mean when we say "relax"? Most of the time we are trying to help the actor discover the need to be aware, present, in contact, centered, and concentrated. In this way their energy flows naturally through them. Their organic thoughts, feelings, and bodies are able to respond intuitively, and to spontaneously express impulses. They are capable of being inspired, or "in the zone," as athletes say. Accidentally on purpose.

Preparation is not about eliminating all tension and, inadvertently, all uncomfortable feelings. Meditation is normally used to lower one's level of excitement. The desire to disengage from one's feelings and sensations often dissolves into some universal feeling of well-being. Meditation can be used to help us channel our feelings into a state of readiness. It will heighten our senses and bring us into direct contact with what we feel: sadness, happiness, hunger. Relaxation only occurs after one has fully expressed one's feelings.

Preparation is a state of active rest. We may feel excitement, anxiety, even fear; but we must not block the flow of energy to the microcosm within or the macrocosm without. One is in a state of readiness, without necessarily being ready to do something specific. In a state of preparation there is no anticipation, which can be eliminated by the willful capacity to concentrate on being in the moment. This can be done with a blank mind, or a mind that concentrates on some specific object or reality in one's personal dream space. What preparation shares with relaxation is the elimination of blocked energy and the habits that cause it. I define the preparation process as learning to intentionally develop a state of being in which one can be spontaneously inspired; in which one consciously directs oneself to express what one perceives and feels about a particular reality. Accidentally on purpose. Preparation is one of the most important aspects of work to study and develop. Artists and artist-scientists speak about this state of being "illuminated"; technicians don't.

When I first started working it literally took me hours to get ready to walk onstage and say, "Hello." It's exactly what I felt when I played the sailor in *The Rose Tattoo*. I had to work extremely hard to get myself sufficiently under control, as I lived so much in a state of depression. That doesn't help when one wants to give in and let go. I would get simultaneously excited and anxious. I used to feel that at any moment I would walk off the stage and into the audience.

Learning to prepare took me fifteen years. I didn't really feel open and in fluid control until 1975 when I created a role in Lanford Wilson's *The Mound Builders*, at Circle Repertory Company. I had just returned to New York after spending three years in Montreal, Canada, working at the National Film Board, where I directed an actor's and director's workshop. I was divorcing my first wife, an actress named Wendy Girard, to whom I had been married for five years. I had stopped being a vegetarian. I was ending a period of my life that was so ascetic that I had lived alone through a Canadian winter in a house which had no hot water. I heard from Heather MacRae, whom I was seeing, that Circle was looking for an actor. Heather was playing in Circle Rep's hit play, *The Hot L Baltimore*, also by Lanford Wilson. From the moment I went for the audition, I could feel that my working state was different.

While waiting in their old theater on the second floor of a building at 83rd and Broadway, I got up and found a space where I could do some push-ups just because I felt like it. This was something that I would never have let myself do before, because I would be more concerned with what the other actors thought of me than of what I needed to do for myself. I remember thinking that if I saw another actor do what I wanted to do, I'd judge him to be a narcissistic asshole. I sat there and thought for a moment, then said to myself, "Fuck it! I don't care what anybody thinks." My energy was clear, I was open and friendly, and did what I wanted to do in the audition, which was never a sure thing.

Auditions continue to be hit and miss for me because they are approval situations. I tend to think that anyone in authority is going to interfere with my desire to get something that I want, or tell me that I'm not worth it. How well I do depends on how I feel and how I feel toward a prospective employer. If I'm concentrated and working for myself, I will meet my own standards. This isn't a guarantee that I'll get the part, but I've always known when I got a part because of the clarity of my feeling and perception during the audition. Every project I've ever been involved in had a feeling about it from its birth that I trust (like a surfer on a wave of life). I've learned to recognize and take care of that feeling.

I've tried everything, from over-preparing to absolutely no preparation. I once attended an audition for *Enter Laughing*, a comedy directed by Gene Saks. Alan Arkin got the part that I, along with hundreds of others, read for. I was so nervous when I got onstage (which I remember thinking was great for the part, because I was reading a monologue where the character telephones his mother) that I played the entire scene with my back to Gene!

My energy would get so far out that I never had a fourth wall between myself and the audience. They were always there. When that bothered me, I would turn my back and hide, which is very "Method." Work in the-ater-in-the-round gets you over that habit because there is no place to turn without the public being there. The stage is the worst place in the world to try to hide, but a lot of actors are very good at it. I always feel the audience; in fact, when I'm acting, I want them to be there. The only time that actors don't is when they are in acting class, in training, or in re-hearsal, because then their work is private, and it is difficult to be that vul-nerable. Imagine looking over a writer's shoulder when he's working. If the other watchers are going through the same process, you can share in the development of an atmosphere based on truth, knowledge, and a mu-tual love for the work.

To Be Or Not To Be

Without Sense Memory technique I couldn't feel or express anything, or so I thought. The Method didn't consciously teach actors how to con-nect their humanity and feelings about themselves and their lives with their art. Everything flowed through the technique of exercise work.

Some people actually have natural sense memory. The knowledge that realistic technique is based on natural functions is a helpful way of understanding the process. *Educare*, the Latin root of education, means "to bring out of." Natural actors work intuitively; they have the talent and capacity to express what they sense and perceive without formalized tech-nique. Studying will only help them to understand and use the gift more consciously and fully. Marlon Brando is probably the most noteworthy ex-ample of a natural actor associated with the Actors Studio. Everyone as-sumes he studied the Method, but he didn't, and he certainly never learned sense memory in any systematic way with Stella Adler.

The argument about whether to feel or not to feel is even stranger, since acting may be the most human of all art forms. In fact, an actor is not only the artist but in the moment of his creation, he is a living work of art. No one would tell a painter, a sculptor, a writer, a dancer, a musician, a composer, or a singer not to become involved, to play without feeling, or create in cold blood. An artist does need to be objective in order to judge what he or she is doing and thus do it better. People are conditioned to believe that objectivity is a cold, intellectualized process in which we distance ourselves, and our senses, from the reality we are observing. Objectivity is really the ability to analyze the reality that one is, naturally and intimately, connected to by being able to perceive, and coherently express, what one is sensing and feeling. Objectivity is our own capacity to use our mind to consciously contact and analyze intuition, sensation, and feeling in order to determine what is true. Objectivity is an ongoing, always-evolving process of deepening our awareness of life.

What is difficult for any artist or scientist is even more so for the actor: in order to analyze and understand, the actor must be able to observe what he creates without the benefit of distancing himself from a sketch, or a typewritten page, or a mirror, or a canvas. To be objective, the actor is obliged to know himself, to know whether all of his sensations and perceptions are real and true in the moment of doing. This capacity can be aided by film and video, but the actual process of creation for an actor takes place in the moment; no matter how clearly he sees himself afterwards, his observations have to be related to that instant, much like an athlete.

There is a story about the great French actor Coquelin, who was a proponent of the representational school, which champions the lack of emotional involvement and objectivity unmixed with sensation. One night during an emotional scene he was actually moved to tears. After the performance he called the company together and apologized for having lost control; he assured them that he would never let it happen again. Whatever the reason for their rejection of real experience in art, this is what leads certain actors to pronounce that actors who become personally involved, passionately obsessed, or possessed by their work are neurotic, and advocate an art form based on such prescriptions as "Don't become personally involved" and "Don't express real human perception and experience in art," and such premises as "Art is not a means for human beings to understand themselves." They present a false argument that reality and real experience are impossible to achieve regularly. It supposes that a technician is always brilliant, which isn't true. No artist measures a technique by insisting that it always produces a great work of art. We would all love to be able to, but nothing in the history of real human experience supports this mechanical thinking. This distortion of truth is so great that it appears to be a conscious invention of those human beings who are suspicious of feeling and their own humanity. They try to teach us to undermine ourselves with lofty ideas which only hide small-mindedness and the sense of our own inadequacy.

Simply put, an actor has a choice: to be, or not to be. There are two basic schools of thought: the representational, in which the actor's training is based on objectified, visible technique and analysis that separates and distances the actor from the character; and the realistic, in which the actor wants to become completely involved, using his own being, knowledge, and skill to transform himself so that the totality of what he imagines the character's existence to be is brought to life. Their ideas of what being objective is are as different as the principles are.

I have seen actors who do not consider themselves to be realistic who, on a given night, are more real than most actors of the realistic school: John Gielgud, Laurence Olivier, Ralph Richardson. In fact, a large part of the English theatrical community lines up against the Method and the Actors Studio, often confusing the two. Many actors who profess to be "real" think that means expressing feeling without regard to the need of becoming involved in the world of the character and being transformed. They reduce the character to their own comfortable habits of behavior and expression, rather than rising (or falling) to the level of the character. Their acting has only a level of personal expression that, no matter how wonderful, does not contain the perception, intelligence, and mature conscious expression that is the hallmark of all great art.

The basis for reality is not in the actors ability to express emotion, as my father's work tends to imply, but in the actor's capacity to tell the truth. Defining acting as the art of transformation changes the actor's attitude to the creative process.

My father believed that Stanislavski had regressed by the time that he wrote *Creating a Role*. At that time, Stanislavski had begun working directly from the play, using imagination to involve the actor in the play's life. He did not base scene work on Sense Memory exercises. My father concluded that Stanislavski no longer believed in, or used, sense memory. I do not agree. Stanislavski was developing a synthesis of sense memory with imagination and script analysis. I continue to expand this synthesis in my work and to clarify the creative process. My work is rooted in the realistic school, but I have defined the nine natural laws of creativity, and consciously use dreams and imagination, with which we all reach out to know the world.

SCENES WE DREAM AND MAKE REAL

Carolyn Coates, a working actress studying with my father, asked me if I wanted to do my first scene in class, from J.D. Salinger's *Catcher in the Rye*. In the scene, the bellboy of a fleabag hotel in New York, where sixteen-year-old Holden Caulfield registers after being thrown out of prep school, cons him into seeing a prostitute. In the book, she is about Holden's age. He is a virgin having a nervous breakdown, and he invents a story about having an imaginary illness. He ends up not having sex with her, more out of fear than any sense of moral propriety.

We rehearsed in Carolyn's apartment on West 83rd Street near Broadway, first just reading the scene without too much planning or discussion. Her husband, Jimmy Noble, also an actor, often sat in another room which made me feel more at ease. We didn't socialize, which happened so often when people rehearsed scenes for class. I was always uncomfortable rehearsing in people's apartments; I didn't know how to behave, or whether they had to like me in order for us to work together. I didn't talk a lot, and only relaxed when I was working toward some specific goal. I wasn't like some of my friends, whose main goal in scene work was to get their partner into bed. Not that I didn't want to. But I was nineteen, and so depressed that I didn't think anyone was interested in me.

I don't ever remember proposing a scene to a fellow student. I was too insecure to have an opinion about what I thought would be a good scene to work on. Reading and analyzing plays wasn't an actual part of our training. Sometimes my father would assign a scene to someone, but it was always in terms of developing the actor's behavior and expression, which was not necessarily directly connected to the actor's capacity for scene analysis.

I intuitively understood Holden and was not far removed from him. I saw little to laugh about in my life, but could readily laugh at his. Without any conscious planning or designing, I picked out some clothes and toilet articles, which I put into a small suitcase. In the year that I had been observing, my father would discuss the logic of a scene in relation to our choice of what sense memory work we were going to do. I wanted to leave myself open to my intuitive sense. I never tried to direct myself or block a scene. Most actors I've worked with believe that rehearsing is designing a scene: they don't treat their rehearsal process as an adventure, the exploration and discovery of the life of another human being.

My rehearsals never had any apparent sense of direction in the early stages. I was intuitively doing what actors should do: exploring an unknown territory. Intentional dreaming, focusing oneself on the realities of the character's world without prejudice, is a fundamental part of an artist's work. It occupies the most important part of any artist's work, over half of which takes place outside of rehearsal. This open-mindedness is an element of talent and organic thinking. Without it, creativity is very limited—an actor may be very good, and even personal, but he can never be very original, or deeply involved. Artists are known to become obsessed or possessed by what they are doing. I was to discover that this is a normal part of the creative process.

On scene day, I began preparing when I woke up. It was like a sporting event. I was constantly trying to relax and not ruminate over the scene. Whenever I was anxious, excited, or frightened I tried to control my feelings by running them through the labyrinthine habit of thinking I had. The only thing that stops rumination from killing feeling is the intense fear and excitement that gives the habit the energy it needs to run on.

I tried not to let my fear turn into panic. I concentrated on the given circumstances of the Salinger scene as I perceived them, because I had no idea or plan of what I was going to do. I never did when I prepared scenes for classes or at the Actors Studio. I had no desire to direct myself in a scene. I always wanted to discover, explore, and create life as spontaneously as I could. I directed my thoughts towards exploring the imaginary room of this dilapidated hotel: I imagined yellowed walls with fingerprints and dirt smudges. Sometimes the wall became hospital green. What would it be like to wander around New York alone at night, suffering from the exhaustion and fear that is part of the nervous breakdown that Holden was going through? His thoughts seemed so familiar to me. I worked on a sense memory of tiredness. I would try to hold his life in my head, turning the thoughts and feelings over and over. I was afraid that if I didn't do this they would flow away, and I would not be able to get them back. Sometimes, this rumination would kill the reality and I would suddenly feel dull and machine-like. I was as much a mess as Holden, which helped me in the scene; my anxiety over contemplating a possible sexual encounter was as real as his. I was still a virgin, and not much older than he was. At the time, I didn't wonder why I always seemed to be attracted to girls who took no interest in me. Once I did, I realized it was a great way of avoiding contact, or feeling anything other than the constant, habitual pain that I tolerated with ease. There was a need that wanted to explode out of me. When it bothered me enough and I found the courage to make a date, I would normally not show up. I never approached any of the women I really liked. When they approached me, I was so veiled and noncommittal it must have seemed that I wasn't interested.

When the scene was announced, I was alone on the stage of the Malin Studios, in the Capital Theater Building on Broadway at 51st Street. This space was leased by Dr. Sol Colin, who had his own school, the Dramatic Workshop, which had been founded by Irwin Piscater, one of the founders of Epic Theater. Colin had inherited it from him (not by relation, but artistic succession) and he rented space to my father. Sol was a large, pleasant man, with enormous glasses that framed his owl-like eyes. He had a thatch of whitening hair, and a large mouth with thick lips. He spoke with a heavy Russian accent, and had been Pirandello's secretary for many years while he lived in Italy.

I had set the stage with a bureau, a bed, and a chair, and created an imaginary mirror. I felt frantic as I opened an imaginary door, and entered the imaginary room, ushered in by the imaginary bellboy. I can still see him: short, balding, smelling of sweat and alcohol. I could feel my heart pounding. I looked around, put down the suitcase, and sat on the bed. After a few moments, I felt a strong impulse to open my suitcase, take off my shirt, put deodorant under my arms, change shirts, look in the mirror. As the hooker—Carolyn—knocked at the door, I tested my breath. I heard some distant laughter, and wondered what people thought was so funny about watching me suffer. I was frantic. I tried to relax and hold onto myself, to stay "here," to not lose my concentration. My father said that this was one of the principle reasons for making choices: to have a point of concentration with which to anchor reality. It helped me to not fade away into depression and nothingness, as I habitually did in life. Most actors want to learn technique in order to eliminate anxiety; good technique will teach you how to use it. The more important something is to you, the more nervous, anxious, and excited you're going to be. It's a good sign. As a matter of fact, the worst feeling in the world is not to have any desire to go to work. Not being nervous and excited is when you're in trouble, because you have nothing to work with.

As my concentration built, I felt as though I was in the middle of a huge circle of light and energy that radiated out from me, magnifying where I was and what I was doing. My perception of life seemed larger, clearer, and more detailed. I don't know how or why I trusted my instincts, but all during the scene I had the feeling I was inside a fishbowl. One sees the world beyond, but the sensory world to which one is attentive ends at the inner edge of the bowl. Stanislavski called this "the circle of light." Neither Stanislavski nor my father was inventing a style of acting: they were examining, discovering, and organizing the way in which great actors had been working for thousands of years. All real discoveries concerning nature, including human nature, are based on our capacity to observe and experience its essence. All realistic techniques evolve in this manner, and the principles on which they are founded are based on organic functions.

Carolyn was very nervous, but the contact between us was good; we worked simply and truthfully. I felt more personal and intimate than I did in my own life. It felt as though I was living in another world, except when I heard people laughing. When the scene was over, my father was as relieved as I. His critique was very positive, and I listened with a sense of distancing myself, holding back my feelings with the attitude of suspicion I reserved for compliments. Without saying why, he asked to see the scene again. This was not standard procedure, but I was glad to oblige: I was curious to see what it would be like the second time. I think that my father wanted to see if I would work as intuitively and truthfully as I had when I repeated the scene.

My father never encouraged an actor to be emotionally spontaneous, which he suspected as being impulsive; or personally expressive, which he mistrusted as being indulgent and unsystematic. Everything was the result of a consciously controlled thought process. He made it clear that acting might seem like therapy at times, but there was one major difference: the object of therapy was to cure oneself and live a better life. The object of an acting class was not to become healthy, but to become a good actor. Peggy Feury was a wonderful acting teacher who sometimes taught my father's classes when he was ill. Long before she became well-known in her own right she told me that the lower half of my body was dead. She shocked me, as when any teacher makes you conscious of something of which you were previously unaware. The comment made me even more self-conscious than I already was. But Peggy was right; I was cutting off feeling in the lower half of my body.

Great works of art were fused in my father's mind with the idea of perfection. Humanity and feeling, by virtue of their spontaneity and simplicity, are of course excluded from the world of perfection. His goal could only be achieved by learning to dominate one's humanity. Being simply human means never being able to achieve perfection. But his humanity was the source of his creativity.

There is an image of man's estate on Earth, from Cheng Man Ch'ing, a Tai Chi master. Cheng describes us as literally "swimming on land" in the same way that a fish lives and swims in the ocean. This sense of fluidity, of effortless contact and continuous movement, as if in slow motion, became fundamental to my definition of preparation, and the creative state.

Carolyn and I repeated the Salinger scene two weeks later. I felt very differently than I had the first time. We hadn't rehearsed. I didn't have any desire to repeat what had worked well, but I did not trust myself to behave intuitively, as I had the first time, and change what I had done. The scene felt flat. When my father asked me what I had worked on, and what I had really felt like doing, I said that I had really felt like doing nothing: I had wanted to lie on the bed and not answer the door. I hadn't been excited at all, as I had the first time. He asked why I hadn't done just that. I was shocked to realize that I hadn't trusted my impulses. I felt lost and confused. I never forgot the feeling of having ignored myself. Of course, I had been doing just that for most of my life.

This conflict between spontaneity and my belief that control meant being able to hold back my intuitive feelings was always the crux of my creative work. If I could hold back and control an impulse, I would assume that it wasn't real.

Acting is never just being oneself. It is not simply the process of transposing experience. Neither my father nor Stanislavski explained this sufficiently. Stanislavski's books don't communicate what transformation feels like. Most actors approach a role by saying, "What would I do if I were in my character's situation?" The artist-actor would say, "What would I do if I were the character in the situation?" Aside from animal exercises, my father's technique didn't touch on characterization. His class work developed the actor's capacity to be truthful and to express feeling. Or, to be more precise, it was only about expressing one's own personal truth.

I, on the other hand, define acting as the Art of Transformation. We can understand the process by observing the work of many film actors. I don't mean any actor who works in the movies. Until recently, most actors came to film from the theater. If you're theater-trained, you are more likely to act based on what you imagine the life of the character you are playing to be. The rehearsal process implies the actor's exploration of the character. This is how the art form has developed. In the movies, the time and the learning process do not exist. The actor has to know how to develop his character before filming begins. The short-take, out-of-sequence manner in which films are made also makes character work extremely difficult. Under the intense pressure of the camera's all-seeing-eye, most film actors have neither the time nor the training to deal with transformation. Even actors who have done it consummately in the theater will often not risk transformation in films, because it's just too demanding and time consuming. They have all they can do to be able to express their own personal truth.

The three thousand mile abyss between New York and Hollywood is one of the major contributors to the direction of many actors' development, or lack of development. The first question posed by the actor on a bare stage is, "What do I imagine I have to create?" Without transformation and the search for a form that evolves from the play and character (within which one expresses a personal truth), creative freedom becomes an open license, permitting the actor to do whatever the hell he feels like doing and calling it acting. This is based on the belief that acting is only about expressing personal truth.

My second experience in scene work also had a profound effect on my working life. It came after a scene from Steinbeck's *East of Eden*, which I worked on with Zero Mostel's niece, Barbara Mostel. (Zero Mostel was a friend of my family, and a fine painter as well as a wonderful actor. During the years in which he was blacklisted and couldn't get a job, my mother remembered him arriving onstage in the middle of a love scene she was playing in Cafe Crown. He walked in, sat down at a table and ordered coffee. My mother was forced to go over to his table, and take his order, before he let her go back to doing the play.) It's a very simple scene. A girl, Abra, brings lunch to Cal, who is working in the fields. Our scene was well-received, but it lacked something fundamental. I felt distant, relatively calm, and in contact and complicity with Barbara; I thought I was really talking and listening. When it was over, I stopped acting, and began telling my father what I had worked on. As I did, I began to relax. At that moment, he said, "Like now." I asked him what he meant, and he said, "Now you are real." But, I objected, now I wasn't acting. He said, "That's it. That's exactly it. Now you're not acting." It was true. At that moment, I was really present, really talking, really listening. I understood that I hadn't been doing that during the scene. I had actually been out of contact. During the scene I had been in a state of walking sleep. From that moment, I understood that "real" doesn't mean "almost like"; it means real. That's why I really loved acting. It allowed me to discover how I once knew how to be. It taught me about life. My father, who had unwittingly helped to put me into the trap was now consciously helping to set me free, at least when I was acting.

I have always made my life choices according to my inner needs, and not by any measure of any rational or material objective. This has forced me to confront not only myself, but also to recognize myself in relation to my parents. They bequeathed to me the conflict between their respective beliefs. I wish I could say they also bequeathed me their love, which would have made it easier for me to love myself.

My mother believed in the simple pleasures of life and family. She also had passionate inner longing and sexual desire. Occasionally she would even kiss me on the ear with her mouth and tongue, which horrified me and made me feel very uncomfortable. However, at least I knew that she loved me. She also bore an inner sadness and resignation, grounded in a submission of her own desires to everyone else's. I identified with, and re-belled against, this deadening feeling. It still exists in the depths of my old habits, and I do battle with it on the rare occasions when it reappears. My true connection was to my mother's unconscious self, the part of her that reflected on the realities of life which cannot be measured in material ob-jectivity. This contact with my intuitive mind, the third eye, the psyche, and the psychic realities that precede the Higher Mind (Kether in Kabbalah) was in me, whether or not I wanted to admit it.

My father, on the other hand, shared himself only through his work and his passion for knowledge. He was driven by an almost compulsive thoroughness and a habit of analytical thought, which gave his work a sys-tematic pragmatism. His sense of truth helped me to recognize my own. In the long run, that truth proved as valuable as any of the Sense Memory techniques.

I wanted desperately to be myself, but every time I wondered who that was I drew a blank. I only knew for sure that I didn't want to be like ei-ther one of them. Most of my life has been spent finding out how I could be the dreamer that I am and still be pragmatic and successful. Luckily, my own organic thinking led me to recognize the existence of my own personal dream space.

Dreaming and imagining are an essential part of my work process. The dictionary's definition of dreaming comes from the Old English: joy, music, a sequence of images. We hear, see, and feel things that exist if we believe that dreams are real. Psychiatrists, neurologists, parapsychologists, aborigines, saints, ascetics, artists, and scientists all explore, study, and live with their dreams, interpreting and using them to direct their lives. When, as a child, I asked my father about the spots I saw in the air or when I closed my eyes, he told me that they didn't exist. When I had nightmares about the elephants and snakes that surrounded my bed, I was told that I was imagining things. When I lay awake in bed, in terror because I couldn't move or call out—my arms felt so heavy that I couldn't lift them and my throat refused to make a sound—I felt foolish. Whatever my mother might think, my father would curl his mouth into a mocking smile.

My father gave up his dream of having a permanent theater because the economic pressures made everyone into competitors, not collaborators. He blamed the horrible failure of *Peer Gynt* on the set designer, who had designed an old fashioned, realistic set for what is fundamentally a dream play. And this failure drove him out of working in the commercial theater, and away from directing, until fourteen years later when he directed The Actors Studio Theater production of *The Three Sisters*. When I asked him how he could be surprised by the set if a director is always collaborating with the designer, he claimed that the set that arrived in the theater was not the one they had discussed. I don't know where the lack of communication came from.

No one knows exactly what dreams are. Sometimes I don't know if I am dreaming, or if dreams are dreaming me, entities in their own right that float into my consciousness. We tend to believe that we are the center of the universe, so we assume that these phenomena are of our own creation; I am not so sure. I know that some dreams come from my inner self, resolving emotional problems that I'm having in life while I sleep. But there are other dreams: intuitions, premonitions, that visit me in visions and thoughts that travel from some still uncharted part of our universe.

Several years ago, I was living in Paris in a studio apartment where I spent three months a year while I traveled and worked in several countries in Europe, which is how I lived for almost ten years. I kept dreaming about a theater in which I could create the work that individual productions in other people's theaters did not permit. I decided to close my school in Paris (I had closed the branch in New York in 1985) because I did not want to direct an organization that was not a theater. A school attached to a theater (as I had in New York in the 1980s), was another matter, because it made learning an organic process. Two weeks after I closed the school, I was invited to create what I eventually called the Theater International de Recherche, a studio-theater for artists (including myself) to evolve and to create productions. The synchronicity of the offer was startling and difficult to dismiss as coincidence.

These moments of union with the universe are among my greatest pleasures in living. When they occur on a personal level, in life or in my work, I recognize it as a contact with the cosmic life force. I had consciously tried to ignore the wealth of this dream life because when I was nine, that's what I thought that men should do in order to be men. Of course, no matter how much I neglected my dreams, they were an important and natural part of the creative process. Through them I began to listen to myself and become conscious of who I was, though this reality was separate from my conscious work process.

My breakthrough occurred after I had been working professionally for over eight years. Until then, when I dreamed and imagined, I believed that I was just being lazy. I possessed so little self-respect, mocking those parts of myself that my father mocked in my mother, that I held back the development of my creative process for years. Once I began to take myself seriously, revising my habits took another eight years, from 1969 to 1976. I studied acting between 1959 and 1962, and began working professionally in 1961. I get my best ideas at seven in the morning as I wake up, having solved a problem during the nighttime, when the inherent part of my mind is free to function as it is meant to. I have worked hard to learn to behave like this when I am awake.

It's embarrassing to discover that the best work you do is after the scene is over. But it's when a lot of actors relax, stop acting, and begin to do, simply and really, what they really want to do. What they've been trying so hard to make happen, happens when they stop trying. With a good creative process the play will tell you what to do. Mystics talk to God in that personal dream space, athletes compete with inspired brilliance when they enter their personal dream space, great scientists have inexplicable leaps of consciousness and insight when they enter their personal dream space. Some normal, relatively innocent, sometimes unconscious human beings, like you or me, can learn how to consciously enter our own personal dream space. All you have to do is breathe deeply, and listen, as a scientist listens to the universe in order to discover and understand what life is. It is how we learn to inspire ourselves.

Whatever discoveries, additions, and corrections I've made in teaching, acting, and directing have all come out of these seemingly mundane moments. In those seemingly banal, simplistic moments of truth, I understood what I wanted to do. I had spent a lifetime trying to deliberately become able to do what happened accidentally. The life that I was living was simply living me.

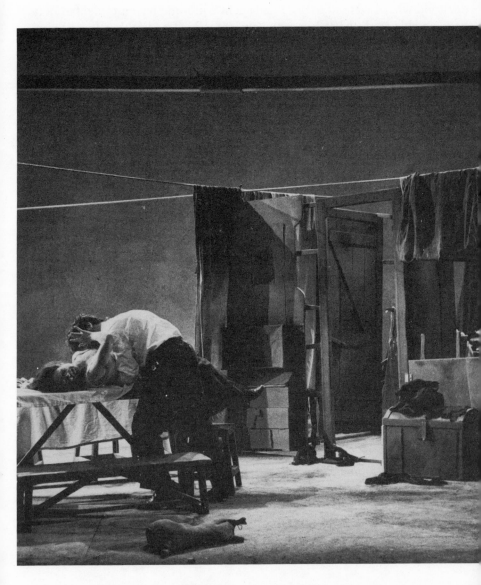

Maria Rosa by Angel Guimbra directed by John Strasberg
at Centro Dramatic de Catalunta (Barcelona) 1983

CHAPTER THREE

DREAMS, BELONGING, AND AWAKENING AWARENESS

I listened to my mother's dreams as they flowed painfully out of her during my childhood sessions at her bedside. I began practicing to be the doctor that I never became, and the teacher that I did become. I eventually settled on the premise that living is a process of trying to make our dreams come true. Susan seemed to have her dream come true by the time she was eighteen. I dreamt of being a war hero, a soldier who rose through the ranks to become a general who fought alongside his troops. In reality, I had lost touch with my dreams as they dissolved in encroaching adolescence.

My father acted as though he thought my mother was a lunatic. Every time I think of dreamers, I see my father's face turning away from me as though I had spit in it. His lips would press tightly together in an attitude of disgust, and a condescending smile would mask his eyes. His right hand would wave me away, as he said, "Darling, if dreams could come true, we'd all be millionaires. Dream a little less, and do a little more." Strange behavior for a man who entitled his book, *A Dream of Passion*, and who inspired his students and members of The Actors Studio to dream. What a fierce, internal conflict he must have gone through during his life. Was he so afraid of his own dreamer that he had to mock the dreamers in his own family? Perhaps that's part of what he meant when he shouted at me, "Who do you think I am, your mother?" My mother was the mystic, according to my realistic father, but it was she who had to borrow money to pay the bills. She merely worked herself to death so that he could practice his idealist philosophy.

❖ ❖ ❖

When I was seventeen, I drove cross-country with my sister, who was recovering from her love affair with Richard Burton. She slept in the back seat of Marty Fried's '49 black Chevy coupe that he and I drove. It was a great trip, during which I registered at the University of Wisconsin. In the Badlands of South Dakota, Susan wanted a dramatic photo of Marty, and she got more than she bargained for. She asked him to step beyond the safety chains on one of the slippery clay hills. He obliged, but after she had taken the snap and returned to the car, Marty lost his footing on the wet ground. He slid down the muddy slope, breaking his fall by digging his hands knuckle-deep into the sodden clay. I was unable to enlist the help of any of the sleep-walking tourists who stood staring nearby. Finally, a man loaned me a long chain with which I was able to pull the terrified Marty to safety. Driving was not only something I loved, the scenery and mountain roads enhancing my pleasure; it also made me feel adult and important in my family. Pop didn't drive, and Mom, who did, would sit beside me, stamping her foot on the brake she wished was there every time she thought we were in danger. She never drove on the Los Angeles freeways because she was afraid that once she got on, she'd never be able to get off.

In 1961, Susan had escaped my mother's suffocating influence. On one of the few occasions that my father took any kind of stand, he had told Susan to go and live her own life. Her apartment in Rome was in a palace behind Piazza Lovatelli, which one found by walking from Piazza Venezia past the house where Sophia Loren and Carlo Ponti lived. I sat next to Sophia one night in a theater in New York. I must admit, I don't remember the play, I only remember that Miss Loren was one of the most beautiful women I had ever seen.

Susan lived in what was called Trastevere, the old quarter. Europe is old to an American, and generally beautiful, but if El Greco could see his view of Toledo today, he probably wouldn't paint it.

People who migrated from Europe to the United States settled in places that had the same environmental traits as their native homelands. The Spanish were in the south, Scandinavians in the north, the Dutch by the sea, the Germans inland. Like all living things, our consciousness is formed by the land on which we live. The dictum from the sixties, "You are what you eat," applies as much to the land of which we are a part.

Traveling made me conscious of a playwright's roots. I suddenly needed to know whether a play takes place in its playwright's real time and place or, if not, how it is transformed in his personal dream space and emotional time. Chekhov, in most productions I have seen, seems English to me, not Russian. Shakespeare is a cosmic voyager: his love stories take place in Italy, and Hamlet is a prince of Denmark, descended from Vikings. He had never been to either place. One word, Denmark, can affect an entire concept and feeling of a play, depending on what it means to you: imagine *Hamlet* set in Italy, or *Romeo and Juliet* in Denmark. The epoch in which a play is written, by whom, and how life affected the artist should influence how we think about the play. Wine from grapes grown on one side of a hill is different from wine from grapes grown on the opposite side of the same hill, and so it is with people.

We are none of us trapped by our own small-mindedness unless we choose to be. Travel allows us to see what we haven't known so that we can discover ourselves. Our closed-minded lives, trapped in old patterns, are erased when life becomes an adventure. This is what happened to me.

We sat at an outdoor restaurant in a nearby piazza where we savored the smells and sounds of life as if they were part of our meal. I fell in love with a dish of fresh string beans that had been cooked, cooled, and seasoned with oil, lemon, and salt. It was as though I had never really tasted beans before. Dinner became a lingering celebration, a shared sensory experience of wine, veal piccata, gorgonzola cheese.

The square was full of people whose hands and arms gestured so freely in the air that I thought they were going to kill one another. Unable to understand Italian, I was forced into direct sensory contact with the world. Italy was so much more pleasurable than Sense Memory exercises! I was shocked, thirty years later, when I conducted an acting seminar at the Festival di Bagni di Lucca, in Tuscany. I had assumed that Italians were natural actors. On the contrary, they were paralyzed with intellectual concepts. I had an unusual ally who helped to dissolve this cerebral atmosphere; a fly who made an unsolicited appearance in every scene by Pirandello or Shakespeare. He would alight on an actor's shoe and force him to interact with his reality. Scenes would often begin to transform under his insectile influence. The actors gave me a key chain at the end of the seminar, on which was inscribed, "Alla Mosche, Piace, Pirandello e Shakespeare" (To the fly, Thanks, Pirandello and Shakespeare). The fly was a very good actor.

Susan took me to a film festival at Taormina, in Sicily, where from the moment of our arrival my senses were stunned by a primal world, pure white and hot in its semi-arid surroundings. We were housed in a monastery which had been converted into a hotel. The soul of its religious past was still alive in the secular body. One had to bow one's head at the doorway to the rooms. The peace and harmony of centuries in retreat in this communal life, in the midst of so much natural beauty, was counter-balanced in my mind by the horrible reality of having to renounce sensuous, earthly love. I was still a virgin then, so I had only hopes and dreams, but after a lifetime of some considerable experience, I still prefer peace and harmony to be accompanied by all the earthly pleasures.

At the monastery, Susan and I sat in a large room with Claudia Cardinale. There were others present, but I was unconcerned with them, absorbed as I was with Claudia's beauty. I bit into my hors d'oeuvre, crunched, and enjoyed making contact with people's eyes. Suddenly, I felt as though my mouth was alive. I looked around, but no one else seemed to be reacting adversely. I thought, "To hell with it," and spit out onto my plate the animated food that seemed to have been walking around in my mouth. I was not mistaken: it was alive with ants! I looked around to see if anyone was shocked at my behavior, but La Signorina Cardinale followed suit, as did my sister, and soon everyone else. Claudia looked at me and Susan and we all began to laugh. It was then that I knew that I really liked Italians.

Susan and I rented a car and drove south through Naples on our way to Capri. Driving through Italy makes one understand why so many wonderful painters were born there. Terra cotta became my favorite color. When I swam in the Mediterranean for the first time, I could see my body in the turquoise and emerald green water; the land and sea had golden highlights, as though the world was framed in sunlight. Lovely as it is, the Mediterranean has always seemed to me to be a beautiful bathtub.

To enter the Grotto Azura on Capri one is told to lie flat in the bottom of a rowboat. The oarsman maneuvers into the mouth of the cave while the tide is going out, leaving the mouth only partially underwater. If the boat is caught on the incoming wave it can be lifted up and smashed against the portal of rock that is the entry way. The sense of danger sharpens our senses, and once inside, the water is so luminous and clear that it seems unreal. It is illuminated by the sunlight reflecting off the bottom of the sea through a hole at the floor of the grotto. The water was so warm and translucent that when I slid into it I hung on the side of the boat as if

I were suspended in empty space. I was literally afraid that if I let go I would fall. After my senses acclimated to the extraordinary beauty, I let myself fall into a world that I never imagined existed.

Bikinis were so small that to a repressed young man from a puritanical country they seemed non-existent. Everyone else pretended to be completely blasé about the scantily-clad women walking by, but I believe there is more going on in most men's minds than meets the eye.

I had been in Italy for two weeks when my parents arrived in Rome. The four of us went on a driving tour to Florence, Siena, Assisi, Ravenna, and Padua before arriving at Venice. I was the very willing chauffeur. Susan and I made it a gastronomic tour of Italy, testing each hotel chef's expertise in making a harlequin soufflé for dessert. At the Grand Hotel in Florence the soufflé fell as it arrived at the table. Over our protests, the maître d' refused to serve it and made us wait a half an hour for a second. It was well worth it. We needed our nourishment, as our father expected us to tour the several kilometers of the Uffizi gallery in one day. He felt compelled to see every "great" painting he could find. I hated museums for years afterwards. It was a long time before I could reenter one. My head aches just thinking about it. Eventually, I learned to look at one or two painters or rooms, seeing for myself what touched me personally, rather than being driven by the world's "correct" taste.

We arrived in Venice, where in the Piazza San Marco we ran into Stella Adler, of all people. Ever the center of attention, she appeared as an amalgam of characters from Tennessee Williams. She was dressed as a cross between Princess from *Sweet Bird of Youth* and Blanche from *Streetcar*, and was accompanied by two strikingly handsome young men, like Maxine from *Night of the Iguana*. Gazing at the glamorous trio I wondered who was doing what to whom. Stella's expansive personality was well suited to the magnificence of Venice; she felt neither dwarfed nor humbled by the glittering triple domes of the Byzantine cathedral in front of which we all stood.

I don't recall much of what Stella said, dazzled as I was by her jewelry, make-up, and beautiful companions, but in the middle of the polite conversation she suddenly invited my parents to lunch. She magnanimously supplied a boat to bring them to the palatial Hotel Cipriani, where she was staying. My parents were clearly ambivalent about going, but my mother, who saw possibilities in everything, held sway and they went. Stella and my father renewed their endless argument about acting technique.

As for myself, my obsession with sex found an outlet on an expensive gondola ride I shared with a young woman from Texas. She was my age and we met at the Danieli where, like me, she was staying with her family. We passionately necked in the boat, but my hands were denied access to her flesh by the most sturdily-constructed girdle it has ever been my misfortune to encounter. The result of my aquatic amorous adventure was a premature ejaculation. To rub salt in the wound, I had to ask the gondolier to make a stop so I could urinate.

We took a day trip from Venice to Asola, the mountain home of Eleanora Duse. Gabrielle d'Anunzio wrote all of his plays for her. Only the French critics, who were weaned on Sarah Bernhardt's theatrics, failed to appreciate her strength and subtlety. She would often transform her inner being, which would reflect itself in her physical appearance without the use of make-up. It was foggy when we were there, probably not unusual for the place. It was preternaturally quiet, and as the eye wandered from mountain top to mountain top it felt like standing at the end of the world. If a good wind came up, you felt carried off like a cloud. It was a beautiful land which made me feel sad and reflective. Duse was buried in the mountains overlooking the clouded valleys to the north of Venice. It was at moments like this that I could feel my parents' love of a fellow artist, their reverence and their appreciation of who she was. Observing the land where she chose to live, so full of longing, I felt that she was drawing me into the theater, a world I had long refused to inhabit.

From Venice we went to Athens where I stood amongst the pillars of the Acropolis, the oldest building I had ever seen. The air danced before my eyes with a light so pure that I could see it moving. The place, and the men who built it, made me stand erect for the first time in my life. I admired the Greeks for their brilliant culture, the product of a tribal people who rose above being warriors and pirates. When we visited Epidarus, our guide demonstrated the wonderful acoustics of the magnificent outdoor theater that seats up to fifteen thousand people. From that moment, I couldn't stop wondering if the scholars who speculated that the Greek theater masks were constructed to aid voice projection had ever visited the physical theater. Our main difficulty with Greek plays is that we think of the Greeks in terms of statues and philosophical city-states. We would do better to imagine a warlike, tribal people who also possessed the intellectual and artistic capacities to express their extraordinary depth of perception and knowledge in artistic forms.

Greece offered me what I can only call one of the purest memories of my life. My father and I went to Delphi to see the oracle, which sits on the tip of a mountain. My father sighed a wish to bathe his feet in the stream that bubbles through this temple of western civilization. He turned away to leave, too timid to put his feet into the water. I stopped him, knelt down and removed his sandals, and then mine, and we sat on a rock and bathed our feet together. Our selves, and the air, sparkled. I wish our relationship had always been that moment. We smiled in the serenity of life and each other. The oracle had given us a gift so silently that we did not notice. We sat in companionable silence as we gazed across a valley of olive trees, our feet cooling in the ancient stream of time.

Elias, our driver, who spoke English he had learned from Robert Mitchum, took us from Delphi to a restaurant near the crossroads where (according to Sophocles) Oedipus killed his father. At the bottom of a flight of wooden steps, under a large weeping willow tree, a stream ran through the middle of the eight or nine tables. A little wooden bridge linked the two halves of the restaurant. In the distance a huge rock jutted out of the earth like a dome, at the top of which was a cave once inhabited by monks. We pointed to the food we wanted to eat: fresh bread and feta cheese, shish kebab, salad, watermelon for dessert. We toasted our health with retsina wine. The meal was as fresh and wonderful as the day. Somewhere, I have a photo of me with my arm around my father's shoulders, father and son smiling out at the world. For that expedition, I became again what he had called me when I was little: the sunshine of his life. It's the only day of my life when I can be sure that my father and I loved one another.

We planned to be in Berlin for two weeks. Our purpose was to visit the Berliner Ensemble, Brecht's theater, located in East Berlin, and to attend a theater festival taking place in West Berlin. Although West Berlin at the time was a showcase of freedom, wealth and poverty existed side by side. Within a five-minute's walk of the new Hilton were bombed-out zones that had remained abandoned since the war. West Berlin was surrounded. We however, ate luxuriously in the restaurants: wild boar, pheasant, and duck, accompanied by light Rieslings and Moselles.

Amidst reports in *The New York Times* of imminent war, we rented a VW Beetle and drove to Checkpoint Charlie. This was no act of courage; we simply would not allow the Strasberg family vacation to be interfered with by an international dispute. When we were within two blocks of the border, we saw American tanks and armored vehicles lined up near this notorious gateway between East Berlin and the American sector of West Berlin.

The East German tanks stood guarding the border; one of their cannons had a flower in the barrel. A large American captain stood with his toes on the borderline facing the German and Russian soldiers. As we passed through the checkpoint, we sensed a strained politeness from the East German and Russian officers that barely covered a suspicious, hostile atmosphere. On our numerous crossings, however, we were never harassed. Some of the East German soldiers were younger than I, and their youthful, rosy cheeks seemed totally incompatible with war. Crossing the border was like entering a time warp. Everything in East Berlin was gray. In total contrast to the Western Zone, there were no flowers on windowsills! Cafes and restaurants seemed to be hidden, the silence was oppressive on the barren sidewalks. One felt watched by people who didn't exist.

An aging actor in West Berlin looked at us sadly and said, "Everyone knew what was happening under Hitler, but your government is putting all of the same people back in power. It's crazy. You're giving them back the guns." It was true. America was so afraid of Communism that even Nazis looked good.

My father was more excited during those two weeks than I ever saw him. He had known Brecht when the great man had emigrated to America during World War Two. My father said that Brecht loved to go to the movies and particularly adored gangster films. Gangsters symbolized the revolutionary spirit that he espoused in his own work.

My father and mother had seen the Ensemble in London in 1956. Brecht died later that year. At that time, my mother had been working in England with Marilyn on *The Prince and the Showgirl*, with Laurence Olivier. My parents had been surprised to discover that Olivier was envious of and competitive with Marilyn. According to them, he did everything in his power to undermine her. He was not only severe during rehearsal and filming, but he photographed the scenes to his advantage. My mother was particularly depressed and tired during the filming. She was probably beginning to feel the effects of the as yet undiagnosed cancer which would lead to a mastectomy and chemotherapy. She had already begun to slowly die of the disease, and of the loneliness, heartbreak, and resignation that accompany, or, just possibly, create it.

In 1961, we met Helene Weigel, a superb actress and Brecht's wife, in

Brecht's study, a room crammed with books, whiskey, and the smell of cigars. It was a place for thinking, writing, and talking. We talked for several hours about the crisis of the Ensemble since the Wall had been erected. Half of the company lived in the West and did not want to reenter the Eastern sector for fear of not being allowed to go home at the end of the day. Weigel, now head of the Ensemble, was desperately replacing the Western contingent of the company. Ekkhard Schall, who was married to Brecht's and Weigel's daughter Barbara Berg, was a theatrical and brilliant actor, whom we saw in the title role of *The Resistible Rise of Arturo Ui*. Schall created a brilliantly theatrical parody of Hitler, approaching the level of Chaplin and Keaton. When he was a child in Berlin, the Americans came and took away his Nazi Youth uniform. He had cried bitterly, as he loved his uniform and felt the soldiers to be cruel. He looked at us and said, "I was a child. I didn't understand until much later what the uniform represented and what had happened during the war." Perhaps some of the brilliance of this work related to his own personal shock and discovery of the man he had adored as a child.

I had never seen a theater like the Berliner Ensemble. When we went backstage, my father pointed excitedly at the props. "Look at that," he would exclaim, as he grabbed me like a child. "They're all real." We looked in wonder at the ancient brass scientific instruments. The set of *Galileo* was covered in hammered copper, whose reflected light shimmered with the terra cotta color I had just seen in Italy. The floor of the stage was tiled in such a way that people's footsteps sounded as if they were on cobblestones. The sight and sound of the play was utterly real. In one scene, Ernst Busch as Galileo was served a fresh, hot chicken to eat. I had never seen anyone really eat on stage. There was a simple reality in watching this great scientist say he wasn't hungry, and then devour his chicken with a voracious appetite. We understood the man's love of life, and the conflict that was going on between the man and the scientist's search for truth, now being threatened by the Inquisition's objection to his discovery, without a word being spoken. The genuine sincerity of the moment made a statement about society, and a man ruled by forces greater than himself. It was theater being practiced as an art. It was unforgettable.

One day, we watched a replacement rehearsal for *Arturo Ui*. A new actor had been hired to play the role of Dolfuss, the gangster boss. They spent three hours rehearsing his entrance. He had to take off his hat, walk across the stage to Ui, and very simply deliver his line. The director, Manfred Wekwerth, would constantly interrupt, saying, "No, no, no! Just come in and say 'Hello.' Don't act." The actor would nod and come in again, but there was always some little tell-tale movement, a little flick of the hat, or some tick he thought was "interesting." Wekwerth came over to my father, who spoke some German, and said, "It takes us two years to untrain them. Actors acting would drive Brecht crazy."

All of the intellectualization about epic theater is, pardon the expression, bullshit. Perhaps theater scholars love to write about "distancing" and the elimination of real feeling from the theater because they have so little real feeling.

The Brechtian actor merely tells his story. Brecht didn't want an actor's emotion to obscure the essence of the drama; it is the story that counts. I am stunned by the fact that most "Brechtian" productions are intellectualized, academic theater. These long and boring evenings are in total contrast to the Ensemble's wonderfully theatrical evenings, in which we are entranced by Brecht's arguments because we're having such a good time.

I recently conducted a workshop on Brecht in Paris. I invented an exercise in which I asked each actor to recount a major emotional crisis in their life as though it had happened to someone else. I thought that "distancing" themselves from the event would produce the kind of profound emotional simplicity that Brecht wanted. It worked, and was actually one of the most popular seminars I ever did. In Paris, people's idea of Brecht and "distancing" is largely cold and didactic; the work produced in the seminar was anything but.

Artistically, Berlin was full of life. An international theater festival in West Berlin happened to feature Roger Planchon's production of Molière's *George Dandin*. This was the first time that I actually enjoyed Molière. When the Comedie Francaise had come to New York in the 1950s, I'd been surprised when a young actress began to recite and then cry. I'd turned to my mother and said, "She's crying." My mother leaned over to me and whispered, "Glycerine." Sure enough, as I watched, the "tear" froze to her face.

There was none of that chicanery in Planchon's production. He successfully created a seventeenth-century provincial family's life: their relationships, feelings, and class differences were explored with a simple theatricality, using frozen moments highlighted by light changes when characters spoke their inner thoughts. The production is engraved in my memory. Like all great art, it exists in its own personal dream space and emotional time, meaning it is timeless and ageless. Molière's sensitivity and understanding regarding a woman's desire for love, freedom, and equality are hundreds of years ahead of Ibsen. Planchon's production made all of Molière's thoughts so present that it was clear that French society had not yet caught up to the playwright. Molière's thoughts and feelings had been so fully realized in this production that the audience could truly feel all the sensory realities that we call daily life.

Our European trip was the only time that I saw the vulnerable and open child in my father, and the only time I saw what his dream-come-true might be. It wasn't power or fame; he didn't even envy National Theaters. He considered them to be government-sponsored production houses, the majority of which had no clearly defined artistic principle—producing organizations, not theaters.

This memory of his child-like enthusiasm makes me feel that I am my father's son. I believe that a man's greatness is a reflection of his ability to dream and then make the dream real. The oracle at Delphi awoke my dream and Italy brought my senses to life.

Ghosts directed by John Strasberg
Compania Julieta Serrano at Festival de Oroño (Madrid) 1992

CHAPTER FOUR

CHAOS, DOUBT, AND CONFUSION—
THE BEGINNING OF THE CREATIVE PROCESS

People can be side by side and dream and live in worlds apart. I came back from Europe with new insights into what was becoming a growing passion for my work. More than anything, I wanted to be in the theater.

My father's actual teaching method was based on four hours of training per week: two hours of Sense Memory and two hours of scene work. In the latter, he saw and commented on two scenes per class. When I studied Sense Memory, he handled five or six people at a session. Originally he had done this work on an individual basis, and eventually he handled up to twenty people at a time.

It has never been emphasized that my father's class work was not the same as the work he did at the Studio, where his work was passionate and inspirational and involved his analysis of individual acting problems and discourses on theater in general. He did no basic training there, though he often lamented that many Studio members lacked technique. Ironically, most of the free technique classes offered at the Studio over the years were poorly attended. My father was the spiritual guide who stimulated creative imagination and pointed out problems in technique and logic. The solutions were up to the individual who, at his own discretion, took classes with someone outside the Studio.

I didn't feel completely lifelike in my work. I had a feeling of self-manipulation that came from a dependency on the self-conscious use of exercises and preparations when I worked. They produced real enough sensation and emotion, but intuition and spontaneous inspiration was missing. Technique was separating me from the art of acting. I needed someone to give me permission to trust myself. I needed to learn that technique was not some perfect way of avoiding mistakes: technique, it turns out, is being able to learn from those mistakes.

THE ACTORS STUDIO

My father is credited with having trained every member of the Actors Studio and with having taught the Method to every actor at the Studio. He is also thought to be the founder of the Studio. It is also assumed that every member learned to act in the Actors Studio. Wrong on every score. Even members of the Studio sometimes think it is a school. Do they think that artists don't continue learning all of their lives? The name clearly defines what it is: a place where an artist works. This confusion has been very destructive to the Studio, especially now, when it needs to redefine itself.

The Studio was never a school for beginners. It was a movement of talented artists who shared the mutual goals of exploring their own personal dream space and expanding their artistic capacities. That is the Studio's true uniqueness.

My father was a teacher who loved and nurtured talent, and who had an extraordinary knowledge of acting and the art of the theater. But the Studio was not where my father performed magic on the uninitiated. Many of the actors associated with the artistic success of the Studio were inspired by him, but they were not novices when they became members of the Studio. My father's passionate belief in reality as a fundamental part of theatrical expression and his dedication to the maintenance of this standard were both central to the Actors Studio. He kept everyone focused on their love for the art and the work. He managed this while being surrounded by the business of theater and film, where one's feelings about art and creativity need to be kept hidden. The Studio kept people's artistic dream space alive. That mission is sadly missed at the moment. Whether we are for or against the movement, it stimulates everyone and is good not only for creativity but for business.

My father was a Scorpio, a tough, selfish man, determined to be successful. The one area of work he mastered was teaching. He was in his late fifties when he began to receive the recognition that he wanted, but even then he was overshadowed by my sister and Kazan. He lived well, but he was not satisfied. He suffered from personal insecurity, and his feelings of not being sufficiently recognized were never fully resolved. During the height of the Studio's success, in the fifties and early sixties, he received a very small salary which, more often than not, wasn't paid. The Studio was always broke or in a financial crisis. He was given credit for the success of a whole generation of actors and directors who were more famous and making more money than he. We live in a culture full of successful people, many of whom achieved their success through cleverness and the theft of power, and in which wealth and social recognition justifies any form of behavior. The only thing my father did wrong was that he wasn't rich enough. He fixed that at the end of his life.

The Actors Studio, along with the Comedie Francaise and the Moscow Art Theater, are three landmarks in the history of theatrical organizations. The Comedie Francaise was the first permanent theater, meaning that the life of the organization continued in perpetuity, existing longer than the life of any one artist, generation of artists, or benefactor. The Moscow Art Theater was the first ensemble theater, meaning that the actors and directors shared a common principle and basis of training in production; they were not just a group of artists with diverse methods and principals of work, as is usually the case in theater production.

The Actors Studio institutionalized the realistic principles that are the basis of many actors' creative processes. Before its creation, talent, imagination, and a sense of truth were believed to be individual phenomena; results of an individual's personal involvement. Without the Studio, the common thread that links these qualities to the work of Stanislavski, which the Moscow Art Theater was based on, would not be understood in the proper historical and social perspective. The work of Marlon Brando, Montgomery Clift, James Dean, Elia Kazan, and many others in the American theater and cinema has had a revolutionary effect on theater and film in every country and culture in the world. We have still not seen the end of it. Talent, and the creative process that leads to this particularly intimate and personal expression of talent, can no longer be considered an accident or a mystical gift. Its nature can be studied, and we can all learn from understanding why great human beings are great. Whatever the future of the Actors Studio, its legacy will never change.

The Studio home had been a Greek Orthodox Church, a white brick building at 432 West 44th Street, between 9th and 10th Avenues, which it now owns. On Tuesdays and Fridays, from 11:00 A.M. to 1:00 P.M., my father moderated the acting sessions in which members presented work. I saw Paul Newman work on Petrucchio, and Eli Wallach do Richard III. I witnessed Geraldine Page do Gertrude in the scene I mentioned earlier, directed by Walter Beakel, with Kevin McCarthy as Hamlet. It was as alive and powerful as any theater I've ever seen. Like so many rehearsal moments, it had an intimacy that makes theater art. I would love to see an entire production with the sweep, force, and humanity which that scene had! The behavior and physicality created an excitement that gave one the sense of watching real people in a real situation. Walter extracted a quality of spontaneity that made the language come out of the behavior, so it was immediate and understandable. In Hamlet's "Speak the speech" monologue to the players, the advice seemed to be given to actors whom Hamlet really knew. We knew their relationship, and there was a sharing of knowledge which made us feel that we knew each actor. This reality came from the fact that all the players were members of the Studio: it is what ensemble theater is based on.

Realistic acting is based in behavior, not illustrative technique. The spoken text is an expression of the behavioral life that the actor and director have created. When that principle is applied, acting becomes involved and personal. It is centered in the body and soul, not in the head.

The Studio in those days was throbbing with life. Geraldine had auditioned seven times before she was accepted into the Studio. When I asked her one day about doing all those auditions she shrugged, and said, "Oh, I guess they just didn't think I was good enough." Gerry was one of the few who had real humility. I had the privilege of both her friendship and her professional expertise. We worked together many times, not only during the years of the Actors Studio Theater, but in our collaboration at my school. I do take credit for convincing her to teach, though when I first asked her, she looked both excited and scared. She said, "But I don't know how. What would I say?" She finally agreed that at least she would come and watch a class, and afterwards she said, "Well, I think I can do that." Gerry was also an integral part of the Mirror Repertory Company, where I directed her in five productions between 1983 and 1985.

The first time I saw her work at the Studio she was standing on stage with her hands at her sides. Every time she moved her hands and arms my father would command her to stay still. After several tries, in which she always managed to make some kind of gesture, he asked the Studio's stage manager, Lee Marsh, to tie Gerry's hands behind her back with a rope. There came into her eyes a look of fear and desperation, like that of a trapped animal. She finally became very still, and when she began again she was completely simple. Deep emotion filled her body and voice and expressed itself in the most personal and intimate manner. She made me lose all sense that I was watching someone act; it seemed impossible that she could consciously will herself to be this vulnerable. These are the moments when one understands exactly what realistic acting is: no more theory, no more acting, no more ideas. There is just a person who becomes a living work of art.

Paul and Eli were already famous, but they worked on parts as would any other student. There was an atmosphere of learning and humility that I have also seen in some martial arts masters, dancers, and athletes. There was no arrogance or attitude of superiority; no one tried to hide behind an image. Hard work was done in a spirit of pleasure, for the love of excellence and the pursuit of knowledge. People who love what they do like working hard. The Studio removed the sense of "specialness" that surrounds the majority of successful working actors. Everybody had something to learn, and everybody had problems that they could work on without feeling ashamed. The air tingled from the aura of reality and the sense of truth.

I've never encountered such an atmosphere of obsession and love, of determined dedication to learning, in any other theatrical institution in the world. Failure is only an effort that one learns from. Success is impossible without it. Unfortunately for actors, their mistakes are almost always made in public, and after too many errors one may find oneself out of a career.

The Studio broke all the constraints and rules. It changed the atmosphere that created the urge to cover up, and encouraged actors to take chances. It was precisely that risk-taking quality that many of the best and most successful actors are known for. It was a workshop of peers and top professionals who, in the Studio, could continue to be creative, to practice, and to make mistakes. The work was sometimes boring, self-indulgent, or mannered; sometimes it was stunning, and exposed a reality that I would pay good money to see. Those moments dominated the underlying politics, pettiness, and mediocrity that tend to choke the life out of any institution, even one which originates in love. The Studio was a place for dreamers and dreaming.

Before I auditioned and was accepted I acted in several Studio projects. *Who's Happy Now?* was an Oliver Hailey play, directed by Andreas Voutsinas, one of my father's students. I played the part of an interlocutor, a character who talks directly to an audience. The idea of having to make direct contact with the audience so terrified me that I worked harder than I ever had before. I had no technique, emotion, or exercise to cling to, and nothing to hide behind. I simply had to be there and talk like a human being; the point of concentration was to be personal and present.

I remember how the stage lights in my eyes created the sense of otherworldliness that is so particular to being on stage. I was speaking slowly and deliberately across the magic of time and space. On the other edge of the light and darkness, where spirits join the stage and the audience together, were people I knew. When I talked to them with the words and thoughts of this other person they also became transformed. My personal dream space and my real life became one thrilling reality; I could speak to these people more simply and intimately than I had ever been able to before. The experience left me with a love for plays which use an interlocutor, especially when the narrator is the playwright, as in Tennessee Williams' *The Glass Menagerie* or Brian Friel's *Dancing at Lughnasa*. Don't we often feel this intimacy as a public, too? Don't we often feel that we know an artist better than we know our own family? That there is a shared sympathy, an understanding? I've had nights, as an actor, when an audience was more familiar and intimate to me than the people in my own life: I was there for them, and they were there for me.

In the fall of '62, Terry Hayden, a member of the Studio who had seen me work, asked me if I would like to act in a play that she was directing off-Broadway. I didn't understand why anyone would offer me an acting job. I had no professional experience, and even less sense of self-worth. Nevertheless, I accepted. I made my professional acting debut in *Five Evenings*, the first contemporary Russian play to be presented in New York. It was a little play, but I had a good part. Terry had also cast Simon Oakland, Frances Heflin, Maria Tucci, Joy Geffen, and Vernon Weddle. Contrary to the play's title we ran for four evenings before we closed after a total of six performances. We opened on a Thursday and played Friday night and two shows each on Saturday and Sunday. We were paid thirty-five dollars a week. On our only Sunday matinee two old ladies talked all through the performance. During one blackout, as I was trying to prepare for the next scene with my personal object exercise, they began to discuss the actors: they thought I was nice, but that Maria was much better. My hearing homed in on them, like the radar operator in a submarine in one of those war movies. I couldn't stop listening to them. They taught me a memorable lesson in concentration.

I was teased in the dressing room about doing a preparation. With or without it, I was terrified to go onstage. Many actors are disturbed by anyone who needs to prepare or who takes their work too seriously. I learned to prepare in private. I've found that onstage is one of the best places to be alone. No one ever looks there for the strange reason that they never expect anyone to be there unless they have to be.

My next Studio project was *Marathon '33*, written by Studio member June Havoc. The play was based on June's experience of the notorious dance marathons of the Depression, at which people would compete for money by dancing for days, even weeks at a time. The rules were very strict: the dancer's knees were not permitted to touch the floor, and they could only take one five-minute break every hour to use the toilets or to shower. Couples slept in each other's arms, eating, having haircuts, even getting dental or medical care, as they moved across the floor. After a childhood career in vaudeville collapsed with the onset of the Depression, June, the younger sister of Gypsy Rose Lee, ran away from home to participate in the marathons. She was only seventeen when the events she described in *Marathon '33* took place.

June co-directed the project with Timmy Everett, a dancer-choreographer. We began work by improvising for three days a week, and then doing extensive Sense Memory exercises, which the play's reality demanded. I was partnered with a diminutive but extremely strong dancer by the name of Lane Bradbury. Over a period of a year we worked the play as only an ensemble cast can, presenting the results for the view of the Studio members. The play went on to be the second fully-fledged production of the Actors Studio Theater, and was a Broadway success in 1963.

Auditioning for the Studio

In the spring of 1963, I auditioned for and became a member of the Studio. For my audition, I chose the scene from Clifford Odets' *Awake and Sing* where the young man comes home after his girl friend has jilted him and discusses the situation with his grandfather. It's a very emotional scene from the beginning, which I liked because the Studio had a five-minute time limit per scene. The last thing I needed was to be worrying about the time. Auditioning is what I dislike most about being an actor. I am dependent on someone else letting me do what I want to do. I always expected to be criticized by authority unless I'm having a really good day, in which case I don't care what they think because I'm working for myself. The situation affects many actors' concentration. As a director, I learned that some actors are great at auditioning and nothing else; they will never be as good as they were in the audition, except possibly opening night. I wonder how many wonderful actors have never been discovered due to this process.

I was thinking about who would do the scene with me when my mother announced that she had already talked to Jacob Ben Ami, one of the great actors of the Yiddish theater. He had agreed to help. Jacob was one of the few people my father spoke of with reverence whenever he mentioned having seen Jacob's performance of Samson in *Samson and Delilah*. Maybe I should have been flattered, but I was furious that my mother had acted without consulting me first. I was insulted that she thought I wasn't capable of making my own decisions. She was interfering with my work life, the way she had interfered with Susan's. When Shelley Winters arranged for Susan to meet George Stevens, who was to direct the movie of *The Diary of Anne Frank*, Stevens did not seem inclined to use Susan. As a director, he wondered what artistic contribution he would make using an actress who had already brilliantly created the role. Shelley pleaded with my parents to let Susan go to Hollywood and meet the director alone, so that he could see that she was open to change and wanted to be directed by him. Shelley knew that if my mother went, Stevens would realize that he had no chance to direct Susan. Heedlessly, my mother went along. Whether that was the reason Susan wasn't cast, or whether Hollywood didn't want a Jewish girl in the role because it might hurt the box office, my mother's behavior seemed insulting and disrespectful.

I felt trapped, but I met Ben Ami at the classroom studio in Carnegie Hall one afternoon at about five o'clock. He didn't seem like Samson at all. His eyes were fiercely direct, but his appearance was more like the kind of Jewish doctor that Paul Muni would play. He had salt and pepper hair and a deep voice that was very mild, but resonant. He was as nervous and uncomfortable as I. I don't know what my mother had said to him, or why he had agreed, but she had got us both there.

We talked a little and read the scene once, after which he started to ask me what I thought about the character and the situation. These were the kind of questions that I absolutely hated; I felt interrogated and tested. At that time it made me feel stupid to ask myself the kind of questions that I now routinely ask myself and everyone else. I kept my thoughts to myself, because I was afraid I would lose whatever intuitive connection I had made between thought and feeling. I was also afraid of being ridiculed, so I would simply say what was expected of me, not what I really felt. In this confusion, my silence was a shield of protection.

Whenever I browsed through my father's collection of working scripts of great actors, I would see that they had notes written in the margins. I imitated this as a part of my desire to be great and to find the perfect method. However, everything I wrote seemed banal or stupid, inconsistant or obvious. I also have to confess that, because of my secretive nature, I was afraid that my mother (or someone like her), who read other people's letters and writings, would spy on me and find out what I really thought. (One of my wives actually did open my mail.)

As an actor, I only knew things by how I felt. Analysis of my thoughts felt like the intellectualization of a process that, when it worked best, was spontaneous, thoughtful in an organic way, and intensely personal. I thought, like a lot of artists, that if I were conscious I would separate myself from my feelings and that would have the opposite effect of what being naturally conscious is. The belief that asking questions is dangerous to the creative process is still a major obstacle to many artists, a fear I understand, having had it myself. However, there's no other way to know. Imagine if human beings never asked questions.

Towards the end of the meeting, which lasted about an hour, Ben Ami asked me who was going to play the grandfather. I turned red with a feeling of utter shame and rage, and said that I thought that he would. He said that he had agreed to direct or work on the scene with me, but that he wouldn't act in it. I didn't know if he had decided he didn't want to, or if my mother hadn't told either of us what her plans were. I suspect that she had lied to both of us, as I knew she could. I'm sure her efforts were made in the name of love, but love is not shown by unilateral decision-making.

It seemed to me that an audition piece for the Studio was not one which ought to be directed. I've always insisted on being judged on my merits alone. I didn't want to do whatever it took to get in. I told Ben Ami that I didn't want him to direct. He was very polite, and said that if I wanted to meet again he would be glad to help.

I asked Salem Ludwig to do the role. I explained that I didn't want to rehearse too much because I didn't want to have time to think myself out of my feelings. Spontaneity is especially important for an audition. Salem agreed to be my partner.

On the evening of the audition, I arrived about an hour before my scheduled time. The ground floor of the Studio had a large room to the left of the entrance, a staircase leading up to the main auditorium and the office, which was to the right, a green room with bathrooms labeled "Romeo" and "Juliet," and a small kitchen, a library, and a back rehearsal

room where a spiral stairwell led upstairs to the stage. All the actors
waited in the first three rooms until their scene was called. It felt like being in a herd of cattle in a corral, being funneled into the slaughterhouse.
One almost chokes on the fear and anxiety. I can think of no better way
to create mass panic than to throw actors together in the same enclosed
space when they are about to audition for something that may affect their
entire careers.

I found a quiet corner in the office and lay down on the couch. I began to prepare a private moment and an emotional memory. The emotional memory was from a time when I was about eleven; I heard my
parents fighting in the kitchen next to my room. I remember clutching at
my door and pleading in a whisper for them to stop, that I was sorry for
what I had done, and would they please stop fighting. The argument was
of course not over me and I had done nothing to provoke it, but I've never
forgotten that moment. I chose it because feeling alone and abandoned
seemed to parallel the feelings of the jilted Ralph in the scene.

As my private moment, I looked at myself naked in a mirror. I would
create the feeling of standing naked before the world to make myself feel
particularly vulnerable. Who would I be if I were naked in the desert? I
worked on these two exercises and went over the given circumstances
prior to the scene. I had worked for over half an hour when they notified
me that we were third to go. Scenes were strictly limited to five minutes
with one minute for scene change and set up. Whether or not you were
set up, the clock began running.

I moved into the back room, wading through waves of terror and anxiety. I asked Lee Marsh if there was a way to go up through the spiral
stairs at the back of the Studio. I didn't want to risk losing my concentration and wanted to be in my own world. I didn't want to pass in front of
the judges, who sat in shadow behind lights which were directed toward
the stage. (It seemed medieval to me, even when I became a judge at these
same auditions; black hoods should have been worn.) This was an unusual
request and the stage manager said that he'd ask the judges during the
next change. The judges included my father, Cheryl, and several other directors and actors who had conducted the preliminary auditions. To my
relief, they agreed to my request.

I felt frozen as I waited, as doubt, panic, and then despair engulfed
me. I had prepared too far in advance and given myself too much time to
think, and I felt like an overwound spring. I was afraid that nothing was
going to happen and that the audition was going to be a disaster. I listened

to the scene before me, and remember hearing only desperate screaming tones from one of the actors. I heard furniture being moved, then my name and the scene were announced. I remember thinking that if my emotions weren't primed by the time I got up the stairs, the scene wasn't going to work. I was terrified that my thoughts would inhibit my feelings.

I felt like I was standing outside myself, a spectator to the process, but about half way up the stairs I started to fall apart. I could barely control myself; it felt wonderful. Cheryl said later that I played the scene a bit too emotionally and my voice got a little out of control. Afterwards, I felt I had done more or less what I had wanted to do and that I had a good chance to get in. Later that night, I was phoned with the good news: I had become a member. The reasons for my being accepted might have been tinged with nepotism, but I felt that I had earned it. The work in the scene had adequately represented my sensitivity, talent and emotional capacity. Although my technique was irregular, I had been real.

MM and *Desire*

Can you imagine how I felt when my parents' drafted me to do a scene from *A Streetcar Named Desire* with Marilyn in my father's private classes? "Young man. Young, young, young man..." I was instructed to do everything I could to help her. My soul was now indentured to serve their relationship with Marilyn. At twenty-one, I felt that my career had already been erased.

Marilyn and I had known each other for almost eight years. We liked one another, but I was always shy. Being alone together was painful. The only other person with whom I've had the same reaction was Montgomery Clift. I know now that they were as shy as I was, but at the time I couldn't separate their feelings from mine. Nor did I realize that I had a talent for sensing other people's thoughts and feelings. Marilyn, Monty, Kim Stanley, and my second wife, Sabra Jones, are the only people I've personally known who trembled (physically) in real life.

We rehearsed in the new studio at Carnegie Hall that my father had rented for his private classes. The Capital Theater Building, where he had held his classes for the past several years, was being demolished. Carnegie Hall is enormous: the corridors are labyrinthine and the floors seem to be of different heights. The studio—Room 1013—was at the end of a long corridor, in the corner opposite the men's room; a large, relatively narrow rectangle. Light streamed through the high windows unless the red velvet curtains were closed. Those curtains were borrowed from the warehouse where Cheryl stored scenery and costumes from productions of hers. My parents loved furniture that came from plays. Our house had a sofa that had been used in *The Rose Tattoo*. Later, after Marilyn died, they added the white, baby grand piano that had belonged to her. The room had a platform/stage at the far end, which ran the fifteen-foot width of the room, and risers for five rows of chairs. The room held about forty people.

Marilyn and I leaned against a window frame, and she asked me what I thought she should do. I suggested that we read the scene together and see what happened. After several read-throughs, we discussed what the Kowalski apartment might be like. I didn't care what it was like; my character didn't live there and would not have seen it before the scene. Marilyn seemed anxious; she wanted and expected me to help her, which was strange since she was a star with much more experience than I. What did my parents think I knew that she didn't? Marilyn and I liked one another, and once we began to work, our shyness ebbed. Work gave us something to share, a common point of concentration. Once she got over her initial anxiety, she was very capable of doing her own work.

I never rehearse scenes to be done in a class too thoroughly. I always devote my scene work to the initial stages of creation, when one is intentionally dreaming and imagining what composes the character and the world of the play. Scenes are never at performance level. That should be done in Performance workshops, and only with sufficiently trained acting students who can apply their work to the rehearsal process in which performance is the goal. Most actors are taught that rehearsing is a process of planning how to illustrate one's ideas of a scene. They assume that these ideas are the life of the character and the play, and that rehearsing necessitates the collaboration and mutual agreement of their partners. They believe that the rehearsal process involves a mechanical working-out of the technical aspects of the scene and, without realizing it, they start thinking like a director. They work on things an actor has little control over instead of the fundamental creative process.

To intentionally dream about the world in which the character lives is work which the actor must always do alone; it is then that he establishes the link between himself and the play. This is what I now recognize takes place in the actor's personal dream space. What most people call rehearsing is really a superficial form of directing and performing. I always knew this intuitively and I never cared about designing a scene when I did scene work in class.

Marilyn and I rehearsed in the tentative fashion that is common when actors are exploring a new world. We did a lot of anxious searching in one another's eyes. This longing for eye-contact is one of the things I remember most about her, as she trembled with the desperate hunger of a child for life, comfort, love. Beneath whatever mask I was presenting to the world, I trembled in the same way, but no one ever saw it, not even me.

In the midst of this confusion and doubt, with chaos yawning beneath us, we were investigating the situation and relationships of the scene. We threw ourselves into this imaginary world full of strange people and places, synthesizing ourselves and the reality of the rehearsal into the reality of the play. When this transformation is successful actors often experience simultaneous sensations of terror and ecstasy: like falling in love, the experience transports them to another reality and dimension of existence.

Each time we would finish going through the scene, Marilyn would ask me if I thought that it was OK. She wanted to know if there were other things she should be doing. She was desperately insecure, but a very hard worker and nobody's fool. The dumb blonde persona may have been founded in reality—the nervousness in her mouth and lips were genuine symptoms of personal problems—but it was clear that she was aware that she had created a female character in the tradition of the sad sack tramps of Chaplin and Keaton. When she came to New York to work with my father it was because she wanted to be recognized as being more than the mask. In their cruelty and arrogance, people condemned her.

Our rehearsals were sketches of life, character, and ideas. There are rooms in museums devoted exclusively to artist's sketchbooks like the one devoted to Turner at the Tate Gallery in London. I love them as much as I love really good rehearsals; there is an essence captured that is the quintessence of art. One always hopes the production will be able to sustain that level of intensely intimate reality. Of course, watching most good rehearsals is boring; nothing appears to be happening. Everyone seems lost in thought, preoccupied with something that only they can see. This is the discovery which makes rehearsal time so essential. Many actors and directors don't know what rehearsals are for; they jump into rhythm and design as though there is nothing else. I guess that for them, there isn't. I never had problems learning lines, which is what many people think is the most difficult part of acting. Being creative doesn't mean that I couldn't remember a direction or repeat blocking. None of these basic realities of acting are problems if one has a good creative process. If you have a solid foundation, acting becomes profoundly involving and pleasurable, even after many performances. Actors who get bored after a few performances aren't serious about their work.

My biggest problem was repeating emotions. I was trained to solve this problem by using sense memory techniques; it was effective, but a solution that I wasn't satisfied with. My aversion stemmed from the need to plan an exercise so that I would be able to release a feeling I knew was going to happen on the next page. The technique seemed mechanical, and because it anticipated what was going to happen, concentrating my work in it pulled me out of the moment. My father said it was like a musical partition. In the moment of performance, artists and athletes have to be able to respond spontaneously. Even their thought processes must be capable of responding in the moment of action. Planning exercises like this separated my thought process from those of the character in the play. Despite the emotional power and consistency which is the strength of my father's Method, I felt as though I was manipulating myself. Even when I mastered the technique and could do exercises quickly, without diverting my concentration from the play, two things happened: the life of the play was reduced to a series of sensory and emotional exercises, and the exercises would wear out and need to be replaced by others. The entire technique interfered with my intuition, imagination, intentional dreaming, and spontaneity. It made it harder to get involved with the play, because my habits were trained to concentrate on a technique that stopped the natural, organic thinking I had in my personal dream space.

In the *Streetcar* scene, a young man collecting money for selling newspapers knocks on the door, and Blanche invites him in and begins to flirt with him. She is so desperate for company that she needs to be with someone, anyone, rather than be alone. The boy doesn't really know what to do, and wants to leave. On the day of the scene, I prepared in a quiet corner for almost an hour. When the scene was announced, I entered from stage right and knocked on a pole that served as an imaginary door. On the pole hung a curtain, beyond which I could see the room Marilyn had created with objects that she had brought to involve herself in Blanche's world. I didn't want to focus on anything I saw, though my cursory glimpse took in a make-up table full of cosmetics and clothing spread all over the stage. Marilyn opened the "door." Her make-up was almost grotesque, as I'd never seen her. Her eyes were liquid, full of a mixture of terror and longing; she was trembling more than I have ever seen anyone tremble.

The scene felt as though life were moving in slow motion, we were so hypnotically attached to one another. The atmosphere seemed thick and waterlike, as though we were "swimming on land." I didn't know what either of us would do. She enticed me, flirted with me, and I felt speechless and horribly uncomfortable. I hovered near the "door," anxious and terrified, wondering if this person, this Blanche of Marilyn's, was going to faint, fall apart, or attack me. At the end of the scene, the boy leaves. The bizarreness and fear I felt seemed very real; I was relieved to get out. Blanche is left alone. Marilyn took a long moment by herself to finish her sketch and the scene was over. The whole room breathed a sigh of relief, as though everyone had been spellbound.

We talked about what we had worked on. I said that I had worked on the humid, sensual heat of New Orleans, and on the relationship. My father spoke to Marilyn with deserved praise, pointing out details of her behavior to clarify what he had liked in her work. (My father had hopes of directing her in this play and in *Anna Christie*.)

At the end he turned to me and, with controlled fury, announced that I hadn't done any work. I sat there, shocked and stone-faced. I didn't argue. I didn't even feel angry. I was stunned and ashamed, but somewhere I knew that his reaction seemed unreal; I didn't understand why I was being attacked. There was no apparent logic for it, but fifteen years later, in the mid-1970s, I told Sabra about this experience. She pointed out that my father was probably jealous of any man who got too close to Marilyn, a thought that would never have occurred to me. I can see now how most people who got close to her became, not just protective, but possessive of her.

At the time I discussed the incident with Sabra, I was trying to make peace with my anger over my father's infantile selfishness, which had caused so much unnecessary damage to my ego. My anger was holding me back from parenting myself in the way my parents hadn't; I needed to trust my burgeoning perceptions of life. I was finally beginning to see my father's jealousy and competitiveness towards me, which had been impossible for me to perceive until I had worked through enough old rage. I had thought of him in terms of his inability to openly recognize my talent, and his lack of generosity about Susan's enormous early success. But not in terms of Marilyn. How could he attack me over her, when I was never a rival for her affections?

THE ACTORS STUDIO THEATER

Fifteen years after the Studio was founded, the Actors Studio Theater came into being. It took a tremendous effort to establish a permanent, serious theater in the United States following in the footsteps of the Group Theater or, on the other side of the tracks, the Civic Repertory Company and the APA. The AST was motivated by the fact that the Studio was not made a part of the new theater at Lincoln Center, for which Elia Kazan was invited to be the artistic director. My father assumed that Kazan would want to include him and the Studio in the new organization. He was mistaken. Kazan resigned from the Studio to avoid a conflict of interest and, emotionally, I don't think he ever came back. My father's bitterness was such that he did not speak personally to Kazan for almost five years.

According to my father, Kazan said that Lincoln Center wanted only the star members of the Studio, not the whole organization. My father said that it was all or nothing, and that no artistic organization could be dictated to by a Board of Directors.

In his own book, *Elia Kazan: A Life* (1988), Gadget stated that he didn't want to work for my father. He wanted to be the artistic director he felt he deserved to be. In America, we often can't work together because we're all so obsessed with power, success, and being number one.

Given these circumstances, my father capitulated to the growing pressure from the membership of the Studio, particularly the efforts of the newly-formed Members' Committee headed by Rip Torn and Geraldine Page, to create the Actors Studio Theater. I remember discussions between my father and members of the Committee, which included Mendy Wager and Frank Corsaro. They needed to agree on a project, and had to get my father to clarify the conditions under which he, as Artistic Director of the Studio, would agree to go ahead with the AST. My mother, dressed in black down to her Bally slippers, was involved in all this, though she never had any official position.

Starting wasn't easy, because my father would change his mind whenever it seemed that things were close to being settled. The fantastic opportunity of a new play was lost when Geraldine, unbelievably, refused to do *Who's Afraid of Virginia Woolf?*, which Edward Albee had offered to the Studio on the condition that she play Martha. When I found that out, years later, I asked her about it. She said that she hated the play then, as now, finding it vulgar and lacking in artistic merit. At the time, I wasn't sure that I liked the play either. Recently, I have seen it in my own personal dream space, and I think it's wonderful. What I've never seen in a full production is the abundant love and humor between George and

Martha. When my father told me that Gerry hadn't wanted to do it, I asked why he hadn't insisted. He shrugged and said that she was bothered by the fact that the husband was younger, as was the case in her own marriage with Rip. Maybe he couldn't have convinced her, but it was worth a showdown. The history of the AST might have been totally different had it begun its life with that play.

The bargaining was lengthy and tedious. One had to wonder if my father really wanted to start a theater, or if he was being pushed into it by people who did. The discussions centered around the desirability of staging a new play, a classic, or an American classic. It had to have an all-star cast, a first-class director, and be a play that had not been recently produced. The choice finally narrowed down to O'Neill, of whom Tennessee Williams said, "Eugene O'Neill created the American theater. He also died for it." O'Neill is definitive of American culture: intensely personal with intimate moments of truth. Whether by accident or design, my father had settled on an almost impossible choice. The O'Neill estate was controlled by his widow, Carlotta, and there was almost no one to whom she would give the rights. Without my father's knowledge, Rip and Gerry approached Jose Quintero, who had directed Geraldine in *Summer and Smoke*, and was the only director that Carlotta trusted. They secretly secured the rights to *Strange Interlude*, O'Neill's massive nine-act psychological drama.

My mother now plotted with Rip and Gerry to force my father's hand. My parents were en route to California to be with Marilyn. My father was very anxious when traveling, always afraid he'd be late or miss the plane, so my mother planned to catch him then, when he would be most vulnerable. At the airport, my mother told him to call Rip and Gerry on an urgent matter. He said that there wasn't time to call, but my mother put the dime in the slot, dialed the number and handed the phone to him. Rip and Gerry asked him if he would once more go over the conditions under which he would agree to form the Theater. They said they wanted to have it absolutely clear during his absence. One by one they asked if it had to be an American classic by O'Neill, and not recently done; with a star cast, headed by Geraldine, and a star director, which Jose was. After he had said yes to each clarification, they triumphantly announced that they had secured the rights and fulfilled all of his conditions. He was stunned and asked them to repeat everything, but my mother told him that the plane was leaving and made him hang up the phone. And so the Actors Studio Theater was born.

Out of the six productions done in three seasons, I was involved in four. These experiences, coupled with the trip to Berlin, all happened in the first four years of my career life. They have had a deep and abiding influence on my personal dreams.

First Season

Strange Interlude

Strange Interlude opened in March, 1963, at the Hudson Theater on 44th Street, east of Broadway—the side of Broadway that commercial producers don't want to be on. The set change involved a turntable that revolved with excrutiating slowness, a serious problem for a nine-act play with a set change for every act. It was ultimately decided to make the changes in front of the public, using the curtain only at the beginning and end of the two part evening; we hadn't yet seen the massive movement towards the no-curtain, open staging of plays. There was a dinner break of one hour after Part One, which began at five and finished at seven-thirty. Part Two played from eight-thirty to eleven-thirty. We ate at the Algonquin Hotel down the street.

The all-star cast comprised Geraldine Page, Ben Gazzara, Betty Field, William Prince, Pat Hingle, Jeffrey Horne, Jane Fonda, and Franchot Tone. The membership grumbled over the casting, having hoped that the Studio would not fall victim to the star system. This was a constant complaint with which I didn't really sympathize: too many of them thought that AST was going to give them roles that they couldn't get in the marketplace. They misjudged my father who, in his own insecurity, craved success and would surround himself with as much power as possible. The production was flawed, but so was the play. The uniformly good cast was not yet a real ensemble, but they did share common principles that were at the heart of the Studio's future. It was a beginning for a theater that Cheryl and my father expected to be judged by the overall choices of plays and not, as commercial theater is, by each individual production. The Studio had a matching grant from the Ford Foundation for the first two seasons; whether or not it would be renewed depended on their accomplishment.

Franchot played the father, a professor who is ill and dies at the end of the first act. He was so believable that one critic complained that a producer had no right to allow such a sick man onstage.

One evening, people in the balcony began to talk during the first act.

Two, then ten, then twenty, quietly at first, eventually building into a steady ripple of "We can't hear!" Finally, Geraldine stopped, turned out and said, "What did you say?" The irony broke the whole theater into a fit of laughter followed loud and clear by "We can't hear!" "Oh," she said, "not at all?" "No," they chorused. She looked around at the other actors, all of whom were frozen in time and space, wishing they were somewhere else. Then she said, "We'll start over." The curtain came in and they started over. It's one of my favorite memories. The surprise and intimacy of the relationship of artist and public is part of the particularity of live theater.

Although the Studio was criticized for its maiden choice, I loved *Strange Interlude*. The play is long, as many of O'Neill's plays are, and somewhat melodramatic, but it's the first psychodrama, and it has his passion and poetry. O'Neill used his knowledge of Freud and our inner consciousness in the monologues, which today may seem a bit outdated, but it is an undoubted American classic. Ben Gazzara played a doctor in love with Geraldine's character. They have an affair, but he goes to Brazil to do research, leaving his best friend, Pat Hingle, whose family has a history of mental illness, to marry Gerry. I can still hear him as he leaves in Act IX, saying, "Oh God, so deaf and dumb and blind. Teach me to be resigned to be an atom."

Marathon ' 33

Marathon '33 (which I mentioned earlier) was the second show that the AST produced. Cheryl Crawford had made a deal with the owner of the ANTA Theater to mount two plays in that theater. My father and Cheryl had always thought that Frank Corsaro would direct the play. Frank knew how to work with actors, and also might be able to help June Havoc to strengthen the play's structure and dialogue. This function used to be the producer's, but directors like Kazan changed that. He was instrumental in Tennessee's rewriting of *The Rose Tattoo* during production. Eli Wallach and Maureen Stapleton used to talk about how the actors would all get together in Maureen's hotel room to rehearse their parts, while Kazan was locked up with Tennessee.

When the time came, June, who had written *Marathon* and functioned as director during the improvisations at the Studio, insisted on directing it on Broadway. This had never been clarified in earlier discussions. The Studio was busily negotiating, as they had already committed to the project and were going into rehearsal. Young as I was, I wondered why these things were happening. Hadn't it always been clear that Frank was going to direct it? There were also cast changes made for the Broadway production. Julie Harris was always supposed to play June; she had come to see the project at the Studio. Julie, waiflike as she seems, had enormous piercing eyes that I can still feel. We never knew one another very well, but the connection we do have is lasting. The play had vaudeville skits, music and dancing. Lee Allen and Iggie Wolfington were not part of the Studio membership but their particular vaudeville skills justified their being cast in major roles.

The set was designed by Peter Larkin, a top designer who counted *Teahouse of the August Moon* among his credits. The set had two side thrusts for the resting quarters, and a large center thrust into the house with two areas reserved for actors who played the audience members. The play began at eight-fifteen, as Phil Kenneally, who played an attendant, would begin sweeping the stage and putting up ropes that made the set seem ring-like. Phil had once been a boxer, and still bore the scars. The production was visually innovative. Tommy Tune said it was the first show he saw when he came to New York. He loved all the ensemble behavior that was crammed into the play and he never forgot the thrill of its theatricality. For five minutes every stage hour we would relax, shower, use the toilets, synthesizing all the months of work that had created the environment of the play. (I know Tommy from when Pete Masterson gave me a desperately needed job as Assistant Director on *The Best Little Whorehouse in Texas*, in 1979–80, when I was dead broke. I had lost what little savings I had on producing plays and trying to maintain one apartment in New York and another in L.A., where Sabra was trying to work.)

Transferring the play from the Studio workshops to Broadway effected several other significant changes. My long-time partner, Lane Bradbury, was assigned to Timmy Everett, the show's choreographer, who also played a major role. I was teamed with Libby Dean, a singer who was the wife of Lee Allen, but there was none of the depth and intimacy that Lane and I had achieved over the months of work at the Studio. (Timmy, incidentally, was to commit suicide some years later, tragically echoing the fate of his character in *Dark at the Top of the Stairs*.) Lane was as disappointed as I was that we were separated, even though she ended up with a larger role. All of the ensemble spirit that was the strength of the Studio seemed to be dissipating. Even June got nervous, unleashing her anxiety on the actors as she blustered, "Don't give me any of that 'Method' crap now." She may have been justified in some of her criticisms, but the company, like it or not, had worked hard to achieve a specific style.

Where there had once been a warmth and camaraderie there was now a lack of intimacy onstage which shocked me. As I looked around at the other actors I was only able to make contact with Julie Harris, Dick Bradford, and Jim Rado (who went on to fame as the writer of *Hair*). It saddened me deeply to see the actors trying to hide their real feelings. The show retained some technical virtue, but it had lost most of its former emotional power and camaraderie. Perhaps a different director could have salvaged some of the ensemble spirit and strengthened the story; it might have been a truly magical theatrical experience.

Two weeks before we closed, I was watching television in the prop room with the stagehands. We liked each other and they had even paid me the compliment of allowing me to work on take-ins and take-outs of other shows. Suddenly Marty Fried, who was the production stage manager, burst in and dragged me out into the wings. I struggled to free myself and angrily asked him what the hell was going on. He hurriedly whispered there was no time to explain, just that I was to find Julie onstage and do what she told me. He then pushed me onto the stage. It was the final sequence of the play; a strobe light jittered across a nightmare dance between Julie and Timmy, who played the boy with whom June ran off when she was just a girl.

I groped around blindly onstage until I heard Julie say, "Johnny, here. Put this on." She connected us by ropes around our wrists, and we spun around the stage awhile. Then she said, "Run off stage," so I did. It turned out that Timmy had fainted as the result of a whiplash accident in a cab. The next day, he came to the theater with a neck brace, but couldn't play. We worked out a shortened acrobatic solo for me to do, and cut his more complicated routines with Iggie and Lee. I finished the last two weeks of the run playing Timmy's role. Who would think that a Strasberg would actually dance on Broadway? I should have been Fred Astaire's kid; I think I would have been happier.

Dynamite Tonight

Dynamite Tonight was a wacky operetta, with book by Arnold Weinstein and a fascinating modern musical score by Bill Balcom. I liked the music and I liked Bill Balcom, who remained passionate and calm throughout the entire turbulent production. It opened in the York Theater at 72nd and Third Avenue, which later became a supermarket. The production was directed by several people. Mike Nichols was even brought in as a last-minute play doctor, but the "baby" died.

The play starred Barbara Harris, George Gaynes, and Anthony Holland, and had a Second City improvisational quality to it. This was natural, as many of the people associated with it came out of that Chicago comedy troupe. It was an anti-war play, in the vein of Joan Littlewood's *Oh, What a Lovely War*. It was seriously funny in the style of Monty Python, with many scenes acted in gibberish to indicate that the soldiers of different countries didn't understand each other.

Arthur Waxman, the Studio Theater's general manager, asked me to assist Peter Hunt, who was the Lighting Designer on the show. Peter later became a director whose production of *1776* won the Tony for Best Musical in 1969. He now runs the Williamstown Theater Festival. At the York we did all the electrical work ourselves: running cable, focusing, patching, whatever. Off-Broadway theaters were not unionized at that time, so we often worked sixteen hours at a time doing whatever was necessary to get the show open. Unions do an admirable job of protecting their members from injustice, but I disapprove of their creating conditions that make it economically impossible for people to be creative and do the work that they want to do.

It was panic-time which, in the theater, never helps. Everyone knows that something is wrong and everyone has ideas about how to fix it, disregarding the fact that they are adding to the chaos. To be honest, two hours of gibberish, no matter how interesting, is not going to work. Two days before opening, in this awful, fear-filled atmosphere, with no director, I was asked to replace the stage manager and to run the show opening night. I felt awful, because while Don Moreland, the SM, wasn't a friend, he'd been there every day and we had worked well together. Why did they suddenly think that he couldn't do the job? And why hadn't they known before they hired him? Opening night went very smoothly, and when the curtain came down nobody had died. But, unlike the other two plays in that first season, which had had mixed, but basically positive, reviews, this one was a disaster.

I've never been bothered about doing whatever needs to be done. I like cleaning a stage. It's what preparing a canvas or cleaning an instrument is to a painter or musician. The toilet in the men's room was clogged at the Studio one night at an hour when plumbers are impossible to find. Liska March, the Studio's coordinator, and the secretaries had the strangest looks on their faces when I said I'd fix it. They were stunned at the idea of me or any "artist" unstopping a toilet. I imagine they thought that artists don't do menial things and never get their hands dirty. I found a large diaper had been left in it. I still wonder whose, because it was enormous, and would only have fit a baby elephant.

Second Season

The three productions in the 1963–1964 season were *Blues for Mr. Charlie*, a new play by James Baldwin, directed by Burgess Meredith; *Baby Wants a Kiss*, an original comedy by James Costigan, starring Paul Newman and Joanne Woodward; and *The Three Sisters*, directed by my father. It was his return to directing, twelve years after the failure of *Peer Gynt*, starring John Garfield, had driven him into directorial exile. The spirit of the Studio members was optimistic. Everyone was willing to give generously to a cause of genuine value. Stars such as Julie Harris, Geraldine Page, Paul Newman, and Joanne Woodward worked for less than they would have under commercial circumstances. The foundation for a permanent theater had been established.

Blues For Mr. Charlie

The Studio chose to do *Blues For Mr. Charlie* as the first play of the second season. The play is set in the deep south, and was written by James Baldwin, an angry, articulate, homosexual African-American. It preceded the Watts riots, the Black Panthers, and our recent efforts to raise our consciousness beyond tribal identities as the basis for our social intercourse. All of the fear, hatred, hypocrisy, violence, and confusion that exist in the southern United States were dealt with in the play. It had a wonderful cast: Rip Torn, Pat Hingle, Larry Blyden, Ann Wedgeworth, Diana Sands, Al Freeman Jr., and Percy Rodriguez, along with many other good actors. Most of the black actors were not members of the Studio, since few of them had taken the audition. I guess they didn't think the Studio would be a home to them, though several became members during the production.

During the second week of rehearsal, Arthur Waxman called again and asked me to take over the role of production stage manager from Ira Cirker, who was now Burgess' assistant director. Arthur said that they were concerned with maintaining control of the company. He made it seem that the situation was potentially explosive.

Emotional outbursts are a normal part of the creative process. Creating is not just easy and fun; if it were, everyone would do it. Directors and producers, who themselves are given to explosive outbursts, are responsible for creating the atmosphere of the work environment. Burgess was a creative, temperamental man with whom I got along well enough, though he had the kind of temper that could turn on you at any moment. So did Rip and Al Freeman, Jr. The company was palpably talented and volatile. Diana Sands, who was luminous, died so young, before the world knew enough of her talent.

Temperamental outbursts in this type of creative situation are not to be taken personally. Being mature doesn't equate with being unemotional. The creative leader needs to tolerate the levels of anxiety and fear that burst out in negative, infantile behavior.

I didn't think I was in a difficult position, because I didn't feel any racial prejudice in myself until the late 1970s. After being looked at with hatred by enough African-Americans or Hispanics solely because I was white, I became conscious of a problem that I don't know how to solve on any large-scale level. Until we accept that we are all prejudiced (and this is verified by examining how all cultures behave towards outsiders), I just wish we would begin to accept the difference between noticing that people are different and hating people because they are different. People, after all, are people.

The sets and lights were designed by Abe Feder, one of the great designers. Abe lit the show beautifully. It was an open stage production with a pyramidal ramped platform, set in a large black box. He cross-lit it with huge lamps in the wings. When I first met him, he looked at me and said, "Aren't you too young to be a PSM?" I said that as long as I could do the job, my age didn't matter. He said, "Well, we'll see."

The level of the acting was very high, and Burgess' direction was good. But he didn't inspire the company, and I sensed that he was in it for himself. For instance, on the night of our technical rehearsal he sat in the house with Abe Feder, at three in the morning, having a great time doing the lights. They were joking around while the company stood listlessly on stage, waiting to finish and go home. I said so, and they snapped to and finished. I know they were tired, and maybe Burgess had had a few, but it is the little things, moments of respect or disrespect, that one remembers.

Baby Wants A Kiss

Baby Wants a Kiss played at the Little Theater on 44th Street. Paul Newman and Joanne Woodward worked for Equity scale, and it was the only production that was a financial success, a tribute to their talent, generosity, and commitment to the Studio. Every theater needs to have a hit and an audience pleaser. Without it, you won't find an audience, and you won't get your funding renewed. *Baby* was written by James Costigan, who played the other man in this three-character play.

The Three Sisters

Three Sisters was different. My father was the director, and had the actors' love, loyalty, and respect. He knew them all, had invested a great deal of time in his casting choices, and held pre-rehearsal meetings, individually and in groups, to gain precious time, as rehearsals in New York for a straight dramatic production were restricted to four weeks. To a realistic director with the desire to create a production that lives with the inner fluidity of human life, casting is at least 60 percent of his work. Kazan has put that up to 95 percent. Any realistic director believes the foundation of any production is: a play, a good idea of what you think it means, actors who can create living characters, and a lot of hard, meticulous work. No amount of money or pyrotechnics will cover the lack of organic life that only actors can provide. Recognizing this is fundamental in defining what theater is.

Physical elements are important, but only insofar as each illuminates and adds to the basic human truth and meaning of the play as you interpret it. Flash and theatrics that seem beautiful often only cover up the fact that there is no foundation of human expression in the director's technique. If there is a serious mistake in casting, no matter how brilliant the director's blocking or design concept is, he will never be able to achieve the production of which he dreams. It will lack the spontaneous life that productions with the right cast have night after night. Organic casting, fitting the actor to the role and creating a family to give the play a foundation of life that will continue to grow and deepen, is a conscious part of a realistic director's craft.

The main cast of *The Three Sisters* was: Kim Stanley as Masha, Geraldine Page as Olga, Shirley Knight as Irina, Kevin McCarthy as Vershinin, Gerald Hiken as Andre, Barbara Baxley as Natasha, Albert Paulsen as Kulygin, James Olsen as Baron Tusenbach, Luther Adler as the Doctor, and Robert Loggia as Solyony. Jimmy was a casting choice my father was particularly excited about because it was unconventional and demanded a great deal of composition work that would show what the Studio as a theater company could do with and for actors. The rest of the cast was: Tamara Daykarhanava, Salem Ludwig, Janice Mars, Brooks Morton, David Paulsen, and Pete Masterson.

In the commercial theater and film environment, actors are cast to type. Only in an ensemble repertory situation, such as in the English theater (where actors are weaned on repertory), in the Berliner Ensemble, and at the AST, have I seen what is to me the natural environment for theater. Actors think in a completely different way about their work. They begin to look beyond what gets them a job, what they sell or do best, and begin to think in terms of character transformation. They look for ways that they can be different in each role, because they want the public to recognize them as actors, not just personalities. When I applied this system during the short life of The Mirror Repertory Company, it was exciting to watch actors begin to think about how they were going to be different in each role, rather than seeing them just play their personal truths. Real repertory is the natural state of actors and theater.

Luther Adler had been in the Group Theater. He was Stella's brother, and a wonderful actor (maybe a little hammy once in a while). He taught me a lot. Most important was his advice not to be afraid of doing too much, of overacting. I was afraid that I wouldn't be truthful. It's a common problem for a sensitive actor with what sometimes seems to be an overdeveloped sense of truth (or an underdeveloped habit of behavior that expresses what the actor/character thinks, feels, or does). We are afraid of doing what bad actors do. The habit of underplaying, playing it safe, creates a trap that makes it impossible to fully realize a creation or characterization. The period of sketching and discovering is stifled and inhibited. Work habits are too small and careful. The actor is thinking about details before he knows what he wants to create. Without trying and failing, it is impossible to find the true being of a character. The work becomes too mental and smaller than life. This is reinforced by movie work, which demands an intense, but simple and truthful, reality.

Most "method" actors are so afraid of not being true, and of overacting, that they never do enough. This results in the habit of making truth seem little. Reality is pulled down to their own personal knowledge and behavior. This is wonderful in movies, but not so in theater. They don't learn to involve their imagination in what they are doing, to rise to the level of the character. There is no transformation, and the actor has no ability to handle classical characters. Most characters, especially pre-modern ones, have much more interesting lives than the actors who play them. Most of us live through fewer moments of high intensity, crisis, and action in a lifetime than a character in a play experiences in two or three hours.

Casting is so important because if you make a mistake, you have to spend an enormous amount of time trying to teach or change too many habits, which most actors will fall back into after you are gone. If you don't involve the actor in your world, in effect you are saying that you consider your work as being totally separate from the actor.

The actor my father had the most conflict with was Kevin McCarthy, who had not been his first choice. Kevin is a very good actor, but my father saw Vershinin as a dreamer, and thought that Kevin's Vershinin seemed too charming a lady's man. I watched my father struggle over this during rehearsal and asked him why he didn't insist more on what he wanted, which was the sense of a lonely dreamer, an unhappily married man who loves his children but has sacrificed his personal pleasure. This is what draws him to Masha, who herself has married a man she didn't love. If he is a dreamer, the relationship takes on another level of reality and illuminates the quiet despair that Chekhov seemed to know that so many human beings suffer in silence. If Vershinin doesn't have this dream quality, then he seems vacuous and empty, and the relationship loses its depth and intimacy. Kevin made Vershinin charming, but he lacked the dreamy sadness that my father imagined in the play. When I asked my father about this, we were in the third week of official rehearsal (actually the fourth, because all the actors had come to the house to begin reading and working through the play one week before the official start of rehearsals). He said that it wasn't the right moment, that he was going to wait a little longer to see if Kevin would begin to do more. He would make suggestions rather than giving a definite direction. He always taught directors never to demonstrate to an actor what you want them to do because they will only imitate you and not do what you really want, which is live their roles. Kazan said that what was so special about Marlon Brando was that he never did exactly what you asked him to do. He always did more. My father's rule was based on the director not influencing or cutting off the actor's creative and emotional force.

This attitude drove some actors crazy. One day my father went into a long discussion with Kim about how her character felt, and why she was motivated to move in a certain way. Kim seemed very confused for about five minutes. Then she said, "Lee, do you want me to cross faster?" (Cross means to walk across the stage.) My father was startled by the directness of the question. He laughed and said, "Yes," with a rare candor and spontaneity. Kim then said, "Please just say what you want. Don't psychologize. It drives me crazy."

A director's first responsibility is to create a good working environment. He must have the ability to communicate and involve everyone, beginning with designers and actors, and ending with the audience. You simply cannot just tell an actor where, when, and how to walk and talk. Since people are not machines, you will never get what you want that way, unless you are lucky or smart enough to have cast actors who know how to involve themselves. I try to direct a play to be actor-proof, composing as detailed and interesting a production partition (the composing of the charcter's lives, like notes of life) as I can, so I am as sure as possible what the audience will be seeing every night, whether I am there or not. My father created a frustrating, labyrinthine situation in *Three Sisters*, one that interfered with the direct contact and communication that is so fundamental to any collaborative art form (especially when there are problems). Interestingly enough, as a teacher this was not the case. He felt that you were in his space, and he could be open, direct, and demanding, as long as contact didn't become too threateningly personal. Most students are vulnerable and needy of approval and love; more so than professional actors, who, even if that is the case, are also working for themselves. So they are more subservient in a teacher/student relationship than in a director/actor relationship. My father was afraid of equal exchanges. When I analyzed my father's rules about direction, I found the same problem—the fear of contact, control, and expression—that I discovered in the Method.

As a director, I saw that I obtained much better results by being specific about what I imagined the character doing. Being specific and to the point helped the actor to better understand the character, and to deepen his or her emotional expression. If an actor is limited, as most are, a concept of a character may have to be imposed during production. You have to direct the play, communicating what you imagine and know about the life of the play. The result can be a holistic production, which happens organically when a director is capable of creating the family of actors and designers that will express his vision. If they are creative in their own right they will contribute qualities that make their characters personal, as the actor will have a particular perception of the character's world. Kazan had this ability, though he was stronger at picking men than women. John Ford created his own acting ensemble. Ingmar Bergman did the same. Peter Brook is capable of inspiring his actors to involve themselves totally in his world.

My father made the kind of mistakes that an inexperienced director makes from fear of contact. His procrastinating resulted in a loss of control over aspects of the production where he needed to be assertive, such as mood, rhythm, and tone (they are like musical notes to me; in this case a tendency to get depressed, slow and "Chekhovian"). My father wasn't inexperienced. This seeming helplessness came from his pattern of expecting people to submit to his authority, and giving up when they didn't. In class, when an actor didn't understand or couldn't do what he wanted, he occasionally reacted with an anger that was vicious and destructive, as though he felt that the actor was deliberately not understanding. I used to think this reaction was normal for a teacher, as I saw it in a lot of them. I did it too, until I realized that people's misunderstanding wasn't resistance to me, and that it was possible that the actor didn't understand or wasn't capable of doing what I wanted. My work improved when I realized that I was capable of making more direct, personal contact than my father was.

The first act of *Three Sisters* is a party for Irina's name day. My father worked hours on that scene, with a verve and a relish that fueled the actors' sense of ensemble. For one thing, everyone really ate. After Berlin, what else? While it may seem obvious, in most plays a scene like this would be faked. There's a big difference between fake eating and really eating, and I've never seen anyone fake eating convincingly. During the run of *Three Sisters*, one could tell what kind of show it was going to be by the interest the actors showed when the food was being placed on the table before the curtain went up. You could see them getting involved. (I remember seeing the Abbey Theater's production of Brendan Behan's *The Hostage*. I got to the theater about fifteen minutes early, and was sitting in the eighth or ninth row. As I sat down to read the program, I heard music, and then voices of people laughing and talking. I realized it was coming from behind the curtain, and was surprised that the stage manager wasn't controlling this. This din went on until the curtain went up, and the effect of seeing this ongoing party was so exciting I'll never forget it. Their involvement immediately drew us into their world.) Real vodka? I'm sure some of the actors in *Three Sisters* would have loved that, but they have to be paid to use their imaginations for something, and several of them stocked up before coming to the theater.

My father approached the development of each character with an enthusiasm for detail I will never forget. It was like watching a painter paint a scene, during which he spends hours on each figure. A good group of actors is like a good team of athletes who play together with, not against, one another. It is a kind of healthy competition. That scene, while it didn't work every night, was fantastic on the nights that it did work. Since I stage-managed the show, I saw the play every night. Most shows lack the spontaneity, surprise, and passion that keep them alive and interesting. The first act of *Three Sisters* had those qualities.

My father's direction set a very intimate tone, and the actors understood that the production relied on this intimacy. Kim Stanley was the most naturally emotional actress I have seen. Kim trembled. Maybe even more than Montgomery Clift and Marilyn, because she worked in the theater, where the demands on the actor, night after night, force her to practice the art of acting with a force and energy that movies don't. Theater is the actor's natural home, where the rehearsal process allows him to learn his art, and practice it freely. He is king once the curtain goes up. Film is a director's medium, where the actor has to prepare his character by himself, before filming, and where he is at the service of the king.

There were critics who were irritated by Kim's emotionalism. The emotion was so powerful that in the second act love scene with Vershinin she would sometimes gasp for breath, her passion was so overwhelming. Some of them found this excessive. Too real. I wonder if they would have said the same of Beethoven, Goya, and Van Gogh. In the immediacy of a theater, without a safe distance from the artist's creative passion, death, and fame, life can feel uncomfortably close. To me, it is not that she was overemotional but that her emotions were sometimes disturbing, especially if someone doesn't particularly like being so immediately moved by another human being's pain and longing.

Geraldine, on the other hand, was a superb character actress, and, essentially, a great clown. Gerry was special; like Orson Welles and Charles Laughton, she created characters that were bigger than life, characters that smaller actors couldn't make credible. They made us believe them because they were such enormous forces themselves. In the fire scene (Act III), when Natasha comes and asks her for the keys to the house, which are the last vestige of the sisters' hold on the old life, Geraldine had an attack of hiccups while her Olga, who takes all the shocks and pain so resignedly, shook with more rage than she could express, and finally did give the keys up. It is impossible to sufficiently describe the surprise, and then the pleasure, of recognizing the human truth that her art illuminated.

I remember observing her skulk around on stage in rehearsal one day, when no one was around, trying to slip a photo into the frame that contained the photo of the character's father. I overheard her tell the prop man, Joe McCarthy, that it was of her own grandfather. She made him promise to take particular care of it and to remember to give it back at the end of the run.

The second act of the play takes place in the winter. Everyone had to create the sense of coming into a warm house from the frigid Russian outdoors. Kim asked if she could have a bit of ice left offstage near the door through which everyone entered the house. Kim hated sense memory. (So much for the idea that all realistic actors use sense memory.) Joe McCarthy, our propman, got a large bucket and filled it with water and ice every night. Waiting in the wings for their entrances, the actors used to gather around it. They would stick their hands into the ice and stand there, whispering to one another, laughing and joking, in that world of actor-characters one sees backstage and in rehearsal. Their camaraderie was very beautiful to watch. It would occasionally come onto the stage, but rarely with the spontaneity and candor that it had in the wings. I'm always making actors conscious of what they're doing offstage—how alive they are in life, and in the wings.

Kim wouldn't talk much. She would pace restlessly, on the fringe; you could see her dream space. She hated imaginary objects and always had a fresh branch that she used like a riding crop. On some days, I would see her with a flower which she held in such a way that it was clear Vershinin had given it to her. Kim needed these real things to keep her grounded and present because she was so extraordinarily sensitive.

The only one who didn't stand around was Geraldine. During the performance, when she wasn't on stage, she was watching television and making phone calls in her dressing room. It wasn't uncommon to see her streaking down the stairs to make an almost forgotten entrance. It was a habit I forgot about until I directed her twenty years later in the Mirror Repertory Company and had to assign an assistant stage manager the task of being sure that she got onstage on cue.

The production had some beautiful moments, but the production was, in a way, unfinished. Four weeks for Chekhov isn't a lot. The ensemble needed time for it to become organic. Although everyone was a member of the Studio, they weren't used to being a Theater. You can't create a theater in four weeks. This could have happened had the Actors Studio Theater survived, and had my father been a more dynamic director. One can only dream about the theater that could have been created had Kazan not separated himself from the Studio.

In spite of the interest, and the quality of the productions, the Ford Foundation grant was not renewed.

✧ ✧ ✧

The Studio had two provocative seasons. To me, what best exemplified the theater's potential were *Marathon '33* and *The Three Sisters*. It was in these two productions that a conscious effort was made to establish the sense of ensemble playing that had infused the Group Theater and its inspiration, The Moscow Art Theater. My father controlled the Studio too closely, and the AST too loosely. The AST was represented as being the Studio dream come true. The working environment, intimacy, and sharing of common principles had to be integrated on a daily basis into the heart and soul of the theater and its organization. In New York, the sense of doing a series of individual productions, and the financial pressures that undermine the environment, overpowered the need to create the intimacy that distinguishes ensemble playing. While there were more good actors in the same place at the same time at AST, the sense of building a theater family was somewhat missing. The exception was *Marathon '33*, whose production evolved over a long period of time.

The leader is responsible for the personality of an organization. My father's reticence, personal fears, rigid obsession with perfection, and pathological inhibitions held him back when he needed to be determined and communicative. It all added up to his giving up on too many points, making too many mistakes. His explosions of temperament, the inevitable procrastination, and the constant need to have someone protect and do for him created an untenable organization. And when he was in a position of having to take command, his fears of making a mistake immobilized him.

Leadership requires not what is often called compromise, but the ability to communicate, collaborate, and synthesize. The contact my father made as a teacher he failed to make as an artistic director. As a teacher he had someone before him who sought his help. It was a controllable situation. Even there, when someone wouldn't do what he asked, his insecurity sometimes led him to take the resistance personally.

He knew about his problem with contact. He regretted his inability to communicate. But he was too afraid of losing control to change his habits. To avoid failure, he also avoided success.

At the World Theater Festival in London

The Actor's Studio Theater was invited to the London World Theater Festival in the spring of 1965. Two productions, *Blues* and *Three Sisters*, were to play at the Aldwych theater, one week apiece. The English were dying of curiosity about their rival cousin. Competition can be healthy, but this isn't always true of the English-American theater rivalry.

In the early 1950s, the works of Tennessee Williams and Arthur Miller re-vived a stale English theater. At the moment, the reviving is the other way around. I think this kind of healthy interchange is what's called for, not the close-minded "mine is better than yours" that we seem to cultivate when we discuss artistic principles at the base of the creative process.

Burgess, Jimmy Baldwin, Cheryl, and my father met in the Lyceum Theater where we were going to rehearse. Jimmy and Burgess blasted away at Rip's interference and negative effect on the company. They decided to fire Rip without considering the subsequent problem of company morale, never mind Geraldine's reaction. Months earlier, I had asked Cheryl and my father to allow me to bring Rip up on charges to the union for his chronic lateness. He often arrived at 8:25, five minutes before the curtain went up, and after I had gotten his understudy (Ralph Waite) ready to go on. It undermined company discipline and hurt the show. The producers, Cheryl and my father, refused to support me. They opted for action far more extreme, much too late, and at a time when the Studio needed to be as strong and united as possible.

Rip was not only playing a leading role, he was a driving force in the production committee that had organized and created the theater. Not one of these governing authorities was willing to face him for fear Rip would turn violent. They decided instead to cancel rehearsal. They were just going to let him arrive at the theater to find no one there. They would arrange to deliver a message to him. Being the Production Stage Manager, and present during the discussion, I was stunned. Burgess' attitude seemed vengeful and adolescent. Although I was scared, I refused to let them behave that way. Someone would have to stay and confront Rip. Not one of them was willing.

So they all left, and I waited. When Rip arrived, about a half hour late, I stood with him on the stage and told him. He couldn't believe what they'd done. I think that if Burgess had been there, Rip would have hit him. I knew Burgess was capable of being vindictive, but never understood Jimmy's position. It was Rip who had championed the play, which the Studio had been afraid to do because of its volatile subject. They knew it left them open to criticism from too many corners. I felt badly, but not because I loved Rip. He was a difficult guy, and I'd seen him be mean during rehearsal. When he was insecure about his own work, he'd project his problem onto the world. (In the following fifteen years, I would be fired three times. Rip, strangely enough, was involved in two of the three productions.) Rip looked at me with a mixture of anger and sadness, and thanked me for having been there. I think the moment cemented a strange, mutual understanding between us, if not friendship.

The result of their action was that Geraldine, who also was pregnant at the time, withdrew from the London production of *Three Sisters*—Rip and Gerry left the Studio for years. More havoc predictably followed as Shirley and Barbara (playing Irina and Natasha) became unavailable, and Kevin, due to Kim's insistence, was replaced.

George C. Scott replaced Kevin as Vershinin, Sandy Dennis replaced Shirley Knight as Irina, Shelley Winters replaced Barbara Baxley as Natasha, and Nan Martin replaced Geraldine. For a theater that was based on the idea of ensemble playing, even these individually wonderful actors could not replace the ensemble spirit that had begun to develop. It was not the same production. This cast, with eleven days of rehearsal, who had never worked or played together, were to present the AST production of *The Three Sisters*. However, I can understand not declining the invitation. For the Studio, success in London could have been an enormously important factor in future funding.

On the opening night of *Blues*, there was a political demonstration in the balcony. I honestly don't remember if it was the right or left that was demonstrating. I think it was the right, because the play had some very strong things to say about societies, culture, and racial prejudice. The play was politely received, both by the public and the critics. But the English theater community and public was waiting.

Three Sisters was in a lot of trouble. George disappeared for three days. It was rumored that he was having an affair with Ava Gardner, and Frank Sinatra was threatening him. George had a bodyguard with him at all times when we did see him. We rehearsed in some of the Queen's guards barracks near Albert Hall. Kim hated George, and longed for Kevin, in spite of the fact that she had insisted on having him replaced. Sandy Dennis sucked air through her teeth on every sentence. When my father mentioned it to her, she claimed that it was nerves. He let it go, hoping it would go away. It didn't. The pressure got worse. Because of scheduling problems and union rules, the cast did not get onto the stage until the night before the opening for a technical rehearsal. I was up all night making the sound tape to have it ready for the one rehearsal that they would get before the opening night public.

The opening night performance ran over an hour longer than the play had ever run. The pauses, the waiting for feeling, all of the classic ills of the realistic school were there, down to Sandy's nervous sucking. The audience booed. Kim was furious, and only Luther's pleading, and professionalism, kept her onstage for the curtain call. I'd never before heard an audience boo or catcall. Underneath, aside from the culture shock, the show had been awful. When Sandy said a line in the play, "This has been a terrible evening," an audience member shouted, "It certainly has been."

The press destroyed the production. My father hadn't helped our reception by his comments about how "stultifying" English theater was. Then my father came into the theater to talk to the actors. He was apoplectic. He began screaming, blaming the company for what they had done. It was their fault. Not a word about the cast changes, lack of rehearsal, emotional pressure, or tonight's performance. Luther finally tried to stop him, but my father was out of control. Then George, who is a large man and not one to take that sort of thing from anyone, had enough. He started to come off the stage into the aisle where my father stood screaming, at which point my father turned and practically ran out of the house. It's the worst scene I've ever seen in the theater. That night, George refused to go on; an understudy walked through the role holding the book.

Back in New York, Kim told Bobby Lewis that she would never go on the stage again. She never has. Both Sandy and Kim blamed my father's bullying for causing health problems.

My father never apologized. It was his decision to go to London. There was no one else to blame. That is pretty much how the theater died. The grant was not renewed. They didn't try to look elsewhere. They didn't try to do anything. I got some of the best practical experience in the world, and I was paid to boot. What did I learn? If you're going to try to make your dream come true, you need luck, courage, organization, and a will of iron. Love, too, is part of what a dream is made of.

Maria Rosa by Angel Guimbra directed by John Strasberg
at Centro Dramatic de Catalunta (Barcelona) 1983

CHAPTER FIVE

WHAT DREAMS MAY COME

The most difficult thing for me to learn as an actor was to laugh on purpose. I could work up a smile, and a "hah!," but I wouldn't laugh, because "it doesn't feel real." My misguided sense of truth meant that being real required doing something familiar or comfortable. But, of course, realistic acting is not about pulling the characters down to your own reality, but opening one's imagination, consciousness, and capacity to the dream space of the play. I once worked on a scene in class from Clifford Odets' *Golden Boy*, in which Joe and Laura are in the park talking after he has finished his workout. "Those cars are poison in my blood. When you sit in a car and speed you're looking down at the world. Speed, speed, everything is speed—nobody gets me!" I felt like the artist Joe is, but I became obsessed with making myself feel that I could be a fighter. I went to the YMCA on 63rd Street, and worked out in the boxing room almost every day. I never questioned my need to do whatever I felt intuitively compelled to do.

I blocked that impulse when it came to laughing. I can hear myself practicing, "Ha, Ha, Ha, Ha, Ha, Ha, Ha" in laughs of seven, like an early version of a computer voice. I can hear my father playing a record of Supervia, the great Spanish soprano, singing a laugh on the notes of an entire song. On key. "Ha haaaaaaaaH Hah: Ha Haaaaah hah- ha haa ha ha ha aaaah-" to the end. Several minutes worth of brilliant technique. I studied laughing. It's contagious, almost like a disease. But I'd spent years becoming immune to tickling, having suffered several horrible bouts of being tickled when I was young. I thought it was a good choice for a tough guy. "Bad choice for actor," as Charlie Chan would say. And for life.

"That's how I am!" I've heard it from twenty-year-olds. Change is unpopular. Luckily, life helped me out, because the more I suffered, the more my sense of humor developed. The greater the sense of humor the more you have suffered. Humor becomes a choice and a matter of survival. Also, I was helped by orgonomic therapy, which made me physically conscious of how and where emotion becomes blocked. Reich discovered that liberating blocked energy dissolves neurosis, and establishes a natural and healthy flow of energy. I became sensitive to my body, as one would if one studied acupuncture, or massage. I learned to feel where emotions reside in my body, and where they are blocked. Now, I can just about laugh on cue, and sometimes cry, or become angry, because I know where to focus my intention. This doesn't feel like mechanical, mental manipulation to me. It feels like a skill—a highly developed awareness, like an athlete or dancer. This is due to the organic nature of the therapy.

EXPANDING CONSCIOUSNESS

I was in the apartment of friends. It was the winter of 1962, and cold, as New York winters can be. It made being indoors with friends even more special. I sat on the floor, feeling more alive and full of love and awareness than I had ever let myself feel. I took out my wallet, and began looking at the things that identified me to the world. Driver's license, union cards, my new Actors Studio membership card, and the green bills with old-fashioned faces on them . . . just Washington's and Lincoln's, because I only had a little money then. It seemed as though it were the first time that I realized who these faces were, and they now seemed much more important and valuable than the money itself. I took out my credit cards from gasoline companies and American Express, which had suddenly become unimportant and false. I began to cut them into pieces, much to people's amazement, pleasure, and, perhaps, a bit of dismay at what I might feel later. I made a collage of the objects I was destroying. I looked at the money, and at Pat Quinn, an actress friend who lived with Dick Bradford. I held a dollar bill up and asked Pat if she wanted it. When she didn't take it, I burned it. As if Nature (or God, call it what you like) spoke directly to me, the bill stopped burning, as if it wanted me to understand something, leaving only the portrait of George Washington with frayed, burnt edges. It reminded me that real success is the ability to express our humanity, not the narcissistic accumulation of power and money. The rigid and impermanent monuments to material success are almost always reduced to ashes eventually. The alternative is the universal, eternal celebration of our expanding consciousness, which becomes a part of what some call God, or, as Reich called it, cosmic, orgone energy. In the early morning, we were all hungry and still high. No one wanted to go out, and there was nothing to eat. No one wanted this experience to end in the shock of the cold and bleak reality of New York, with its winter winds whipping through the side streets, sometimes with such force that one could actually lean into them and not fall. Perhaps to prove that I was strong and not afraid, or in an effort to discover myself, or just because I felt generous, I said "I'll go." I walked down the brownstone steps of the building on West 44th Street, beside the Actors Studio, sure that at any moment someone would walk up to me, point their finger and say, "He's high. He's taking drugs. Probably on LSD or something." I forced myself to raise my eyes and look at the world. To my shock and surprise, no one was looking at me. Everyone was in hiding.

I walked joyfully to Smiler's, the deli around the corner, with my newfound knowledge and freedom warming all of me except my nose, which stood, frozen, somewhere at the fringes of my face. I entered Smiler's and in a glorious fifteen minutes chose all the breakfast foods of childhood for our celebration meal: Wheatena, Oatmeal, and Cream of Wheat with the picture of the chef on the box; eggs, bacon, and sausage; pancake mix and maple syrup; and milk, butter, and bread. It was a breakfast fit for the kings and queens that, in that moment, we felt we were. Our humanity seemed as beautiful as the Rocky Mountains, or the Atlantic Ocean that I have swum in in February, or the snowstorms that bury the fears and hatreds of New Yorkers. My labyrinthine thinking stopped for awhile, and I was at peace, in harmony with, and unafraid of, life.

This magical interlude was my first LSD experience. Time and space, thoughts and feelings, flowed together in an otherworldly way that seemed unfamiliar and unreal. I was thrust into a world so much freer than the one I was used to, in which things flowed together, and everything appeared to be a part of everything else. The separation through which we normally perceive the world dissolved. This new perception is impossible to forget. It permanently alters one's sense of who one is, where one is, what one is doing.

I tried acting with alcohol and marijuana, but it was impossible for me to intentionally direct my imagination or emotional life into experiencing and expressing my personal dream space in real performance time.

In all of my drug experiences, this sense of accelerated motion and a flowing, holographic sense of time and space, was accompanied by a synthesizing of thought and sensation into experience. It created an even greater schism between my dream life and what we consider normal reality; work, striving for material success, power, and status. The world of my dreams seemed more important. But dreams, I thought were something only psychiatrists took seriously. People who went to a psychiatrist were sick, so dreams were a sign of sickness, not of health. Until I stumbled out of this maze, thinking like the child that I was, and am, and discovered that dreaming is a part of real life, my life had no meaning. I was lost, and nothing I did in work or love or with any object-oriented goal was ever really begun with a purpose, because nothing was initiated from the deepest part of me. And so I wandered through life, acting classes, the Actors Studio, working as an actor and stage manager, and the Actors Studio Theater.

In 1963, when my father was sick, my parents asked me to take over his class. I was shocked, to say the least, and blurted out, "I don't know anything." Which wasn't very far from the truth. I'd been working professionally for two years, and studying for four. I was a member of the Studio, but so what? Many members weren't very successful. A lot of people stopped growing once they had gotten into the Studio. Their careers stagnated, or decayed, and the same was true of their inner work. There was no magic, nor was there a systematized study program. It was a studio, in which you did the work you felt you had to do.

I'm often asked about working for my parents. I never considered it a problem. I studied with my father because he and Stella Adler were the most important teachers in New York. I once thought about going to Stella, but that did seem like stirring up a hornet's nest. I also thought that she wouldn't see me for myself, but as the son of my father, whom she detested. This fact of being a Strasberg, rather than John Strasberg, can still pop up. After thirty-four years of professional experience as an actor, director, and teacher, after winning awards, and being known internationally in my own right, some people will still introduce me as "the son of."

I faced the sour expressions of students who wanted the word of God, and were stuck instead with the son of. One actor declared he didn't want to work. "Listen," I said, "if I'm lousy, maybe you'll learn something from your own work, or your own sense of truth. Every time you work you learn something. The only thing you'll learn by not working is that you don't like me, and you already know that. And imagine what'll happen if

I can help you. We'll all be shocked." The class went well. It ended without anyone dying. Afterward, my parents asked me to teach an exercise class on Tuesday evenings for students who couldn't come in the daytime. I was paid $12.50 an hour, $25 a class. My father was still paying his teachers that thirteen years later, when I became Executive Director of the Lee Strasberg Theater Institute.

I was to begin shooting a western for Columbia Pictures, *The Long Ride Home*, in which I would play a Mandan Indian in the Confederate Army. Walter Beakel had gotten me a job teaching contract players in Columbia's development program. I had also gone up for Richard Brooks' *In Cold Blood*; my test was a fifteen-minute improvisational sketch of the character. Richard Wilson ultimately played the part, but my test generated a lot of excitement. Brooks seriously considered using me. When I found out that he didn't want recognizable names, I offered to change my name—if people liked me, they'd find out who I was. I meant it. His assistant, Tom Shaw, showed me the test, and told me he loved it.

My reaction to seeing myself on film for the first time was to go and get drunk for three days. I saw everything I hate about myself: my cartoon voice, big nose, narrow chin, large Adam's apple, and body skinny from drugs, particularly amphetamines. (That is a problem I'd love to have now. I'm not talented enough to be as fat as Orson Welles.) Well, it was the sixties. Everyone was doing it. God, in California shaking hands was a more personal act of contact than making love.

After my mother died, I drove back to L.A., stoned out of my mind, with her .38 and the two boxes of ammunition at the top of the suitcase in the backseat. I drove eighteen hours a day. Screaming and crying over my mother's death, I drove the racing-green Morgan 4+4 at 80 miles an hour. I stopped somewhere in Texas at about 10:00 P.M., to adjust the side-view mirrors mounted on the front fenders. Out of the corner of my eye, I saw a guy get out of a pickup truck and walk towards me. He took off his belt and wound it around his hand. I got back into the car. Leaning against the roof, he asked whether I wanted to buy a belt. I reached back and got the revolver and put it in my lap. I politely replied that my pants were secured just fine. I started the car and drove off, leaving him standing by the side of the road.

The last time I took LSD was on Thursday, June 2, 1966, four days before the movie was to begin shooting. Almost a month after I arrived in L.A. I was still in crisis. I hadn't slept in three days. I was perpetually taking amphetamines, seasoned with other assorted pills, and, of course, marijuana. My weight had dropped to 135 pounds from my then normal weight of 151. I wanted to go home and sleep, but I felt I had so much to prove that when a guy named Dale offered me some acid, I took it, even though I wasn't really in the mood. After a while we started tripping. We went to Pat Quinn's hotel room on the Sunset Strip. I kept taking my clothes off, which upset Pat, because she took it as sexual, which it was and wasn't. I kept putting them back on but I wanted to be naked and free. My behavior irritated them, so they said they were hungry and wanted to get something to eat. As they were leaving, I stood next to Dale and said, "Please don't leave me." I suddenly felt terribly alone, and so closed off, while the LSD was opening me up. I wanted so desperately to be free, to get out. That thought went through my head over and over again.

They left me alone with her pet ocelot, who was in the bathroom, and a glossy photo of Marlon Brando in the lower left hand corner of the mirror in the main room. I looked at Marlon and he looked back at me, with that glassy-eyed impertinent soul of his, and I said, "I'm a man, too." I began to write on pieces of pink message paper I found on a table, about love and the significance of the number 7, which leads to 8, which if turned sideways is the symbol of infinity. I got scared and didn't want to be alone. I went to the phone, wondering whom to call. I would be forced to talk to the hotel operator, to a stranger, and I was afraid of being incoherent. I sat there, thought about Susan and Christopher and Dick, and then decided that there was no one to call. I felt there was no one who cared. I looked around, feeling caged. I imagined myself to be as trapped as the poor ocelot, who was living in the bathtub of a hotel on Sunset Strip. I felt myself breathing anxiously, and took off my clothes again. The walls seemed soft and wavelike, and there was a yellowish gray color to the air. Nothing seemed solid.

The light coming through the large sliding glass doors made them seem like an open and clear space. It was nearing sundown, and suddenly, impulsively, I ran towards the light. Slamming against glass I didn't see, I broke through the window kicking and screaming and bounced off the screen door. I saw the brightest red I've ever seen; and yellow stars and violet planets. My back was pierced by a large piece of glass that remained in the doorframe. I remember feeling it, but it was all part of an otherworldly experience. (The doctor who saved my life told me, later, that I had made a perfect surgical incision.) Everything turned red. I can't say how long I screamed in that window, but people saw me from the street. Someone said that my scream was beautiful, like the screams they felt trapped inside themselves. Finally, I must have passed out.

When I came to I was lying on the floor, still naked, in the middle of blood and glass. A young Hawaiian guy, a hairdresser with really sensitive, intelligent eyes, who lived in the same apartment building I did, was leaning over me. He looked at me, with contact and concern, and said, "Hang on. The ambulance is on its way." For a moment I was totally conscious and present. Someone tried to stuff a towel into my back. I could smell the drugs in my nose, which was ice cold, as it always was on acid. I relaxed into the floor and could hear, more than feel, pieces of broken glass crinkling under me. Lying there, I felt like a large, balloon-like sack. I had no sense of having bones, and suddenly I thought that if I inhaled any more deeply I would explode. It hurt to breathe, and I felt very tired. When I exhaled, I felt I was going to dissolve into the floor. I began to believe I could die, and as quickly knew that I didn't want to go. Not yet. Breathing became harder and harder. So little air for so much effort. I concentrated, gathering force to breathe through the pain each time. It seemed as though very little air was entering my lungs. I knew I had a hole in my back, and was told I probably had some broken ribs. (The glass had punctured my right lung, which had collapsed, and I had broken ten ribs, mostly on my right side. Several of them grew back into a knot, where there is only an everlasting numbness, from nerves that have been permanently severed.) I felt like a large, pulsating jellyfish.

The ambulance ride was like a long dream. In reality, it lasted almost 40 minutes, as the nearest hospital refused to take me, not having the facilities to treat my emergency (or perhaps not wanting me to die in their hospital). The ambulance had to get on the freeway and take me to County General, in downtown L.A. I only thought one thing, "They're not going to kill me."

I came to in the pre-operating room. There were hospital lights overhead and hospital green walls. A young doctor was looking at me. He asked me what happened, and what drugs I had taken, telling me that he needed to know in order to determine what drugs and anesthetic they could use. I said "None." Is this what good spies and other frightened people do? I felt strangely relaxed and lucid. A nurse told me to sign the hospital release form for operating. I asked her what would happen if I couldn't. I was surprised it was hard to hold the pen and write. I heard the doctor say to his assistant, who was Asian-American, "I'll take the top and the lung, you clean up the legs. Then we'll turn him over. Take your time, there's a lot to do." I could hear a calmness in his voice that told me I was going to be O.K. I didn't remember the priest who administered last rites, just in case.

They told me they were going to move me to a gurney and asked me if I was capable of helping. I slowly began to turn onto my side. It hurt a lot. Broken ribs feel awful, and my ribcage was floating. I tried to sit up and was surprised at how weak I was. Suddenly, the nurse signaled to the others, and they grabbed the sheets that I was lying on, and moved me, while I screamed for them to wait a minute. Several days later, when the head nurse reached across me to get something, I noticed that she had a large, black-and-blue mark on her bicep. I asked her what happened. She looked at me strangely, and then asked if I really didn't remember. No, I didn't remember that I had bitten her on the arm when she moved me. I was in surgery for about five hours. They gave me nine pints of blood, and including the dissolving ones, I had close to three hundred stitches.

I woke up in intensive care, in the heart and chest section. I saw my father standing at the foot of the bed, his arms folded. He looked dazed, and his lips were drawn and tight. Poor guy, first my mother's death, and then me a month later. The plane trip must have been an ordeal. This was a man who was used to everyone taking care of him. Ralph Roberts was next to him, looking kind and stoic. Roberts was a family friend, actor, masseur, part Indian, the youngest Major in WWII, and Marilyn's friend and confidante. He would play a part in my 1982 production of *Joan of Lorraine* by Maxwell Anderson, with which Sabra and I started the Mirror Rep.

Susan and Christopher, who played Jesse James on television and was in *Ryan's Daughter*, were there, too. Outside were Dick, Pat, and Dale. Susan looked frightened. Chris looked curiously puzzled.

I felt extraordinarily peaceful. Relaxed and cleansed. I looked at them. What could I say? They were all standing there, close to me, seeming so far away, inside themselves. The emotional walls were visible to me. I was relaxed, wide open, still in an altered state, or just more conscious, and was perceiving several levels of reality at the same time. I could see that they wanted to be relieved of their uneasiness. I knew they all assumed I had tried to kill myself.

That was not what I had intended at all. I had felt alone, and I had wanted to get out. I needed to let go, to express a lot of deep sadness and anger that came from feeling alone and abandoned. I wanted to be free of my old self, get out of my personal prison, my own refusal to permit myself to live my life. Everyone was clearly puzzled and anxious. I was a problem. Life was a problem. Death was a problem. I just wanted to begin a new life. Mine.

Dick told me Pat and Dale were there, and said they wanted to see me, and asked if I wanted to see them. I said no. They swore they had not heard me beg them to stay, but I was no more than three inches from Dale's face when I said, "Please don't leave me." I have had problems with voice projection, but to that degree?

My father offered to move me to a private room in the hospital. I declined. He didn't understand why. For most of my life, I had fought not to feel special, not to fall in with my mother's desire to create the sense that we were artists, different and more important than others. I also never wanted to depend on my parents. That meant accepting their special world; accepting a world of lies and deception, of duplicity and confusion; a world in which my mother's warning, "Remember who you are," rang in my ears. ("Who am I?" I always wondered.) A world in which I had to be careful about being myself and saying what I thought, because when I did, it upset the balance and harmony of their lives. I did not want to return to that same world. I wanted my freedom, and was prepared to pay any price for it. I know that I had what is called "a bad trip," but in a real sense it wasn't. The shame is that there was no one to help to comfort and guide me. But then, most of us have that problem.

In the bed next to me was a boy of sixteen who had just had open heart surgery. His chest was covered with a large cross of stitches that dwarfed the one in my back. Someone in the four-bed intensive care room had died during the night. The nurses placed a screen around the bed until the body was removed, as though death were disturbing or that we didn't know. The following day, a child of five joined us. The head nurse, the one I had bitten, confided to me that she hated when the young ones came because it was impossible not to care and get involved. I fell in love with another of the nurses, a Mormon girl. There was no hope for us, but it didn't matter. My blood was the gift of strangers. Who knew where it had come from or what life it had lived, and how it would affect mine? I felt reborn.

Christopher quickly turned the experience into a potential TV movie, and declared that I would be forever famous on the Strip. I would become a prophet. I could have all the women I wanted. I was amazed. I would never think of exploiting this crisis to obtain work, power, to seduce a woman, or place myself in a position where people would admire me.

Hearing him, on his way to being the next James Dean, I actually believed my unorthodox reaction was a flaw in my character.

I left the hospital after eight days, and went to live with Susan and Christopher. I was back working at Columbia in two weeks, behaving as though nothing had happened. The doctor counted the 278 stitches he took out. I sat in the waiting room next to a man of fifty who was smoking a cigarette three weeks after he had had a lung removed. But now, the depression that veiled my consciousness and intelligence and perceptions seemed to have dissolved.

I began to really see, without rumination or doubt. For the moment, I no longer needed permission to be free. If I were going to be really free I would have to give up needing to be loved by people who were incapable of loving me in the way that I needed. When my mother died, I could feel my love without having to be who she wanted me to be. To completely overcome the habits of this trade-off for love, however, would take another ten years.

When a voice with an old cadence, from behind my left ear, began hissing, "Who do you think you are, anyway?" which sounded strangely sounded, "Remember who you are," I realized that what I wanted was to live with the same truth and spontaneity I had experienced in accidental moments of life and work. My life suddenly had a goal, though one that still doesn't seem to be on the list of the 100 most successful professions.

Teaching at Columbia Pictures was a bizarre experience because the actors were terrified that someone might discover that they still had something to learn. Actors with long-term contracts swiftly became bureaucrats who pretended there was nothing more to it. I soon tired of trying to coax these fear-ridden hopefuls to work. Instead, I would perform cold readings of Shakespeare soliloquies. I would flip open the *Complete Works* to whatever soliloquy presented itself. My aim was to become spontaneously involved with whatever dream space the text evoked in me. My work had a presence, spontaneity, and force to it that surprised me. Without my usual extensive preparation exercises, I listened and reacted to the words from within my dream space. I would breathe, and enter into the dream space (my reflection on how one intentionally involves oneself with, and creates, the given circumstances of the character) concentrating myself in it, to bring the text's life into being. Without trying to control my thoughts, imagination, and feelings, I let myself go and fell into the situation like one falls in love. The separation I normally experienced between logic and emotion was, at least temporarily, dissolved. Without losing contact with who and where I was, I was able to become involved and be transformed.

Images became living holograms, spiraling in emotional space-time, with the intense, slow-motion perception that is common to transformational states. I bypassed the intellectual cross-examination of every impulse, a habit that fed on fear. The tremendous release of blocked energy I had undergone gave me new, unconditional contact and energy. The near death experience freed energy that used to hold those very habits that inhibited free, natural movement and expression. I avoided the labyrinth by following my natural impulses. My thoughts were action.

As long as I remained in this state of contact and being, there was no need to control thoughts, or to criticize myself. There were no mistakes. There was just the sense of living.

I wanted to prove to myself that I could handle anything, and was perfectly in control. As an ultimate test, I plunged back into the use of amphetamines, barbiturates, marijuana, and alcohol (but excluding LSD), trying to prove that I wasn't afraid. Of course, the need to prove oneself is based in fear.

I now began to commit myself to the exploration of spontaneity and my capacity to consciously create a state of being inspired, accidentally on purpose. Talent was still too painful a subject for me to consciously think about. Independent of acting, of my family, and all the elements of the world of my childhood, free of all the confused realities that impeded my knowing myself, I needed to know who I was.

I dropped out. Again. I left Columbia Pictures and stopped teaching. How could I teach when there was so much I didn't know? I made a marginal living as a fair-to-middling carpenter, building closets and laying floors. Laying a level parquet floor is satisfying work, and I loved the peace and anonymity. People would stand and have intimate conversations while I was working, as though I weren't there. It was the first time I felt the difference between the pleasure of being alone and the pain of being lonely. (I turned down an offer from a friend to make more money by participating in paid orgies. I thought about it. I would have made in a night what I didn't always make in a month.) Jerry Brandow, my former girlfriend's brother, got me a job as general factotum on a television commercial house gig with Toyota, at the start of the Japanese invasion of America.

Location shooting was fantastic. We drove nine Toyota Corollas past Bakersfield, over the pass, and dropped down into the desert to film on the salt flats, where we baked in 110-degree heat that forced us underneath the trucks to get some relief. The air-conditioned trailer was for the model actors and actresses. This was not a luxury. It was essential to keep the dry heat from undoing their hairdos and makeup, which would start to dissolve the moment they stepped out of the trailer. They seemed so much like what Hollywood seems at its worst—plastic imitations of life that the desert would melt in a matter of minutes. I did whatever basic carpentry or grip work was needed, from electrical work to holding reflectors. I liked working with my hands. The concentration was pleasurable, simple, calming, and soothing. It helped to center me and brought me close to the earth. I was reminded that my grandfather (mother's father) had been a carpenter.

We leaned into the hurricane wind that the helicopter churned out, turning our faces away from the dust that swirled about. The director screamed to keep the reflectors still. The Toyota swayed in the air, sitting on the platform that was chained to the helicopter, and then, as if in slow motion, I saw the chain break. The red car began its unscheduled descent. It landed before we could scatter, with a force that flattened a couple of the tires, and the chain landed on the roof. The life of that Toyota was over. The director said, "Shit," and we were dismissed until tomorrow. We went back to the motel. The food was lousy, the company uninteresting, the models like plastic toothpicks. I got high and went to sleep. In the morning, all that was left of the car was the dented frame and one of the wheel hubs that had been squashed beyond hope. The two large Highway Patrolmen thought the producer was crazy when he asked them to investigate the incident. We watched them disappear into a spot trailing dust across the flats, up a ridge, never to reappear. They knew the desert rats who scavenged the car for parts to build dune buggies were far away.

Working gave support to my determination to confront a horrible fear. I was the only member of my family who was not a success. Being in Hollywood made it worse. Hollywood has a boom town attitude. The only thing that matters is striking it rich. There's no way to avoid feeling pressure, whether you want to be a part of it or not. It's in the air.

I saw my family infrequently. My relationship with Susan was deteriorating. I actually saw Christopher more than I saw her. He divided and tried to control us. He enjoyed the power, and he needed people to serve him. No wonder Susan loved him. He was much better looking than our father, but had the same ego needs. And he was successful. On the way up. Susan's career was stagnating. She wasn't taking care of herself, and nobody else was, either. One night, at one of her gatherings, when everyone had left, Shelley said, "Stay away from Christopher. He's dangerous." It was said with such love and pain that I knew she was right. She was lying on the floor, tired, drunk, a pill too many, and she looked at me as I bent over her, and she said, "You're a poet, Johnny."

Susan and I were both following our parents by equating talent with neurosis. We seemed to have so little to say, or were afraid to say the little we thought we had. When my father came out to L.A., our talks inevitably ended in an argument. Communication, a word my mother loved, was a battle. My father hated the world we were living in. I scared him anyway; knowing the drugs I took increased his fear of me. He came to L.A. more frequently to see Anna Mizrahi, an actress just slightly older than Susan and myself. She came from a wealthy Venezuelan family, and was on a mission to establish a career in Hollywood. She seemed clever, vivacious, and polite. He dated several women soon after my mother's death, all actresses, and all much younger than he. It was good for him. But when I tried to talk to him about life, or about the past, he would clam up. He never remembered saying or doing any of the things that I asked about. Susan has this same memory.

I recently found a letter I had written him after one of these trips:

Dear Father,

It is 11:30 at night here. I've just come home from working on "Judd," a TV pilot in which Chris guest stars. I have a small but good part and it is a good beginning. I'm very tired but I feel good. I got your letter this morning. I'm glad that you wrote back. As hard as it is we must communicate with each other. We have seen each other or at least a side of each other that we don't like but which is part of life as I feel I want to live.

I'm sorry that when you were here I didn't touch you more. Yelling and screaming come from feelings of isolation that only touch can break. But I was afraid to touch you because of my fear of your not touching back and I was afraid that I might hit you from that anger and fear. I don't want that anymore than you do and I felt that you were afraid of me on a physical level. And I was afraid of you which shows how ridiculous and pre-conditioned we both are.

I feel things now and it scares me sometimes but it is my choice to allow that in myself. Each human being has a choice in life; we choose freely and can change if we want to. We are responsible to ourselves first.

I hope some of this comes through in my acting. I think it does but I'll be able to tell when other people see it. I'll let you know when it's going to be shown.

As for Chris being a black magician and ogre, I disagree violently. I feel he's beautiful, human, he feels, that's what happened between us; we talked and communicated with each other and I discovered that everyone has feelings, not just myself and so I want to communicate them with you. I remember Mother using that word a great deal. I will always love her. No one can replace the contact we made, but room is made for more; different feelings, other human beings. Life is now, not then. I cry over her every now and then. I hope I never stop looking and feeling. It is a strong choice for I am vulnerable but I choose that and work for more openness; with you, for instance. What I say to you is almost meant to get you angry for I feel that when the anger comes out contact will be made. And not violently either, if both people are responsible. I feel responsible for my feelings but I don't know if you are for yours. You have been very passive for a long time and I am not sure if you will be responsible for what you feel or if you will blame it on me. I do not, have not, and will not tell you how to feel; I only ask you to feel.

I am going to bathe and sleep now. I go to work early tomorrow and then I'm getting another car. A used one but it is what I would like to own and I'll make the money to pay for it.

If you want the money for my doctor bills I'll give it to you when I earn it. I do not care that much about money. It only buys things which I can live with or without. I like things but I don't need them anymore. I used to.

I met a girl today on the set. She's eighteen, young and pretty. We talked and touched and just before I left I told her that I wanted to make love to her. She said no and wouldn't give me her phone number. She was afraid. She said that I lived too fully and she was engaged. At eighteen! She knows that she is stopping looking and feeling so as to be safe and protected. Not too little life nor too much. I wished her luck and left.

> Your son,
> John

One night, Franchot invited Susan, my father, and me to dinner at a fancy Beverly Hills restaurant. The maitre d' let me in because I was with them, despite my black leather jacket, which protected me like the armor of knights of old or the magic shirts of Indian warriors. Franchot ordered his usual double vodka on the rocks, which he was forbidden to drink. He had awful kidneys, and a smoker's cough. "At least I can look at it," Franchot laughed. At one moment, he stopped, looked at me, and out of the blue said, "You're going to be fine, Johnson" (his nickname for me). I asked him what he meant, and he said that he wasn't worried about me at all. "I've always known you'd be fine," he said. I couldn't help but ask him how he knew. He said, "I've known you all your life, Johnson. You're a good person. And I love you. And if you ever need anything, you ask me." I was overwhelmed by the love. I asked him why he would help me, and he looked a bit surprised, and said, "Because I'm your godfather, and you can always come to me if you need something." I wonder what my father had said?

During the dinner, I asked Franchot about himself, and then, to my surprise, I asked, "What about women?" It was the first time I had ever asked anyone about women and/or sex. When I was ten there was a conversation about sex going on at the kitchen table. I got up and left in disgust. Susan followed me into my room and asked me if I knew about sex, and I growled, as best as a ten-year-old can, "Yeah. Sure. I know all about that stuff."

(That was my sex education, until my mother gave me, at age twelve, a copy of *Fanny Hill*. All the guys in that book had enormous penises, and I worried that mine wasn't big enough. My father and I had never talked about women, or about love. How could we without bringing up my mother, who had created a barrier between us when she took me into her confidence and made me swear not to tell my father as she complained bitterly to me about the lack of affection and attention he gave her.)

Franchot smiled, leaned towards me, and said, "I always had a lot to prove with women. All my life." And then he laughed, adding, "Now everything's fine. I have nothing to prove anymore."

It was the last time I would see Franchot. He died in 1968, while I was rehearsing Irwin Shaw's *A Choice of Two Wars*, directed by Jack Garfein for the Actors Studio West. Delos Smith Jr. (the faithful family friend who had taken copious notes on our family and its work since he met Susan and mother during the filming of *Picnic*) called me while I was rehearsing at Jack's Actors and Directors Lab on Robertson Boulevard. I went down in the basement to be alone, played my guitar and cried. It would be a long time before I met anyone as kind, honest, and deep as he.

My father stayed with Anna at the Chateau Marmont when they came to L.A. A lot of New Yorkers preferred it to the Beverly Hills Hotel for its sense of old world, bohemian elegance. On one trip, they arrived from Paris with a brown, snakeskin, St. Laurent jacket they had bought for me in Paris. The haunting face of Brando in *The Fugitive Kind*, and his picture in the hotel room, passed through my mind. It was the only gift anyone had ever given me that frightened me. My father told me that he and Anna were going to get married. It was awful how much fear was floating around whenever we made contact. The threat of an explosion was always present.

My mother's warning rang in my ears. "Don't argue with your father. If he gets mad, someday he might have a nosebleed and die." (I always thought, as life went on, that it was a wish of hers.) I told him and Anna that if they were happy that was all that mattered, and wondered why my approval seemed to mean so much to them. He seemed happy, and she seemed to love him.

I became more and more withdrawn over the last months of the fall of 1969. I moved around in California, lived in borrowed apartments, played the guitar, and felt so tired, especially of people obsessed with success. I was tired of taking drugs, listening to people lying, and seeing people live little. lives while they waited for the world to make them famous, which was the only thing that they believed gave life a meaning.

I discovered that "friends" had been hiding drugs in my apartment in the sleeve of my Jerusalem Bible. When two of them sat on my couch arguing about a drug deal, I pulled the revolver from under my pillow, cocked it, and told them to get out. I stood there with the gun in my hand, realizing what I was doing, and turned my back on them until they left. It took me five minutes to calm down and stop shaking enough that I could safely uncock the hammer. I decided to destroy the revolver, taking it apart and battering it with a hammer. Then I fled and went to stay with an actor who lived in an apartment overlooking Barham Boulevard. I loved the place because when you opened the closets the walls were the rocks of the mountains. It felt like a Roman cave. A few days later, I scattered the pieces of the revolver and the ammunition in an area which several days later caught on fire.

Walter Beakel had become an agent, and he pleaded with me not to leave. He said that success for me was just a matter of time.

Well, one night as 1969 drew to a close, I sat in a house in Laurel Canyon all night long and watched people take drugs and play emotional games with one another: little, tentative moves for contact, or flirtations, just wasting life away. As the sun rose, a new inner voice whispered in my ear, "What the hell are you doing here? Get up and get out." The drugs seemed to be a way of pretending to be something one wasn't, and what I had experienced positively with drugs I now wanted to experience without them. I got up and walked to the door. Opening it, I stepped out into the sunrise. Just as they do in the movies, I walked away and never turned back.

CHAOS, DOUBT, AND CONFUSION

New York was blanketed with two feet of snow on Christmas Eve, 1969. It was the same wonderland it had been in 1947, the last time that I had returned there from California. Storms make turmoil inside seem natural. Snowstorms dominate New Yorkers and remind them nature is the most powerful force. She humbles the city dwellers, Nature versus human power and control. People who are brave enough to venture out in such conditions are temporarily re-humanized. They are momentarily awakened by natural forces greater than any that human beings have invented. Barriers are momentarily penetrated and dissolved.

I returned to New York and decided, eight years after beginning my professional life, to take my work, and maybe myself, seriously. Not career, not money, none of the objective, material measures of reality. I wanted to be an artist, as difficult as it is to use the word in the theater, where it seems to mean someone who isn't serious about his or her career.

When I returned to New York, my father offered me a job at the newly created Lee Strasberg Theater Institute. My one stipulation was that I must be allowed to come and go if I found work as an actor. Though it was contrary to policy, he agreed. He loved and respected me more than I had ever realized. In retrospect, I think he was glad I was back, and that I seemed to have ended a period of my life that had so deeply upset him. It's hard to tell, because he so rarely expressed any of his real, personal feelings.

People who idolized my father treated me like a prince. Those who hated him assumed that I was like him, and often wouldn't be interested in meeting me. I don't know which attitude was more disagreeable. Regardless, I was treated as an extension of him, an identity I refused to accept. I was angry about this for a long time. It was even difficult for me to accept compliments from people. I never believed they were genuine. This painful problem is almost totally gone now, though the scar remains.

It has probably contributed to my need to understand and define talent. People even asked his permission to hire me. Over the years, I discovered from a few directors that he had even refused parts in my name. The reality of the Biblical curse, "the sins of the father," is understood by anyone who has experienced how being part of a family influences how one is judged by society.

I found work as an actor almost immediately, being cast as Duperret, the aristocrat who has a constant erection in *Marat Sade*, at Washington's Arena Stage, to be directed by Alfred Ryder. Alfred was an actor-director and member of the Studio. I left for Washington during the blizzard that hit the East Coast during Christmas week. Rehearsals were six hours of pausing every five minutes while Alfred went to the bathroom. At the end of three weeks he hadn't yet blocked the first act. At the beginning of the fourth week, he announced that we were going to have a run-through, and he wanted it to be at performance level. Everyone was shocked and frightened. Alfred was scared and drunk. I said I would be glad to do a run-through after I had gotten a chance to rehearse. Alfred fired me two days later, claiming that I didn't speak well enough. I wanted to give him the beating he deserved. Only the fact that he was so sick stopped me.

I knew he had given false reason, but it was the first time I had been fired. The pain and shock pushed me into working on my voice and speech. I read Shakespeare out loud almost every day for the next two years, making sure I enunciated.

I met my first wife, Wendy, during that production. She was nineteen. During the first reading, I watched her from my slumped position at the far end of the table. It was a large cast, a long table, and I played a major role, so I sat down at the talkers' end. I followed the way she walked in her white blouse and sailor pants. She had gray-blue eyes and was thin, almost boyish. The third night we were together, the telephone rang as we were making love. She answered it and had a long conversation with a married man with whom she had been having an affair. Inside me, a voice said, "Leave." I ignored it and we moved to New York and were married that summer on Cape Cod, where I was working in a theater. During the five years of our marriage I always felt that if I tried a little harder the separations between us would dissolve. I was responsible for whatever problems we had.

We were young, and we shared an interest in life, became vegetarians, and renovated an apartment on Seventh Street between Avenues C and D, on the lower east side of New York, in an area called Alphabet City. We exposed the brick walls and the original ceiling beams and blow-torched generations of paint off pine kitchen cabinets, carrying everything either up to, or down from, the entire fifth floor (penthouse walk-up for the piss elegant) that the apartment occupied. Children lived on the street. Occasionally, there was one as young as six or seven who was shooting heroin. People peeled apples in the street with enormous switchblade knives. There was a gang that stripped and burned stolen cars. The police did not interfere. Riots were a normal way of blowing off steam during the awful New York summer heatwaves.

We could have been on another planet. We saw men land on the moon and experienced a full solar eclipse, all of which moved Alphabet City as little as the dead body we discovered hanging in the trees as we sat drinking our morning coffee and looking out the kitchen window. Only the influx of young, middle class people like ourselves looking for large, cheap apartments seemed to stir up the inhabitants. We were there because we wanted to be there, and they were there because it was the only place they could afford. This is just north of the part of New York where the latest immigrants come to live. My father's family lived there, further south (below Houston Street), when they arrived from Galicia, the part of Poland that was then part of the Austro-Hungarian Empire.

As soon as I returned to New York, I went back to the Studio. The Studio is the only place of its kind in the world where a professional actor or director can have the public privacy a theater artist needs.

Scene work in my father's classes was almost exclusively devoted to contemporary plays, novels, and short stories. Easily accessible material allowed actors to develop habits of expression that would serve them in the American professional theater world. Contemporary material was closer to them, and required minimal work to achieve understanding and transformation. This focus allowed my father to develop the emotional expressiveness and simple truth of the actor, while circumventing the problem of transformation and character composition. Classical material is still rarely produced in the top levels of American theater, and rarely acted by the top actors, which does nothing to change the general belief that realism is only suited to contemporary plays and films. However, at the Studio, you chose whatever material or problem you wanted to work on. At the Studio, one could work on one's dream. I chose to work on the "To be or not to be" soliloquy from *Hamlet*.

I was up second that day. I went up the spiral stairs at the back of the stage, as I had at my audition. I hate entering through the audience. My father was commenting on the first scene. I couldn't stand being downstairs and waiting to be called up; I wanted to walk around in the space where I was going to live and act. (My favorite moments of rehearsal often are when I can just walk about or sit on the set when no one else is around. I have never found a better way to concentrate and begin to transform myself.) I stood off to the side, pacing a little, wanting to have the stage to myself for a few moments before I began. I had not consciously planned or made choices. I chose to work as spontaneously and moment to moment as I could. I wore dance tights, and had a simple kitchen knife which would barely cut butter, but which gave me an object to intentionally focus my imagination. I cannot work on Shakespeare without feeling that everyone is armed.

It was late, and there wasn't the normal ten-minute break between scenes. I heard my father's voice, which seemed to come from far away. I looked at the brick wall at the back of the stage, and began to imagine that it was the wall of the castle. The brick helped. Suddenly, a thought popped into my head. I asked myself what it would be like if my father, the king, were dead. The thought, synchronized with the reality of where I was, went through me like a shockwave. I became involved as soon as I recognized the impulse, and I was terrified that waiting would produce anxiety that would undermine my belief. I began to feel desperate as I tried to hold onto the reality (perhaps a bit too much with my head), which I recognized was fine for the scene. I was able to maintain the state of being involved because I was accustomed, now, to the conscious awareness of being in several levels of reality at the same time.

I heard furniture being shuffled about, and then my father's voice, "This is a monologue from *Hamlet*." I looked at the back wall and was possessed by a desire to run towards it. Leaping onto the platform pushed against it, I lunged upwards, climbing the wall with a desperate need to find my dead fathers, both the real one and the one in the play. My fingers found niches in the brick wall which, in the spontaneous change of perspective, had become the ramparts of a castle; and I climbed until I believed that if I climbed any higher, I might just fall and die. I hung there, afraid to move or speak; afraid that if I spoke, I would destroy the reality and truth of what I was feeling. I had to force myself to begin: "To be or not to be, that is the question."

I stopped, aware of the pain from so many years of not saying what I really believed. It had created a habit of repression that strangled the truth. Even now, the only time I truly like my voice is when I have a cold and it seems to vibrate with life. I came down and wandered about for several moments. Still afraid to speak, I stopped wandering several feet from the first row, and began to look at myself in an imaginary mirror. As I focused I continued.

Whether 'tis nobler in the mind to suffer
The slings and arrows of outrageous fortune,
Or to take arms against a sea of troubles,
And by opposing, end them?

I drew the knife, placed it on my throat and wondered how and if I could kill myself:

To die, to sleep—
No more; and by a sleep to say we end
The heart-ache and the thousand natural shocks
That flesh is heir to. —'Tis a consummation
Devoutly to be wished. To die, to sleep;

"But really," I thought, and, looking in the mirror that was now part of my world, and in which I swear I glimpsed my reflection, I placed the knife more exactly on the vein in my neck, and waited until I believed, before I continued.

To sleep! perchance to dream.: Aye, there's the rub;
For in that sleep of death what dreams may come,
When we have shuffled off this mortal coil
Must give us pause:

I got lost, and the words became a maze. It seemed to me that I spoke in a relative monotone, which even with tone and resonance lacked what I imagined to be the music for classical texts. British English has more melody than American.

there's the respect
That makes calamity of so long life.

My anger and bitterness over all of the thoughts and feelings that flowed through me connected to the text:

For who would bear the whips and scorns of time,
The oppressor's wrong, the proud man's contumely,

I could feel how involved I was—until suddenly, I ran out of steam.

The pangs of disprized love, the law's delay,

Oh, there is no justice in life, or the law! The greed and lying I had seen, all in the name of success.

> The insolence of office, and the spurns
> That patient merit of the unworthy takes,
> When he himself might his quietus make
> With a bare bodkin? Who would fardels bear,
> To grunt and sweat under a weary life,
> But that the dread of something after death—
> The undiscovered country from whose bourn
> No traveler returns, —puzzles the will,
> And makes us rather bear those ills we have
> Than fly to others that we know not of?

I couldn't follow through to the end. I stopped, relaxed, and became simpler, because I knew what this meant.

> Thus conscience does make cowards of us all;
> And thus the native hue of resolution
> Is sicklied o'er with the pale cast of thought,
> And enterprises of great pitch and moment
> With this regard their currents turn awry
> And lose the name of action.

I walked to a pillar, and looked to where I imagined Ophelia, the dream love of my life, would come from. I looked for her with actual longing, and hoped that something would come through the white, double doors at the rear of the room:

> Soft you now!
> The fair Ophelia. —Nymph, in thy orisons
> Be all my sins remember'd.

I wished that I could have seen her, but there was only the look in my eyes to see. And it was over.

The comments were positive, including a comparison from Lou Gilbert, an actor who had worked in *Viva Zapata*, to Marlon Brando. The comparison shocked me, because Marlon's talent and force seemed to contrast enormously to the "sensitive and fragile" image which I still had of myself, and which interfered with my own talent and spontaneous expression. My father was careful, but very complimentary, and noticed the freedom and expressiveness I had, even commenting on my voice, which I hated. He particularly liked the moment of seeing Ophelia. In retrospect, this was the first time I had consciously transformed, and had heard my voice in Shakespeare. It is an unforgettable moment, as deep as any love we feel. I listened to everything people were saying as though through a filter. People had been excited by my power, and I heard, "You had two wonderful moments." People said, "You went in and out of reality," and I thought it meant, "Not good enough."

The strength in The Method was that it was very organized, simple, and clear. It trained concentration and emotional expression, and helped the actor to create a truthful, sensual reality and behavior. The actor lived a real experience. This, however, was also reductive, mechanical, and used by itself did not train the actor to guide his talent and imagination towards involving himself directly in the play. It taught actors to create a parallel life experience rather than a transformative one. Planning exercises for scenes that prepared them for what they were going to feel on the next page is a process which takes them out of the moment, and hinders their involvement in the play. The time lapse only dissolved when the actor's emotion was powerful enough that he became overwhelmed. This could lead to the accident of being spontaneously inspired and becoming totally involved. So could the passion and dedication my father shared with us. However, this accident, in the long run, is the result of the actor's talent, and not part of The Method. If this accident doesn't occur, the actor continues to function with a reality and truth alongside of, but not in, the play, because of how he or she learned to think about acting.

While my father recognized the problem of anticipation as one of the major problems for actors, he failed to acknowledge his work's reductive logic in scene study as being out of the moment. He believed that sense memory, substitution, and private moments were the notes of music of the play, and that the space-time lapse in the actor's creative process was only a stage of learning. The fact that most actors never got to the point where that lapse disappeared he blamed on the lack of study. He never saw that an artist's creative process also had to train the artist's organic thought process. We were trained to think about what exercises would make our imaginary world real, and that any exercise could be done in less than one minute. Actors in the Group Theater learned to prepare emotional responses in plays in this manner. An actor studying with my father was guaranteed to be able to produce strong emotional results on cue. It was true, and as we all thought that everyone used the Method, it seemed to be perfect and to come with a lifetime guarantee.

My father's approach to scene study reveals a flaw in the Method. No organic process anticipates an action or response before the fact. The actor's work on perceiving and involving himself in his own personal dream space didn't exist, in reality, in anyone's work. Stella did it, but she couldn't break the process down clearly enough to be able to consciously pass it on. You had to have enough talent to have understood what she was organically doing. There is a lot of teaching that involves nonverbal communication, but it helps if the teacher is calm and clear about what is being taught.

Stanislavski's and my father's suspicions of inspiration and fears of losing control dominates their work. They believed an artist's creative process could be reduced to a clear and rational process, based on known laws. They excluded the artist's talent and dream world from technique. It made their laws tend to be mechanical, even as they were applied to emotion and behavior. This thinking like an actor, rather than a human being, is what leads to the mental manipulation in my father's sense memory work. Stanislavski was closer to the truth, but lacked the language to explain it. It is difficult for anyone to explain it completely, because it doesn't take place in our physical world. It resides in the intangible world of the mind, the world of life that we can't see and touch, the world of intentional dreaming, which is how artists or scientists explore whatever reality they are studying; the world of thought experiments, predictions, probabilities, and spirituality. It's no wonder I felt weird, alone, and confused, as though there were something very wrong somewhere. I had to get to the point where I stopped thinking that the something wrong was me.

In this state of chaos, doubt, and confusion, I went back to work at the Institute. The year it was founded, 1968, my father had also married Anna and begun a new life. The convergence is not accidental. Anna is a very good business woman. There was also Carl Schaeffer, a lawyer who specialized in Chapter 11's, who was a devoted admirer, friend, and adviser to my father and to the Actors Studio. Carl became my father's partner, put up the money, and set my father up in business. Many years later, when he wanted to help me do the same thing, he took me to lunch and explained capitalism to me as a system in which the objective is to pay people as little as possible for their work in order to make as much profit as one could from that work. But he was totally unselfish with my father, giving my father controlling interest, and later, as Anna became more central in my father's affairs and the Institute was a financial success, he never asked for anything back other than his original investment. He loved my father.

Teachers were not allowed to work outside the school, and, at the same time, were not guaranteed their jobs if they left to take work as actors or directors. They were paid $12.50 an hour. Occasionally, if a teacher became popular, he might find that, rather than having a class added to his schedule, the reverse would happen. The reason given for this was to "balance enrollment." In teachers' meetings, deviations from conventional Method exercise work were criticized, especially in the teacher's absence. If a teacher became too popular or her work deviated too far from the Method, she'd be eased out, though never fired outright. My father believed that a teacher was there to teach what my father had taught him or her and not to teach what the person might know or be interested in exploring. Some of that is understandable, because some teachers began to explore with techniques like bio-energetics, meditation, and group support that they were not necessarily qualified to teach or use. Some of this was a precursor to many of today's acting classes that fail to differentiate between self-development, expression, and acting. Many actors are trained to express themselves, but they don't know how to act. So, in one sense, I agree with his resistance. However, the reasons for our resistence are different.

My father was resistant to new ideas and thought the Method was complete. He also resented competition, and was suspicious of the direct, personal contact in some of these teaching processes. The rigidity of his thinking, and the ambiguity and half-truths of the Institute's policies, made for a medieval atmosphere. The maneuverings that resulted were obvious to all but those who didn't want to know. There were a lot of people who didn't know, or didn't want to know, how the Institute was run, until the politics of working there affected them. The atmosphere eventually touched everyone, no matter how close they were to my father, or how important an artist they were. I could predict who was going to be forced to submit, or else indirectly encouraged to leave. The few times I advised people to be careful, they looked at me as though I were paranoid—including my sister. Knowing was very painful, and I felt more and more alone.

In faculty meetings, my father was capable of making totally contradictory statements on any subject within the same conversation. If I pointed this out to him he would look at me as though I were crazy. It was a nightmare, especially at a time when I was seriously looking for understanding and direction. It was dangerous to be close to my father because Anna would feel threatened by that closeness unless she was sure of your loyalty to her. Anyway, it took me a while to see all of this, longer to believe it, and longer still to accept that my father was never going to be the man I wanted him to be. The close-minded atmosphere doomed the Institute to a life of institutional mediocrity. My father dedicated his life to his love for acting and to set a standard for the American theater. That standard has been compromised, its movement and growth inhibited, in the name of glorifying The Method and making money. God, it sounds like a religious institution. As I became aware, I also grew away from him in the battle for my own identity. I don't believe in inheritance as a guaranteed right (as it is in some European countries), or even, necessarily, as healthy. Accumulating wealth is rather patriarchal, and it seems to ultimately diminish the force of each generation, which I think should make its own world. So when things got dirty, I got out. I had never expected to inherit anything, and knew I wouldn't.

In 1976, when I became the Executive Director of the Institute, I decided to hire the best available teachers in New York. I also forced my father to raise the salaries to $25 an hour. It made him furious for about ten seconds. But the Institute was doing well, and he could afford it.

Most people who suffered under this feudal system blame Anna for the chaotic atmosphere. Anna's need to be in control was certainly a factor, yet my father knew what was going on and had to be held responsible.

In spite of the prevailing prejudice against it, I began to explore improvisation as a part of basic actors' training. I was convinced that improvisation was part of the spontaneity and inspired quality I had when I did my best work. I wanted to create a state of being in which an actor could be spontaneously inspired, accidentally on purpose. Some of the exercises my mother did involved group improvisation. One was of being stranded in a lifeboat. Each actor had to pick a character, something that he wanted, an object, and a sense memory. As we worked, she would shift the circumstances: the boat sprang a leak, for example. It was fun, and she made you aware that sense memory alone wasn't enough. Acting required imagination and interesting, personal choices. It didn't go as deep as my father's work, but it did create a reality!

Another improv my mother did was of three people searching for hidden treasure in Africa. You enter a cave guarded by a legendary serpent. Each actor has a reason for being there and wanting the money. At the first clap of her hands, we would hear drums; on the second, the drums would come closer and we would also hear voices; and on the third clap, the drums and voices would stop. What you imagined about who you were, what you wanted, and what you were doing there affected and changed the scene's reality.

But of course, my mother had a lot of imagination. She neither lied about nor told her real age. One of her best friends was Tallulah Bankhead, with whom my mother had once shared a dressing room. Tallulah, according to my mother, was a pathological liar. So, when asked her age, my mother always said that she was five years younger than Tallulah.

My father tolerated improvisation, but was uncommunicative when questioned about its usefulness. He considered anything other than systematic sense memory training incomplete and unreliable. Techniques other than his were met with patriarchal disapproval. When pressed, he spoke of his use of improvisation in the Group Theater rehearsals, though I never saw him use it. He seemed to equate improvisation with substitution, meaning replacing the play's reality with something personal to which you more readily respond.

Actors who know themselves and have a good imagination don't need to consciously think a lot about substitution. It happens naturally. The synthesis of an actor, what he knows about life, and what he perceives about the play happens organically when an actor is aware of and able to handle the multiple realities that exist when he is in his personal dream space. Substitution is a natural process of making reality personal to you. A simple example of that is the process of anthropomorphism: a culture imbuing animals, plants, and natural elements with human characteristics. We do it when we attribute human qualities to machines or aliens, as in Stanley Kubrick's *2001: A Space Odyssey* or in Steven Spielberg's films, especially with E.T., the Lassie of the cosmos. *Star Wars* is full of anthropomorphism, with R2-D2 and C3PO (the one with John Gielgud's voice—lucky machine), and Yoda, who I think should have won an Academy Award as Best Supporting Actor. Another simple example is when a character falls in love. It would be unnatural ro an actor not to think about when, and with whom, he has fallen in love. Comparisons of character and circumstance are natural. "This one is much sweeter, prettier, stronger, darker, richer, etc."

If actors learn how to understand and involve themselves in the given circumstances of the play and character, and have a knowledge of life and a sense of truth, this part of transformation and synthesis is natural. Dreaming about a play's world is my favorite part of creation. Many actors feel lost at this stage, because while becoming involved with an imaginary world they don't quite know where they are and become overwhelmed by where they imagine they are. Where are they? With the play, in their personal dream spaces.

As for improvisation, if an actor is talented and trained to think organically, he will develop the ability to live moment to moment. He knows that involving his talent and imagination are paramount. He will become obsessed with consciously directing himself into his personal dream space, to begin to concentrate on intentionally discovering realities of the play that he often perceives intuitively and spontaneously; he can become involved in the world he imagines and wants to create. This concentration and spontaneous, intuitive, moment-to-moment living in an imaginary world is improvisation.

In production, the usefulness of literal improvisation is debatable. If the actor needs to improvise to discover a substitute reality, there is no guarantee that, once discovered, the reality can be incorporated into the play, especially on a night-after-night basis. If he doesn't need improvisation to discover reality, why use it? Once an actor develops his own personal dream space of a scene, becoming involved is pleasurable, and the actor does not feel inhibited by the play. On the contrary, he feels free, because his intentional dreaming involves him personally and opens his mind to almost unlimited possibilities to explore and create. He discovers that the play isn't the enemy of the actor.

A common criticism of the Method is that it compartmentalizes one's thoughts. It teaches reductive, non-organic thinking. An actor learns to think like an actor (what, and how, am I going to act?), rather than learning to enter into dialogue with another human being (the character) living another life. Most systems teach the kind of thinking that separates the actor from the life he needs to become involved with. He learns to label everything. That kind of technique can only depersonalize his relationships. It still amazes me that dreamers like my father, who was so inspiring at the Studio, left dreaming out of their work.

Actors doing sense memory work tend to go away in the eyes, like someone taking drugs or daydreaming. The eyes seem to be looking within or away. Actors will often close their eyes in exercise work in order to concentrate on their imaginary reality. This habit of not being "here and now" was sometimes carried into scene work. The actor seemed to be in his own world, apart from that of the play. This problem of presence and contact is engendered by exercise if it is the primary technique being taught. I found that actors could keep their eyes open, and maintain their focus on the imaginary reality, without shutting out other levels of reality. They could learn to concentrate and still be present and make contact, even with their eyes, at the same time. I achieve this focus through the interaction I use in any moment of the actor's work, not just after the work is over. Through it, I teach them that they can be present in multiple levels of reality at the same time.

I began to wonder why an actor, who offstage is a human being with a personal life and history, loses contact with his own humanity the moment he sets foot on stage. This wasn't a new thought. But I was trying to understand how to solve the problem organically. The actor loses contact with himself, his talent (sensing), and his sense of direction and common sense. It is invariably accompanied by the feeling that he or she had no ideas and nothing to say. Most actors feel this way all of their working time. They lose themselves.

Actors, regardless of their training, begin creating by reading and analyzing the play. This analysis needs to be personal, not just "correct." The actor has to behave like a human being, not like an actor. I mean that he has to learn to think like a human being who is living a situation; thoughts that result from one's contact and presence with the imaginary environment on which one is concentrating. Most actors think about what they can do to represent and express a vision of life that they are fundamentally distanced from by the way in which they think. This deep involvement, in which an artist can become obsessed, or even possessed, by the world he wants to create is the only way the actor will discover the organic life of the character and discover what he wants to do. An artist cannot simply search for behavior that represents and illustrates his idea of the author's words. He shouldn't apply a rigid system of thought, analysis, exercises or techniques that enable him to live an experience that parallels the play.

I didn't just want feeling. I wanted involvement in the play, and transformation. That wasn't about getting lost. It was going on an adventure to an unknown land, and a land that is self-created. Being lost is not the same as being in a place one has never been in before. I realized that if I developed a long-term preparation (state of being) that enabled me to become consciously involved, and able to stay focused, in my personal dream space as if it were here-and-now, I could make use of my knowledge, experience, and talent. I would be able to will myself into the world of the play so that I could explore it, and find my way to create my own personal work of art, by Being Transformed.

I also knew it was important to realize that when most actors become involved, and have a real experience in rehearsal, they are shocked, surprised, and confused by the spontaneity and immediacy of what they have done. They say things like, "But that was happening to me, not to the character. I felt that it was real, but it was me." They believe what an actor should feel must be distanced and separate from them. It seems that we forget we're acting, and we forget that the art of acting is transforming, and we are going to have real feelings about things that are real in our personal dream spaces.

The creative process can only be defined by studying what happens naturally when one is spontaneously inspired. When spontaneously inspired, the barrier between self and art disappears. There is no separation. There is a consciousness of exactly what is going on, on as many levels of reality as one's talent and awareness permits one to operate. The artist is one with the play, or with the brush and paints, or with the music. He does not paint or play; he is the paint and the brush, the music. As David Hockney said, "I just love to paint. I could watch the paint go on for hours." In that inspired state, we feel more alive and more conscious.

The synthesis of realities and worlds is the same as falling in love and getting married. The two objects merge and become neither the one nor the other, but something new. I knew that was what creating a character and transforming felt like. I had experienced those multiple realities; text, lines, real place, imaginary place: an audience who is there but is more than who they are, and myself, an actor who at the same time knows that he is an actor and a character.

The actor begins to imagine the possibilities he missed in his original reading of the text, and his sensation and feelings begin to be organically drawn into the world of the play. Using his knowledge of life and his sense of truth helps to ensure the actor expresses himself in coherent action and behavior. That's why the creative process, and what an artist has to say, depends on what he knows. If you can't see it, you can't do it. Even if a director or teacher gives you a great idea, you have to recognize it in your own soul.

A HOPELESS DREAMER

I felt trapped. The changes, in myself and my work process, were incompatible with the raison d'être at the Institute or the Studio, where my father's word was Gospel. Offers of work from other acting schools escalated my feelings of being held back. It was becoming more and more difficult to ignore my father's limitations and close-mindedness. Every time I experimented, I confirmed what my talent and intuition had already told me. But I judged, and events later proved, that if I left and went to another school my father would have found it an irrevocable betrayal.

Anna supported his ego in such a way as to reinforce his prejudices. She used half-truths and character assassination to distort reality. During a fight with Anna over business practices, I called her, in a burst of temper, a whore. It happened. But the only thing reported to my father, tearfully, was that I called her a whore. And it was all he wanted to discuss. It didn't matter that the argument was actually a broad-ranging one about how the Institute should be run.

During the period of my administration, the school achieved a level of organization and professionalism it had never enjoyed before (or after). I worked an eighty-hour week, including thirty hours of teaching. My father and Anna needed to understand that it was time for the organization to grow up. It was an almost million-dollar business, and couldn't be run like a mom and pop candy store. "He hates me," she'd pout, anxious to portray herself as a bewildered innocent about to be pushed into the cold. Anna's theatrics and the enchanted audience she found in my father would finally push me out. I have Anna's amateur antics to thank for helping me move on with my life.

This final break came seven years later, in 1978. It was the beginning of my effort to resolve the conflict that followed me during most of my professional life—whether to do what others expected of me or to achieve what I demanded of myself. It made me think that I was incapable of doing what it took to be successful. I interpreted my behavior as a sign of inadequacy. I never wanted to hurt or ignore those I love, which is also why, until recently, I never wanted to have children; I didn't want to do to them what my parents had done to me. After many years, I finally began to resolve this conflict and make peace with myself. I admitted to myself that I didn't want to change my personal standard of behavior to suit others, and gave myself permission to be who I am. Interestingly, once that conflict was resolved, I had more success than ever. Once I acknowledged that

I didn't care what other people thought was right, the angels that guide me swept me towards the realization of my dream.

In the spring of 1971, I received an invitation to become director of the Actors and Directors Workshop at the National Film Board of Canada. At the end of August we packed up our things and put them in the used Jeep Wagoneer we had bought and left New York. Canada was an adventure. We rented a hundred-year-old stone farmhouse half an hour from the Vermont border and seventy-five minutes from Montreal, near Cowansville in the eastern townships. It was a world not torn apart by the Vietnam War, sequestered from the sickness, drugs, decay, and decadence of Alphabet City.

During the first three months in Canada, when I wasn't working, I sat in the house, nervous and explosively touchy. I was unable to relax. I didn't want to go outside, even to take walks in the woods that surrounded the farm. I was trembling inside. There was a battle going on between my habit of depressing myself to remain in control, with the familiar sadness and pain of abandonment, and the burning desire to free myself. I was still afraid of openly feeling what I had been depressing. My natural capacity for living was trapped under a frozen ocean of tears. This defense against feeling always held me back and kept me emotionally immature. I was waiting for someone who wasn't there, but I wouldn't give up the desperate hope. I wasn't ready to feel the pain of disappointment, which was the only thing that would free me. I did yoga to channel and sublimate the feeling. I was afraid of my anger and self-destructive capacities. They blocked me from getting to the loneliness and abandonment underneath. I began studying martial arts. I had studied Tai Chi, but Sophia Delza didn't teach it as a martial art. At a Kung Fu school with a young teacher named Kim Wong I began to learn how to consciously mobilize and enjoy my own aggression.

Christmas week arrived and I began having serious asthma attacks. The day before a holiday party we were giving, I began to run a fever. We had invited people from the NFB, along with several friends who had come up from New York. Wendy cooked a Brazilian dinner, having lived in Brazil for a year when she was sixteen. She had been raised in the Panama Canal Zone, where her father had worked as an auditor for the General Accounting Office. In the middle of dinner, I started to feel as though I were going to pass out. I excused myself, not wanting to spoil anyone's fun, went upstairs, got into bed, and began to shiver so forcibly that it frightened me. I lay there alone, feeling angry, miserable, and heartbroken at the same time. Would anyone notice my absence or wonder how I was? I knew Wendy wouldn't, because in her youth she needed too much attention herself to be aware of what I was feeling. One of the actresses in the workshop, Julie Wildman, finally came upstairs to see how I was. I was bundled into a snowsuit and taken to the hospital. I was diagnosed with pneumonia. My temperature was 105°. When I was young, I got sick to get attention. Now, I was getting sick to force myself to pay attention to myself. It's a lousy way to relax or take a vacation. It's a habit I still have, and am still trying to change.

The Film Board felt like a club. They had done a lot of improvisational work during the two years of their existence. It had led them into the kind of verbal cleverness, superficial behavior, and comedic results that are pleasant, but ultimately crippling if one intends acting to be deeply truthful. They were accustomed to the kind of positive reinforcement and approval that often marks group training. Deep feelings, real creativity, and a sense of truth seemed threatening. It was the desire to combat that complacency and develop a professional standard and expertise that had led to my being hired.

I began to teach them about concentration and deep feeling. Few actors like to do exercises. They have little sense of how hard they need to work in order to master one of the most difficult art forms. To fall in love on cue, for instance. Dancers do barre work, athletes work out, musicians practice scales. Actors just want to act. But it's not just about being free, using imagination, and not thinking too much. Their work was all done sort of spontaneously, "you know, it's intuitive, you know." Studying the history of any artist, one traces a progressive sequence over years of research, intent, and exploration, finally reaching a point where the artist is there, completely there, in his art, effortlessly, spontaneously inspired; accidentally on purpose. Art becomes inseparable from technique and art seems effortless. The great artist's technique, his attention to detail that evolves over years of dreaming and endlessly practicing, sketching, and layering, putting on and peeling off layer after layer of life, ends up looking as if the actor is doing nothing.

Success begins when an actor stops working on fear and directs his concentration into doing that which he is afraid he may not be able to do. That's also the difference between an artist and a professional amateur. This is not to say that the artist dominates his fear, or that fear disappears.

Fear is a good energy. The more you want to do something, the more frightened you become. Imagine thinking that mastery means eliminating fear, and desire, and longing, and sadness, and anxiety, and love. An animal who doesn't feel fear is a dead animal. Dominating and controlling feelings doesn't mean stopping them. It means learning to use them, to direct feeling and energy intentionally into what one wants to do. Control is really the ability to consciously give in and let go and intentionally and intuitively direct your impulses and feelings into the reality you choose.

During the second year in Canada, I paid for Wendy to go to Paris to pursue her dream of studying mime with Etienne Decroux. I think I wanted her to go as much or more than she did. Isolating myself was the only way I could try to pay attention to myself. I was alone for nine months. I lived in a house that had no hot water, studied Kung Fu, and became a strict vegetarian. I wondered who I was. A dreamer? A fantasist? Actor? Director? Teacher? Here I was, eleven years into a professional career. If I had talent, I would have to do something with it, if not for pleasure then out of a sense of responsibility for the gift I had been given. I felt I had never taken myself and my work seriously. Here I was complaining about my students' attitude, and I was doing the same thing. Maybe they were teaching me more than I was teaching them. Maybe everyone near me felt as lonely with me as I did. Maybe I was as cold as I accused my father of being with me.

Where did I belong? What kind of man was I? Why couldn't I express my feelings offstage? Why did I always feel as though I were squeezing myself, and why did I ignore people when they complimented me? The three years I lived in Canada felt like one long self-contemplation .

In June of 1973, at the end of my second year at the Film Board, I left everything stored in a barn and flew to Paris. Wendy and I slept together, but it was not a passionate reunion. We felt estranged, and lovemaking seemed an obligation and a way to avoid facing the problem.

We bought a Volkswagen camper for four hundred dollars and traveled through France, Spain, and Portugal. In Bretagne, we visited Wendy's relatives, who put their dog in the trunk of their car when they traveled. The dog was sweet but decidedly crazed, as would be any being who was half fried every time he went for a car ride.

Outside Madrid, between a repair depot for military vehicles and a shepherd's flock, we found Viva, a Spanish spaniel, living wild. She was wonderful, and belonged to no one but herself. We backtracked almost sixty kilometers to take her with us. The soldiers thought we were crazy. "Fea" (ugly), they said. While they laughed at us, we bathed this nearly black dog until she became white with large brown spots, a stub of a tail, and floppy ears, a retriever of exceptional beauty. When we left, we opened the door and she jumped in of her own will, a decision she never seemed to regret. When she ate the dry dog food we occasionally gave her, she would take it piece by piece, biting into it circumspectly like an animal used to surviving on anything. She was one of the best people I've ever known.

When we returned to Canada at the end of the summer, we moved to a house that occupied two hundred acres in its own private valley, one hour from Montreal, near Granby. The relatively new, one-story house wasn't large, but we had the valley to ourselves.

I didn't know how to end the relationship. Wendy went to Washington to look for work. She stayed down there awhile. I felt as lonely living with me as she must have.

That year, I decided to produce Brecht's *Messingkauf Diaries*. This series of discussions among a director, dramaturg, and company of actors was an impossible theater piece, neither intrinsically theatrical nor a play. I believed its content and structure would allow me to work with each actor on a scene, monologue, or song. After all, it was Brecht. No one could complain that we weren't working on scenes. They had to get involved. We were going to do a play. At least that's how it seemed to me.

I had added new members to the workshop but the problems remained the same. Little resistances undermined us. One actor wanted to do a clown monologue in which he had to juggle, but then complained that he didn't know how. He said it in the way that people do when you know that they are not going to work at solving the problem. I got angry and said it was easy to learn to do. I went home and taught myself how to juggle overnight. The next day I showed him how to do it. I was really proud of what I'd done, but no one believed me when I swore that I had just taught myself. They didn't want to believe that anything was possible if you were willing to work at doing it.

Wendy introduced me to an ex-seminary student who wanted to be an actor. He was in the workshop. I liked him. She suggested we all live together. I suggested a divorce, stopped being a vegetarian, and went to California. I decided not to renew my contract with the Film Board. I was a guest in my father's house. It seemed natural to feel like a stranger. I had changed more than I knew.

Wendy called to say Viva had been run over and killed by a driver who hit her in order to avoid hitting Wendy's young man, who had taken Viva for a walk. Eleven years later, when my second marriage ended, a pine tree that I loved died with the same suddenness. I know it seems absurd, if one believes that life is a big machine, for someone to wonder if these signs, coincidences, accidents, or synchronicities of life have meaning. It's just as absurd to me that people don't wonder more whether it is more absurd to believe that there is some intimate, inseparable connection between all living beings, or more absurd not to.

By 1974, I had been acting, directing, and teaching for thirteen years. I was changing. My work was changing. Life and work seemed to move closer and closer together. The spontaneity and joy I sometimes experienced in my creative process, and the dreaming and imagining that happened intuitively, was definitely missing from the Method.

I returned to New York, where I would lie in bed startled by the force of my feelings, which lifted me out of my habitual self. I thought I was going to explode, lose control, or go crazy. Memories of going through the window made my fear real. I didn't know what to do. I had spent too many years controlling myself or exploding.

I met myself by accident, in moments of spontaneous living, in work, and, sporadically, in my private life. It was this accidental bumping into myself that I now knew was the key to the door that would lead me to a conscious technique. To achieve it, I knew I had to trust my feelings, which terrified me all the more.

All my life, I feared that I would lose my parents if I satisfied my desires. I needed permission to be myself, a permission I never seemed to have gotten and couldn't give myself. So I just habitually ignored myself.

The three years in Canada, as frustrating as they had been, had produced more changes than I realized.

I was dating Heather Macrae, who was playing in the Circle Rep's *The Hot L Baltimore*. Friends in the company told me that Marshall Mason and Lanford Wilson needed an actor for Lanford's new play, *The Mound Builders*, which Marshall was directing. I really wanted the part. I was spontaneous, made contact in the audition, and conveyed the right sense of humor. I felt at home on stage. They called me back. I was more scared that time, but they gave me a script and asked me to wait a few days. Richard Gere was just possibly going to do the role. Marshall said I was the better actor but that Richard looked more menacing and Indian than I did. I say this only so that everyone knows that hardly anybody is first choice, and who cares? What's important is to take advantage of an opportunity. I waited anxiously for four days and avoided getting into several fights thanks only to Heather's desperate pleading.

Success is directly related to one's capacity to tolerate anxiety. Most people's lives are dominated by their preoccupation with avoiding anxiety. Actors hope that acting techniques, or preparations, will help eliminate anxiety. However, good technique doesn't eliminate feeling. It teaches you how to use it. The more you feel, the more it means you care, and the more you can express.

I was so excited, and so close to losing control, that I wondered if I was going to go crazy and dive through another window. I called Susan, who gave me Dr. Baker's name. Dr. Baker talked to me for a minute or so, and told me to call back at a specific time in two weeks. He had probably diagnosed me during the conversation, and was already working on me and my anxiety—and finding out how committed I was going to be. I asked if there were any chance of seeing him sooner, and he said, "I don't think that's possible. I'm pretty booked up." The waiting was worse, because by admitting I needed help, I acknowledged all these feelings that I had been trying not to feel for all these years. So I felt as though the dam was bursting. I called at exactly the time indicated, waiting to be sure not to call too early or too late, and he told me to call back in another week. I felt encouraged, desperate, anxious, annoyed, and trapped.

I rehearsed, and opened in the play, in a James Dean part, an outsider, the kind of role I don't think most people would think of me for. Being a Strasberg, most people expected me to be either little, wearing glasses, and an urban intellectual like my father, or very delicate and poetic like Susan. Chad (my character) falls in love with an archeologist (Trish

Hawkins), who is the fiancée of another archeologist, Dan (Jonathan Hogan), whom he considers to be his best friend. This friend lies to Chad and betrays him and his dream. Chad believes his land will be sold for a Holiday Inn resort. In reality, his friend has arranged that the new Interstate Highway will not go through Chad's land, because they have discovered ancient Indian mounds. Hence the title, *The Mound Builders*. When Chad discovers the truth, he threatens the archeologists and returns that night to steal some of the artifacts. When Dan appears, Chad makes him follow him out of the house, and neither of them is ever seen again. I always believed that Chad killed his friend, though Lanford, who wrote this fine mystery, never says what happens.

My "dream" of Chad was expressed in the way I imagined he moved and talked. That's how I perceived him. I had trouble letting myself go for the first week, until a casual conversation at the Studio with my father got me on track. I was hung up about not being masculine and sexy enough for the role, which I blushingly confessed to him. When he asked me who could play it, I said Marlon could, but I was afraid to identify with the power in him. My father asked if Jimmy Dean could have, and I said yes. After that I was OK, because he had a softness to his masculinity that I believed I had, too. As for dialect, I just talked to Lanford, who is from that part of the country. There are two moments of rehearsal I remember best. The first was a love scene with Trish where I played imaginary golf. Marshall helped me have such a good time that when I declared my love to her I was surprised by the reality and by how well the scene played. The second was a moment in technical rehearsal in a scene when I didn't have anything to say. That sort of scene is among my favorites, because we discover who we really are in moments of silence. I was sitting and listening when suddenly I heard thunder. I looked out the screen door, beyond the vanishing walls of the theater, to see what imaginary world my dream space had to offer. I loved that storm, as I love them in normal reality, because nature's storms always make me feel that the surging life exploding inside me is normal. I relax, feeling that being alive is a pleasure, not a problem. I loved working with Marshall because I always believed he recognized, respected, and loved my talent. After we opened, he invited me to come to Circle's membership classes, which I took to mean that I needed acting classes. In fact, it was his way of asking me to become a member of the company. What an asshole insecurity makes me out to be sometimes. So many missed opportunities, simply because I never thought I was worth a dime.

I got wonderful notices. One was from the night my father came. I swore to myself I was going to work for myself, and I did. My concentration was superb. When he came backstage, he had real respect and, more strangely, wonder in his eyes. He said simply that he didn't know I could do that. I had grown up.

I was a success. People began to call and offer me work as an actor. Agents asked me to call them. I agreed to do a dinner theater production of *Butterflies are Free*, because it was a comedy and I'd never done one. Not a smart career move, but what I felt like doing. Stopping by the Institute one day, I casually asked Mitch Nestor, then executive director, if he knew an actress who might play the girl. He said he was directing a project at the Studio the following day, and that the girl in it had played the part in the National company. That girl was Sabra Jones. I first saw an incredible timidity, with eyes that watched like a cat's. I think the director, Alba Ohms, and the producer, from Montgomery, Alabama, wanted another girl, which I couldn't understand because I'd read with them both and liked Sabra much better. Maybe it was because she'd already done it. Maybe because I liked her. Anyway, she got the part and we walked to the Chelsea Tavern on University Place to have a drink to celebrate the project. We began to talk about life, and because of the way I was talking, she asked me if I knew anything about the work of Wilhelm Reich. I said I was in therapy with a medical orgonomist (which is the term used by The College of Orgonomy, the organization created by Reich that trains and certifies doctors to practice). She stopped short and asked me who my doctor was. We were both seeing Dr. Baker. The synchronicity made it seem that we were destined to meet. We discussed living arrangements, and Sabra popped up, "We'll room together." That was how we began living together. Late at night, after rehearsals or after the show, she would spend hours standing in the light of the poolside phone talking to her best friend, Sarah Jane Eigerman, in New York. On our three consecutive days off, we drove to New Orleans for two days, with her dog Bunny, a beautiful poet of a fox hound. We drove through Mississippi (where a farmer offered $200 for this ASPCA dog), Alabama, and Louisiana. The south, which I had always imagined, in my New York way, as being arid and dry, was beautiful. I had a great time with the part, although during the tense, humorless rehearsal week I thought we were doing a tragedy. On opening night, the audience started laughing at the serious, real life I was creating, and I brightened up, thinking, "Oh, it *is* a comedy."

When I got back to New York, I felt successful and in love, and I threw myself into working at the Studio to keep this openness. I did Treplyov in several scenes from *The Seagull*, directed by a man from The Moscow Art

Theater. I also did a Salinger monologue, of a soldier writing home to his girl, which I adapted to the stage and transposed to the Vietnam War by using a tape recorder as the device for making the letter verbal; and separate from the production, a scene from *The Seagull* with Sabra. I began Chekhov's scene (the one in which Treplyov says, "I'm coming more and more to believe that it isn't old or new forms that matter. What matters is that one should write without thinking about forms at all. Whatever one has to say should come straight from the heart.") sitting at the desk. I hadn't planned anything. I left myself open to working spontaneously, and exploring the world while I worked. I suddenly wondered why I didn't really try to write. It was such a simple, obvious choice that I wondered how I could have lacked the common sense to think of it before. I began to really try to write, and as I did I became involved and was transformed. This simple and direct, organic thinking, synthesized with my sense memory work on the place, the chimney, the winter outside, the solitude, and my mother in the room next to mine with the man whom everyone thought wrote better than I did, involved me. Everything seemed so effortless. I picked up a book, and it became one of Trigorin's novels. It suddenly seemed so logical that Treplyov, who made literal comparisons between himself and Trigorin, would have copies of Trigorin's work. He was obsessed by him. After all, his mother loved Trigorin more than him, a situation that was easy for me to identify with. I simply did organically what Chekhov suggested.

Sabra stopped midway through the scene, from fear, I think. It was her first scene as a member. My goal, I said, was to eliminate the sense of manipulating myself when I planned a series of sense memories and substitutions. I had been consciously and intuitively working to change this habit for almost eight years. I wanted to work organically and respond spontaneously to the given circumstances, as I did when I was inspired. I used place to concentrate and develop my sense of privacy. I openly discussed the technique I had been exploring. In this public environment my father was finally forced to respond. I was scared but willing to risk a fight. I was not going to hold back for fear of disapproval. My father thought for a moment, and then, very deliberately said to the attending members, "If I've said it once, I've said it a million times. The exercises are like aspirin. You take them if you have a headache." He went on to agree with me completely, and was clearly proud of my work. Years of searching, feeling lost, in chaos, doubt, and confusion had been effortlessly affirmed.

I wondered if my father realized that, to me, the work I was doing was a contradiction to the systematic rigidity of the Method. I don't think so, because he felt that all good actors were using the Method, consciously or intuitively. Did he understand that these underlying principles of spontaneity and direct involvement with the imaginary world of the play, which were not part of The Method, came from a deep, intuitive perception of the creative process that I was slowly becoming conscious of?

When my father asked me to become Executive Director of the Institute I agreed, even though I knew that it might interfere with my personal growth and my career. Perhaps, at last, he would love me in the way that I still desperately needed.

I took over running the Institute in late spring of 1975, just as a contract had been signed with New York University which allowed undergraduates to attend the Institute as part of their degree program. Between 1969 and 1971, I had developed the Institute's first film acting class. I now developed the undergraduate training program. I ran the business with a staff of one paid secretary, who was also a student, and a group of work-study students. I earned five hundred dollars a week. Along with normal administrative duties, there was the imminent reality of buying a building, overseeing repairs, moving, etc. I asked for, and got, several pay raises. I also raised the fees to teachers to more fairly compete in the marketplace. I wanted to have the best teachers in New York, and while I was Director, the Institute had them. I was a thorough administrator, creating a full-time program, and a Summer Program to fill what had been a slow time for the Institute.

Family businesses are a double-edged sword. Everyone feels taken advantage of. Once Anna saw that I could not be controlled I became a threat, and the struggle that only she could win began. Every time I took initiative, Anna felt threatened and I felt mistrusted. My father thought he knew more about business than I, and vice versa. At the end of the first year, we moved to the then new building at 115 East 15th Street. I decided it would be a good idea to write a year-end report. In it I concluded that the growing business could no longer be run with only an administrator (who also taught thirty hours a week), a secretary, and student office workers. In private, I asked my father to clarify promises he had made to me about an eventual percentage in the business. He and Anna were incensed by that request. They viewed the report as a bold threat to their authority, judgment, and control. Within a year, I would resign, and within a year of that, they had instituted every recommendation I had made.

As time went on, my tenure became a nightmarish, indirect struggle between Anna and myself for credibility with my father. It was a manufactured problem that everyone reacted to as though it was real. It was a sick atmosphere, full of hate and distrust. Anna painted me as the evil, ambitious son.

I decided to leave. I knew it was the last time I would make any effort to win the love and approval of my father. I knew he wouldn't leave me (or Susan or her daughter Jennifer) anything in his will, as he had promised to do. I knew what kind of man he was, and of his utter surrender to Anna's will and desires. It was clear that we had become two families, hers and ours. I also knew that what I was experiencing was not an isolated phenomenon. I knew that, in a cosmic sense, it wasn't personal. Anna would be threatened by anyone she couldn't control or use whom my father might love too much. In the end, the only promise of theirs that still matters to me was the one to provide for Jenny, who works in the Institute in L.A. Jenny, who never had a father that was present, loved mine like the father she needed, and I'm sure he loved her all the better because she needed him. Jenny doesn't use Christopher's family name, because she never felt he was her family.

Funny, Susan sabotaged her career to help Christopher achieve his, and he had that career until she left him because she was tired of being married to a little boy who did what he wanted and couldn't take care of himself. He disappeared from view once she left him, wondering if she were strong enough to survive alone. She's done that all her life.

I saw next to nothing of my father after that. I was not permitted to enter his house. Once, he had a fight with Anna over that prohibition, and he invited me to the mansion they'd bought in Bel Air. But, while I knew it cost him a lot, and that he loved me very much in his own way, his house was no longer my home. I felt as though it never had been.

The last time I saw him alive was at an all day, eight-hour, Sunday Royal Shakespeare Company performance of *Nicholas Nicolby*. During the intermission, he was alone for a few minutes and I went over to say hello. His eyes seemed old, sad, and tired, in spite of all the success and happiness his career and life seemed to be giving him. He was glad to see me. We talked for a few moments, and then I could feel him becoming nervous. He was afraid, but trying not to show it. I remember looking at him, and saying, "Don't worry. I understand. I miss you sometimes. And I love you." His eyes went away, and I thought he was going to cry. I said that I'd like to call and see if we could have a pastrami sandwich sometime, like when we were young and went to the Gaiety on 47th Street, which was the only deli in New York where you could order half a sandwich. He said he'd like that too. This was one of those partings when people plan things they know will never happen. It seems fitting that we said good-bye in a theater. It's what we shared, and where we meant the same thing when we said "love."

I was alive. I could tell from the pain, confusion, and clarity I felt, all at the same time. It was the first time since I was ten years old and lay still, depressing myself, breathing as little as possible, hoping the terror I felt from the elephant's feet and snakes I imagined hovering around and under my bed would go away, that I felt really alive. The dreams that seemed to have been suspended inside of me woke up. I was whole again.

La Señorita de Treveles by Carlos Arniches directed by John Strasberg
at Centre Dramatic de Valencia 1990

CHAPTER SIX

DREAMING IS THE COURAGE OF A MAN

My father died in February 1982, two nights after having danced on the stage of Radio City Music Hall in Alex Cohen's benefit, *The Night of 1000 Stars*. He had a heart attack early in the morning and was taken to Roosevelt Hospital, where he died without regaining consciousness. Anna wouldn't have called me, but she did call Susan, who called me. I was at a 7:15 Karate class around the corner from where we lived on East 46th Street, over Nanni's Restaurant. I ran to the hospital and found Anna, Susan, and Al Pacino, who was like the son my father needed, and who took care of the boys and Anna afterwards. Al and I had been buddies when we played baseball together—as close as two loners can be. That all ended when Anna cast me as pretender to the throne and erected all these walls around the imaginary country she ruled.

I sat on the floor with Al. In those kinds of crises people are either calm or hysterical. We sat there calmly, and even under the circumstances, it was nice just to be together. The doctors wouldn't give out any information for quite a while. Then they came and reported to me, his eldest son. Anna was vulnerable and wanted comfort, even from me. I gave it, wondering why people are most human when they're suffering. She let me go in to sit with him first. His body seemed pale and frail, like a statue made out of almost human flesh. I would have sworn he was made of alabaster until I touched him. I cried right away. It was a relief to just be able to love him without any walls between us. All the problems were solved, and he didn't stop me from simply loving him, or run into any of those far away places he could go. So I felt that was resolved in a way. He had lived to be eighty-one, and he'd done a lot of what he dreamed. I loved him. I wish I'd liked him.

I was glad my voice didn't crack too much when I spoke at the service in the Booth Theater. I saw Paul Newman standing in the back, just one of the crowd, out of the spotlight. I've always liked that about Paul, because he and Joanne always seem to have guarded their humanity and maintained a private life. Anna did bury Pop next to my mother in Ardsley, which I wondered about. Everybody crowded around Anna so that they could get in the photos that would be in the papers. I felt like shelling their minds with bombs of truth, but I didn't want them to believe Anna when she said I was crazy.

Sometime after that I ran into Anna and my half-brothers, Adam and David, at Serendipity 3, a great place for iced hot chocolate and foot-long hot dogs that my mother discovered almost the day it opened. Anna pretended she didn't see me. Maybe she didn't. Anyway, Adam came over and said hello, and I love him and think he's like me. I knew he'd pay for that act. I hope they're OK and wonder what they dream of being.

Jose Luis Gomez, artistic director of the National Theater of Spain, invited me to conduct a seminar in Spain. I looked forward to this adventure, and never had a second thought about not speaking the language. I believed, perhaps naively, that I would understand Spanish actors by what I saw them doing rather than by what they were saying. The experience taught me to trust not only what I perceived, but what was really important for actors to be doing. It reinforced my conviction that acting is what one does, in which the meaning of words is the expression of what the character is living. It also resulted in a major change in my work. In order to talk to the actors, and for them to talk to me, there were translators who translated both the scenes and what we were saying. When I began to discuss the scenes with the actors, to determine what they imagined they should be doing, the lengthy, often intellectualized thoughts they expressed (which are difficult to understand in any language, whether you speak it or not) had to be translated. This process was frustating, indirect, and relatively contactless, because it was all about actors "correct" thinking. I wanted to get to the point, to the essence of what they, and I, perceived about life. I began to ask everyone, including myself, to talk not like an actor, but like a human being, so that we could understand one another, simply and directly. This accident of circumstance revolutionized my work and is what led me to realize that actors do what they think they should do. If I wanted to help them be real, I could do that best by helping them to think organically; instead of thinking like actors trying to figure out what the right thing to do was, they had to think like human beings who wanted to understand how someone felt so that they could live another person's life. I believe that the evolution of my productions, which have become more and more basic, comes from my desire to communicate what I feel as simply and directly as I can, to any human being, using the universal language of our common human experience, which we all understand. What some might consider an obstacle became a tremendous advantage.

(My favorite story about acting comes from Eva Le Gallienne, with whom I co-directed a gorgeous but boring production of *Alice in Wonderland*, which Sabra produced. Once Eva was auditioning for the part of Ophelia and was waiting in the wings while John Barrymore was auditioning for Hamlet. He ranted and raved, declaiming a soliloquy, and as he came off stage, he saw her, and, winking, said, "I did that to get the part. But it's not how I'm going to do it." "How are you going to do it?" she asked. "I'm not going to do anything," he replied. He did get the part and went on to give the greatest performance by an American actor in the role. She said he was brilliant and did "nothing" except play the role with a romantic and simple, profound, human truth—and Le G, as friends called her, was a tough critic. One night she arrived at the theater after finishing her own show next door, just in time for THE soliloquy. As he paused before beginning, the cat who lived in the theater under the guise of being a rat exterminator walked out of the wings onto the stage, perhaps because it felt warmer out there. Barrymore saw him, and stopped for a moment. He walked over to the cat, picked it up, began to walk as he stroked it, and simply continued, talking to him. She said it was the greatest moment she had ever seen in the theater during her eighty-two years of life. It is in accidental happenings that we learn who we really are, and what we really do. One sees an actor's technique in the unplanned moments, when he falls back on what he believes to be his most solid resources.)

Sabra and I arrived in Madrid, which she didn't like much. On the other hand, I felt it was my destiny to be there. But Sabra and I were always pulling in opposite directions, even over pleasure. Every time we'd go somewhere, she'd begin worrying about whether it was the best thing for her to do, because she should be trying to get work. I didn't think it was a defense against pleasure. I just thought that my desire for pleasure, or a vacation, was proof I was a lazy, impractical dreamer. On the weekends, we'd go to Cordoba, Seville, Barcelona—and then to London. And there, Sabra was enchanted. We discovered Fielding's Hotel behind the Bow Street Police Station, near Covent Garden. I left her there for a week and went back to work.

Meanwhile, I was in paradise, falling in love with Spain and its actors. The interactive dialogue that I began having with the actors (assisted by the wonderful translators who were also wonderful human beings—like Luis who seemed an extension of myself, or Marina Saura, an actress who is the daughter of the painter and the niece of the filmaker) while they were doing scenes kept them from thinking like actors working on scenes. It dissolved preconceived ideas about the scene which distanced them from the real life of the character. Whenever I could make them think and talk like people trying to understand another human being's life, they became personally involved, not in playing a scene but in living another person's life. Their passion was freed from the labyrinthine thoughts that imprisoned it, and this led to moments in which they became spontaneously involved. Their work transformed with a suddenness that even I was surprised by. Making them talk personally about simple human reality made everything change, without any systematic technique, without a special code or language, without improvisation, mirror exercises, or sense memory exercises. The work was all about real life. I began to say to actors, "When you don't know what to do, pretend that's it's not a play. Pretend that it's life."

The next weekend, I rushed to meet Sabra at Victoria station. We took the overnight train to Edinburgh to see Arthur's Crag (the hill that overlooks the city) and listen to people speaking English I couldn't understand. This was more than frustrating. I was already exhausted. My head was boiling from living in a language I didn't speak, which forced me to concentrate when I ordered a cup of coffee. I had a great steak and a real Vodka Gibson and drove on the wrong side of the road, so it was fun. But I was working hard and getting sick because that's how I relaxed. Sabra got mad because I wanted to sleep. She felt I was unwilling to share a cosmic experience.

Alice in Wonderland

You can't co-direct a play unless you're friends or lovers. Le G hated my father and was suspicious of me until I convinced her I was not my father. I was younger, taller, more talented, better looking, and obviously had different opinions and perceptions. Back in New York, we cast the play together, and Sabra, who was the show's producer, worked hard to get the best actors to audition.

I used to enjoy the open call auditions required by Equity. While it was truly a cattle call, with hundreds of actors appearing in an eight hour period, I liked to think that maybe I'd meet one or two that were interesting to me, even if I didn't use them right away. However, one day I was talking to one actor who seemed interesting, and I took a little longer than usual. I took three minutes instead of one. The union monitor rushed over and insisted that I go faster. I asked him whether he was prohibiting me from actually being sufficiently interested in someone that I might actually hire. He looked at me with the glazed eyes we see in all the police and armies of the world who keep their own citizens and neighbors under surveillance, and he said that I had to see as many actors as possible, meaning that he wasn't interested in whether anyone got a job. Why should he? He worked not as an actor but as a union employee. He was not concerned with actors working but with the union's published statistics bragging about the greatest number of auditions and interviews for its paying members. Since then, when I direct in New York I let my assistant handle the open calls.

I watched Le G block the play in about a week and was impressed at how fast she worked. As the next few days went by, however, and we rehearsed the scenes over and over without any comments or suggestions from her, I realized that from her point of view her work was done. Now the actors simply had to act. Most of them were waiting for her to work with them. She didn't know how and, what was worse, she was jealous of any effort on my part to work with them. When I did try to rehearse on the sly, a few of the actors (and why are they generally the ones who need the help the most?) refused to take direction from me. The production was sold as being a revival of Le G's Civic Rep production of *Alice*, so how could we fire her? But I could feel the underlying panic and imminent disintegration. I called Tommy Tune and asked if, as a personal favor, he might come and help. In the middle of his own production of *My One and Only*, with hemorrhoids so painful he could hardly sit down, he came to see the show. A day later, he and Sabra and I sat on stage in a circle and held hands. Then he said, "You're so close. It's beautiful, and if you can fix . . ." He then proceeded to talk about moments in the play, both in the acting and in the staging, which needed better timing or new blocking, all of which I was well aware. When Le G found out, she was furious. She couldn't admit that she was incapable of the work without collaboration.

And so the show, which could have been a hit, faded away for lack of direction. Success in production is a measure of how hard you're willing to work to eliminate or change all the moments that don't work. Magic—and 90 percent hard work.

The most successful parts of the show were the set and costumes, created by John Lee Beatty and Patricia Zipprodt respectively. I knew John Lee from Circle Rep, where he was the resident set designer. He adored Le G and the project. Le G wanted the production to look like the Teniel drawings in the books, so that visually, as we moved from scene to scene, it was as if we were turning the pages of a book. John Lee designed a panorama and the apparatus to scroll it; there were about ten of those mechanisms in the world, all of them in major opera houses. The machinery was oak or teak, because these woods were hard enough: they were also absolutely gorgeous. The actors and parts of the set were on platforms that rolled on and off from the wings. The play had original music from the 1932 production she had done; Jonathan Tunick orchestrated it.

Patricia's costumes were nominated for a Tony. They were also faithful to the book, and very well thought out, between her and John Lee, to be sure that the whites were different enough and not tiring on the eyes. The costumes were very heavy and hard to act in, but in the long run, I don't think that weight was a problem. The masks, on the other hand, were an obstacle. If masks aren't mobile, in long scenes you lose the actor behind them. Theater is intimate—more intimate than film or television, or the Kabuki. You must feel the presence of human beings in a theater. There were discussions about cutting away the masks to give the actors access into the play. We needed their active presence and pacing. In a word: animation. It was too inanimate.

FREEDOM

The Institute Europeen de l'Acteur called me from Paris. The same organization had invited my father to teach there fifteen years earlier. Founded by Augusto Fernandez, an Argentine director-teacher, and Lev Bogdan, it had been installed in Bochum, Germany, where they'd run the theater until A.F. decided to return to Argentina, at which time Lev became director of the theater festival at Nancy. He eventually moved from there to Paris.

Sabra thought of Paris as Oriental in its search for beauty and perfection. I found it a place where it rained a lot, where life was simple and sensual, where buying food was a festival of smells and colors that you could taste, where one could walk for hours looking at all the small businesses that dot Paris and show us how the French really want to live. "Le bonheur," as they say—none of which has anything to do with Napoleon, Louis XIV, de Gaulle, or the sense of grandeur that most people identify as being the important part of French culture, unless I imagine Napoleon drinking his favorite Chambertin as he planned battles in his tent, or de Gaulle eating dourade at Le Dome.

It was the first seminar since my father's that French actors attended. The Institute's clientel were mostly German actors. The French didn't seem very curious or open to outside influence. Perhaps it's the language, or the fact that they live very well and prefer to leave well enough alone. The seminar took place in a theater space called La Forge, on Rue de la Forge near Ledru Rollin and Bastille. Going to buy food at the fantastic open markets was difficult because I felt shy and had to talk to people in a language I didn't speak, or be willing to smile, point, and use fingers while they wondered if I was an idiot. At the time, it made me feel stupid. Later, when I realized that if I was going to learn I had to accept, and like, feeling like a child, it began to make me feel innocent. Looking, listening, imitating, being sensual and real. This sense of always changing, always being reborn—I had no idea that that is what is happening to us biologically all of our lives. I thought it was just part of my secret life.

I began to understand that how actors think and what they believe they should do, as opposed to what they really want to do, is culturally based. These rigid habits and thought patterns can be both positive and negative, but merely adorn the artists, and are never part of their organic thoughts and basic humanity, which is a much deeper and truer reality than French or Spanish, German or American culture. The Spanish, I had found, wanted to feel, but had no habit of organizing their thoughts and what they wanted to do. It was the opposite in Paris.

The French gave me detailed explanations for their ideas of a scene in place of being in the scene themselves. Over the years, I found that if I could get them to think organically, their thoughts related directly to what they felt about the imaginary environment, and they would become capable of very simple, real, and beautiful work. It meant getting rid of thought processes they went through with such verve; they were so labyrinthine that it could drive anyone crazy. "Why did you do that?" I would ask. "Because in the moment that the character says 'Blah blah,' he or she is thinking 'Blah blah, blah, blah, and blah.'" "How do you know this?" "Because I think it," they would answer, in their Cartesian way. "And was it real?" "What do you mean?" "Don't you know when you're real?" "That is ambiguous," they would say. And yet, the air crackled with hidden desire. They just didn't have the habit of developing their own real thoughts in their own personal dream spaces. They were trained to work within some mechanical idea of human thought. When I was able to involve their humanity in their work, their talent and knowledge was freed and the scenework became more spontaneous and personal; they began to have real and interesting experiences in their work.

Some actors have natural sense memory—Brando is a good example of that—and some have a good technical base in sense memory, such as Dustin Hoffman. In either case, the good actors are obsessed with bringing their dream space into a common sense, here-and-now reality. Once you've got a dream space, you need brushes and paint, experience and knowledge. I began that process of expression with the actor's desire to explore the play they perceive in their dream space and to intentionally focus on their choices outside that world. It's no more and no less than advanced child's play. Innocence in a mature adult is more beautiful than in a child. It doesn't mean being defenseless. It encompasses a different concept of power. Most martial arts systems are based on a simple and pure, natural innocence.

I worked directly with scenes and no longer taught sense memory work. I told most actors that if they learned sense memory they would have a technique that helped to make the dream space real, but I admit that I can't teach an actor everything. I have neither the time nor the desire. And the personal dialogue I was now using in scene work was producing changes in the actors that I felt was not only much more valuable, it was original, and a development of my own creative process. I also saw that the serious actors who worked with me became aware of which additional techniques they needed to learn with other teachers. Once they knew, it was up to them to learn it. What I love best about New York is that it is the only school where an actor can search out his own program of learning. No one will help you; but, more important, no one will stop you.

When I returned to Berlin for a two week seminar, the wall was still standing, a monument to a prison in which people behaved, desperately, as though they were free. Sabra and I jogged in the park, passing Hitler's bunker. We climbed up a scaffold to look into the Eastern Zone, as East German soldiers casually pointed machine guns in our direction. It reminded me of traveling in Spain during Franco's tenure, and the Guardia Civil directed traffic while armed with machine guns. I had always wondered what would happen if someone made a wrong turn! We jogged past the Reichstag, site of all the gigantic Nazi rallies that we all recognize from the movies. We followed the narrowest part of the river that was now a border. The East Germans had built a part of the wall under water, using barbed wire, and we passed several graves of East German victims, shot trying to swim to freedom.

I woke early one morning, after Sabra had left, in the old hotel room over a bar and around the corner from the Kurfurstendam. I heard people in the bar singing songs that I'd heard in movies, and recognized that force of life that Germany, as a nation, has too often misdirected.

During the seminar I was giving, a young actor clicked his heels and bowed to me after he worked. I'm not the kind to enjoy this type of reaction in people, and found myself in the kitchen during breaks washing dishes, because I wanted them to understand I was human.

Lev Bogdan took me to a performance of *Pina Bausch*, as Berlin was always having cultural festivals. Cultural expression is a sign of a free people, except to Americans, who are too busy trying to be rich to want to think about whether they're happy or not. The audience began talking, because the performance was long and repetitive. I'm always amazed when audiences do this. I like it and hate it, because the contact is direct but rarely positive.

Joan of Lorraine

I was growing further and further away from Sabra. Therapy, travel, my own work, and new relationships made me more and more real to myself. I began to live with a part of myself that she had no time to get to know. She was busy with her own life and could never manage to stop, and I was tired of fighting for contact; she probably felt the same way after a while. It made me feel exactly as I did as a child when I was so anxious to please. She came to London and Paris, and stayed a few days in Berlin, by which time she was restless and eager to get back to New York. I didn't know what her secret life was. I knew what her ambitions and real-time dreams were, but not as a man and woman together. She always seemed unsatisfied. I felt as though I were always coaxing her to share moments of pleasure with me. I wondered if she came to Europe because she was interested in me or because of Europe. My life in Spain became part of my private world. However, while I felt somewhat hurt by this distance between us, I also felt free. Anyway, if you love someone you let her go her own way, as painful and terrifying as that is.

Sabra wanted to become an actress-manager. The Mirror Repertory Company was born out of her dreams and an incredible amount of obsession and hard work. In Febuary of 1983, we produced *Joan of Lorraine* by Maxwell Anderson at the sixty-seat theater of my acting school, The Real Stage, on 46th Street between Eighth and Ninth next to Joe Allens' Restaurant, in a building that the Stagehands Union had bought. They leased the school a floor for a few years while they prepared to renovate it, with the possibility of moving us down to the ground floor. It was an ideal situation. I paid $600 for the whole production. It's an interesting play in which a group of actors is rehearsing a play about Joan of Arc. The twenty-four actors included Sabra, Will Patton, Peter Flood (a teacher at The Real Stage), Ralph Roberts, J.C. Quinn, Elaine Rinehart, Eric Anderson (from Whorehouse), and a lot of good actors who were willing to work for nothing. The play was long and, by contract, we weren't allowed to touch a word. The prohibition notwithstanding, for the first time in my life, I cut a play. I cut an hour and a half, turning a four-hour play into a play that lasted two and a half hours including intermission. Sabra was wonderful in the lead. She has a soul of an actress, whatever she may lack in technique. You've got to catch her on a good night. Anyway, Joan of Arc is her kind of part; a dreamer who lives for dreaming. I guess that's what we shared. More than being lovers, we helped each other to believe in our dreams. It was like helping each other grow up.

As a result of the production, which Sabra's secret investors loved, they gave her money for two productions in the fall. Not a lot of money, $35,000 for two large-cast plays. (There are a lot of great American plays that nobody sees anymore, because you need a lot of actors for them.)

Maria Rosa

Joan of Lorraine opened and I left for Barcelona to direct a production of *Maria Rosa*, a Catalan classic, at the National Theater. The actors had alien training methods, and spoke another language, but I managed to do some really interesting work interpreting a play that was normally treated like a Greek tragedy. I saw it as a drama about migrant workers, with love, treachery, and murder. I imagined a wagon that they pulled, which could be taken apart and become the walls and doors of the temporary houses they occupied as they moved from place to place. It was a modern idea in the spirit of Miro, Dali, Picasso, and the architect Antonio Gaudi. I was suspicious of my designer, a Catalan painter-sculptor named Guinovart, because painters aren't scene designers. I was afraid he would create images rather than spaces in which people live. I arrived in the shop when the wood for the cart arrived, and it was a very low-grade wood. I was stunned because I kept thinking of his wood sculptures in the modern museum that were all made of found woods, noble ones with a soul. That was what the set had to have. He looked at me with eyes wide open, like those of a frightened child. I don't think he understood that a set has a soul; it is not flat. I was always pushing, making them burn the wood, texturing, painting, but it was never what I wanted. It was a child's idea of theater. Even the painted cloths were painted on cheap cloth, rather than on canvas, and they draped badly. He never understood just how real I wanted the onstage world to be. The actors did, because they live on stage. The play was well received by the public. As for the critics, well, as my father always said, "Critics tell you whether you're going to run or not. They rarely tell you anything about the play." My favorite review of that production was that I had directed the play like a John Ford movie. It was not intended as a compliment, but I accepted it as one. I think his films are epic dramas.

I have always had a particular feeling about Greek tragedy. I don't see it as being highly stylized, nor as a representation of a culture of statues, but as a deeply human, almost religious experience. I've dreamt of doing a production with music written by Stevie Wonder. When I was Kazan's assistant director on a production of *The Eumenides* that he did at the Studio back in the early sixties, he sent me off to work with the actresses who were playing priestesses. I did improvisations based on revival meetings, using Greek and Balkan folk music that I played at half speed, to get what I thought was the reality of the trances that priestesses were known to enter, which often involved drugs and sometimes sexual intercourse, as in fertility rites. He hated it when he saw it, which is understandable, because the priestesses were more ferocious than his furies!

I was beginning to be asked if I wanted to direct operas, and as magnificent as opera is, there is nothing more beautiful to me than the music of human beings talking. I began to hear when the actors' music was off-key, even in foreign languages. I felt so attuned to it that I began to give line readings. I behaved as though it was totally natural to me. If I'd stopped to think about it, I would never have permitted myself to proceed. But the more I lived for myself, the more I felt in tune with my talent and intuition. It felt as though I were riding on the crest of a wave of life. This development may have been the result of listening and learning for all those years. I don't think I really began to talk until I was over forty. I was now making up for lost time.

Being able to listen is a measure of talent and a diligent creative process. If you listen, life will tell you what you need to know. In *Maria Rosa*, the migrant workers meet to decide about whether or not to go on strike. It was very hard to get the actors to become really involved, until one day during a break I heard several actors carrying on an animated conversation relating to their own salaries and hours of work. When the rehearsal break was over, I insisted that if they couldn't identify with their character's life, at the very least they could imitate themselves. They connected, and from then on the scene worked. One of the most pleasurable qualities of being real is that life helps. Actors always seem to be desperately searching for reality, and they have such difficulty finding it. But life is always going on. Sharing my capacity to perceive life and express it in a form is what some people call teaching and/or directing.

No matter how much preparation I do for a production, during rehearsal I will discover aspects of the play that will change my direction. The interaction one has with a play and the playwright in the personal dream space is an ongoing, endless process. The spontaneous imagining, perception, and discovery that result from this focused, intentional dreaming is a major element of improvisation. The flashes of insight and intuition, the moments of illumination and understanding that result are a natural part of any good creative process. Your perception and perspective keeps changing as you become more involved. This never-ending process makes me wonder how a painter knows when he's finished a painting—couldn't he paint one painting all his life? This must be why they finally varnish them—so that they have to stop. My wife Anne, a modern primitive (naive or folk art) painter, told me the true story of a French painter who was arrested in a museum where one of his paintings was hanging, with his paints and brushes, determined to add one last improvement.

THE MIRROR REPERTORY COMPANY

The money Sabra raised to start up the Mirror Repertory Company arrived towards the end of September. We had about three seconds to decide on the plays; get the rights; find a casting agent, stage managers, publicist, and general manager; and create the company so that we could rehearse and open before Christmas. There were a lot of groups who claimed to be repertory companies (which means revolving several productions at the same time) but which actually prepared only one production at a time. We would open the two plays as close together as possible. Of course, we had to rehearse them at the same time, too. We decided to do Susan Glaspell's *Inheritors* and Clifford Odets' *Paradise Lost.* (Sabra and I will never agree as to who suggested *Paradise.*)

Several years earlier, Geraldine and Rip had asked me to read Strindberg's *The Creditors* with them, possibly to be followed by a production at the Public Theater. It's a short, savage play, which they saw as having an equally savage humor. Sabra and I had gone to their house, a large brownstone in Chelsea. As we climbed the stairs we passed clean, unpressed laundry hanging from the banister. Rip put on an unpressed, clean white shirt for the reading. Gerry argued with the maid, who wanted to stay and wash the dishes and clean. Rip showed me a window pane with a bullet hole in it and told me that "they" were always watching him, "they" being the government. Rip lived independently, the way he wanted to, and did things like befriend Black Panthers and go to Cuba. We pulled two orange crates together, put a board on top, and sat around this combination living and dining room table and read together. It was strange, an almost enchanted world, in which people behaved bizarrely, laughed a lot, and loved what I did. With love and acceptance in the air, we all agreed to work together.

I was playing an artist who is ill, insecure, and capable of being manipulated and emotionally tortured by the ex-husband and wife (to whom my character is now married). The ex-husband develops a relationship with me, the wife's new husband, without me knowing that he is the ex-, in an effort to avenge himself on the wife and separate us.

One week before the scheduled opening of *Creditors* I was in the stage of rehearsal where nothing seemed funny. I looked up and saw that Alfred Ryder had arrived. I had been fired twice in my life, once by Alfred and once in a production in which Rip had acted, so seeing the two of them together didn't augur too well for me. Three days later, Rip, who grew more nervous every day, and who, when he is nervous, begins to project his feelings onto the world in a distinctly paranoid way, arrived at rehearsal screaming that he'd lost his boots, having left them in a taxicab. I said to myself, "John, you're going to get fired. Rip forgot his boots." I was. I called Joe Papp on the phone and asked him to come see a run-through, because I knew I was doing terrific work, and said if he didn't like what I was doing I'd go without an argument. He wouldn't interfere. I left, with Alfred running after me, saying, "John, I had nothing to do with this. Nothing. You've got to believe me." I didn't want to listen. I didn't want to be around people who were always blaming their problems on somebody else, when I was not in a position to affect a change in that atmosphere. The next time I saw Gerry was a couple of years later, backstage one night after seeing her in *Agnes of God*. Sabra pleaded, coaxed, and pushed me to ask her to teach at The Real Stage. Gerry was intensely pleased, interested, and grateful for the attention. After she saw that I didn't teach a system, but was working with the principles that I'm explaining in this book, she relented. She loved nurturing young actors. A year later, I asked her to become part of the company. She was delighted, and agreed to become the company's artist-in-residence. She felt that we were giving her a home. We loved her and felt that we were becoming a family. She had played so few of the classic roles she should have, and would have, played had she been English (they would have respected her and valued her). The American theater community treated her as a weirdo. She did look and act like a bag lady but boy, could she act. She loved me forever when I told her I wanted her to wear a sexy red dress in *Paradise*.

Paradise Lost

We began rehearsing at the end of November. I had cast the company in about a week. We assembled a great group of actors. Everyone wanted to work with Gerry. They didn't get a living wage, so it certainly wasn't for the money. Rehearsing with Gerry was not exactly what most of them thought it would be like. She drifted around the stage within the blocking that I was doing as fast as I could—we had only three and a half weeks. We'd rehearse one play from 10:00 A.M. to 3:00 P.M., and the second from 4:00 to 9:00 or 5:00 to 10:00. The only one who worked non-stop was me. Gerry, Sabra, Tom Brennan, and Maxwell Caulfield were in both plays but weren't allowed by union rules to rehearse more than seven hours out of eight and a half, five days a week.

We paid so little money ($150 a week and $15 a performance), that there were often days when the actors couldn't be there because they had to earn their livings doing soaps or commercials or an occasional film or TV episode. I had a simple rule: "If you're not there when I'm blocking a scene, your character doesn't move." *Paradise* had twenty-four characters on a stage about 11 feet deep and 18 feet wide, with a full set with furniture, walls, a staircase, entrance way, etc. Not many people could move at the same time.

The play was deemed by the critics to be poorly structured and outdated. Clifford hadn't been dead long enough for his work to become a classic. I think it has a beautiful structure, like jazz, and I directed the play in that spirit. Clifford does overwrite (so does Shakespeare, O'Neill, Lope de Vega, etc.) but the language is colorful, like the language he grew up hearing, the dialect spoken by Eastern European immigrants who mixed words and syntax from several languages in the way some people cook. For this he is accused of writing phony dialogue. He was painfully aware of that criticism.

When he led the playwright's unit at the Studio, he would sometimes present scenes and then ask the playwrights for comments. He was prepared for the perfectly natural response: "The dialogue is awful. People don't talk that way." After one of these sessions, he took out a tape recorder and played a recording of his aunt and uncle talking in the kitchen of their apartment in the Bronx, which he had transcribed word for word and used in this scene with "phony dialogue." If you put on stage or in a film what you see in life, no one will believe you. They'll say you're being too theatrical. As difficult as this is to believe, for anyone who wants to be successful, knowing it is one of the real strengths of "reality."

Gerry would drift around, letting pages of the script fall from her hands as they were spoken, which became a problem when we rehearsed the next day because she could never find her script. When I caught on, I had the stage manager have any number of scripts ready for her. Then she would look at me and smile, and say, "But I need the one I can't find. It's got notes in it." She also ate onion sandwiches. Actors would come to me, furious, saying, "Can't you control her? I can't work with her. She doesn't know what she's doing." And I would say, "Look, some of the problems are irritating, but if I were you I wouldn't worry about her. She's going to do something, and it's probably going to be really interesting. If I were you, I'd stop worrying about her and worry about what you're going to do." This normally stopped them and sent them back to their own work.

The company was very professional, very interesting, and had great energy. Among them were Mason Adams, Brian Clark, Jess Osuna, Ann Hillary, Tom Waites, Maxwell Caulfield, Juliet Mills, Matthew Cowles, Clem Fowler, Bill Brydon, and Jim Pritchett. I didn't know if I was really directing or just moving actors around. I had so little time to think about what the plays were about and to be conscious of what they meant to me and what I wanted to say with them. It was a matter of relying on intuition and hoping I had a good idea, fast.

Paradise was a hit. We couldn't handle all the people who wanted to come. We got letters and donations from a lot of people in the profession: Hal Prince, Steven Sondheim, Nicos Psacharopoulos, Alan Schneider, the Newmans, Dustin, Al Pacino, etc. We were discovered, and New York flocked to The Real Stage's sixty-seat theater, where the lights blew the fuses the night the critics came. Sabra's investors were delighted, and wanted us to move into a larger theater. I wasn't sure. It all seemed so fast, and I thought we should reflect on it, do what we had to do for the rest of the season and see how long the success would last. While Sabra had her doubts, she felt obliged to do what the investors wanted. I acquiesced because I felt that she had raised the money and that gave her the last word. If it happened today, I would not agree that money automatically earns the right of final authority in an artistic organization.

Inheritors

Susan Glaspell was the first female writer to win the Pulitzer Prize for playwriting. *Inheritors* is an interesting but not well-known play about a midwestern girl's awareness of life and prejudice, in particular against Indians. I had my assistant, a bright and conscientious girl named Susan Fenichel, research Indian and Anglo-American views about life, and projected some beautiful sayings on the curtain before the play began. (..."Now we will reconstruct and straighten out your mind... This song hereafter shall belong to you alone. It is called 'I use it to beautify the earth'"...) It had one of those "Joan of Arc" parts for Sabra. Tom Brennan played the grandfather, who is emotionally disturbed. They had a beautiful relationship, and on nights when they were on, the play had a spiritual quality to it. It was not for a large public, but when you do real, revolving repertory, you can have plays like that in the schedule; plays you want to do that will only find a limited audience for one or two performances a week.

Rain

At the end of January, a month after the dream began to come true, we moved to the theater in the basement of St. Peter's, the church in the Citicorp building on 53rd between Lexington and Third Avenues. It was a 199-seat house with a weird stage that had a low roof and little space to store our sets, which were always being changed as we played two, and eventually three, plays in rotation every week. Despite the fact that I had to re-direct the first two plays for the larger space, Sabra insisted we open the third play, *Rain*, by John Colton and Clemence Randolph, on schedule. This was the play based on the Somerset Maugham short story about Sadie Thompson and the Reverend that takes place in the tropics. It has been made into two films, one with Joan Crawford and Walter Houston and the other with Rita Hayworth and Jose Ferrer. Both are good, but lack the depth of this fine play about sexual repression, love, and God. I thought of Sadie not as a hooker but as a predecessor of the hippies of the sixties, a girl who wants to be free and is not afraid of knowing that love and sex are related. The play was written in the era when playwrights were exposing the hypocrisy of Victorian society, more well-known in the works of Ibsen, Schnitzler, and Pirandello.

I was worried because we needed time. Sabra was never well-concentrated when she was in rehearsal. She was always running out to the phone. Any discussions with me were terminated with, "It's about the money. I'm sorry, but I've got to go."

I knew that *Rain* was running twenty minutes long. I didn't know what to do, and had no time for reflection. We opened anyway. I kept rehearsing, because in the old days theater people continued to rehearse a play after opening in the hope the play could find its public after opening. Within a week I saw how to fix it. I cut the play, especially in the beginning where it started slowly, and turned it from a three act into a two act. It flew along to a 10:15 finish. People began to tell me that I directed plays very filmically. I do often concentrate the dramatic essence rather than spreading light and people all over the stage just to fill up the space. I want to be able to make people look at someone's pinkie if I think that is the best way to express the drama taking place. In *Rain*, I had a split set to reveal what Sadie was really doing with the sailors she entertained versus what the Reverend thought was going on. I also wanted a small pool for the love scene between Sabra and David Cryer, because I think that wet is sexy. David is another really good actor that we were lucky to have wooed into the company. He played the Reverend to Sabra's Sadie.

Sabra was so visibly affectionate with David in front of the company, both during rehearsals and backstage, that it made a lot of people, including me, uncomfortable. It led me to believe that they were really falling in love, and I asked her not to act that way in front of us. It seemed disrespectful to me and everyone else. I couldn't say I blamed her, or that she didn't deserve to have some love in her life. Our apartment on East 46th Street, over Nanny's restaurant, had become an office. It was so full of paraphernalia office and animals—two cats and two dogs—that when I wanted to write she suggested I set up a little table in the bathroom and sit on the toilet. Sabra liked that a lot. Perhaps I was recreating the same relationship I'd had with every woman since my mother. My relationships in Europe helped me to stay with her. European women made me feel manly, desirable, and more the me I felt I secretly was. I was afraid to talk about this in therapy, because Dr. Baker knew us both, and I thought he would side with her. At any rate, I felt like the real me was living apart from all this in Europe.

The more I traveled, the more America became a place that I visited rather than lived in. Traveling was freeing me from feeling trapped by the parts of American culture that constrict us all, particularly the obsession with material success and power, and the feeling that to be successful one cannot be oneself. The catch-22 is saying that once you are successful you can do whatever you want. What no one says is that by that time it's too late. You are no longer who you were, and you are trapped with the illusion that money is the measure of the capacity for pleasure.

One day during rehearsal, Gerry, who played a small role of the Polynesian wife of the trader at whose inn the play takes place, came in and set the table during the first major scene between David and Sabra. She stood there and listened to them rehearse. As we continued to rehearse the scene and began to repeat it the third time around, she would occasionally stop them, apologizing for the interruption, and ask if that was the end of the sentence. No one, myself included, realized what she was doing, she was so quiet and thoughtful. I just watched and waited. Then, as they began rehearsing again, she began to set the table, putting down a plate or a knife and fork in the pauses, in the commas, and at the end of sentences or paragraphs. I was watching an artist orchestrate a piece of music. She never disturbed the focus, and made no movement or noise that covered a word of what they said. The opposite. What she did highlighted the scene. In this moment, she confirmed the fact that many talented actors perceive the music and rhythm of a play in their personal space. I've never seen anybody use objects with a more conscious sense of how one's movement, behavior, rhythm, and timing helps to articulate the vision of life you have.

Gerry's love of her art compensated for all of her eccentricities, of which her forgetfulness was probably the most frustrating. One example of this was her vagueness about time. I had complained strongly to her about her never being ready on time, which meant that the curtain would always go up ten to fifteen minutes late. The next evening she'd been the first to arrive at the theater, at six o'clock, to the shock of us all. She shut herself in her dressing room, and was dressed and ready by half hour. When the stage manager called fifteen minutes, she marched proudly out of her dressing room and into the wings to await the play's commencement. The stage manager, who had not seen her, passed by on his routine check of the backstage area, and Gerry smiled and said, "I'm ready." He blanched so noticeably that Gerry asked him what the matter was. He looked at her, as she stood smiling in her Polynesian make-up and costume, and said, "Gerry, we're not doing *Rain* tonight. It's *Paradise*. You're in the wrong costume." Gerry ran back to her dressing room, shedding clothes as she went, in what would be record time, if we kept such records in the theater. As irritating as this kind of thing was, I believe that her child-like innocence was part of her greatness as an actress.

I once asked her if she wanted to play Amanda in *The Glass Menagerie*, a part she could have played magnificently. She thought for a moment, and said, "I don't think so." I was surprised and asked her why not. And she said, "I saw Laurette Taylor play it in Chicago, and I have nothing to add." I still think that her apple would have been a beauty.

During the three seasons the Mirror had in New York, I directed six of the eleven productions: *Joan of Lorraine, Inheritors, Paradise Lost, Rain, Vivat! Vivat! Regina!,* and *Ghosts.* Twelve were scheduled, but one didn't make it. *Sore Throats,* by Howard Brenton, was a beautiful play, the only one I ever read that used foul, sexual language poetically, in a way that illuminated life and the character's inner longings. It was canceled during rehearsal by the director, who either got scared, or thought she was being ignored by us, or both. It was while we were busy moving to Citicorp and rehearsing. It's a shame, because Sabra battled with the Board of Directors, several of whom resigned because they were shocked by the play and she refused to cancel the production.

Ghosts

Sabra and I agreed that I should write a letter to the Studio. We were using a lot of Studio actors, and both of us felt a collaboration seemed natural and beneficial to both organizations. In the two letters I wrote to Paul Newman, who was then president of the Studio, I suggested that one way the Studio could grow, change, and establish its identity independent of my father (who had died the year before) was by creating a school. It had the teachers to create a solid financial base for itself. I offered my help and support, but I never got an answer. I know that Shelley Winters, who was a member of the Board, pleaded for them to include me, but they ignored me instead. I felt like the ghost of my father was still around. Some members were suspicious because in several interviews I had expressed the views about my fathers acting methods that you're reading about in much more personal detail here. The old guard considered this an act of treason. I considered it normal and healthy, an act of love and involvement, not of jealousy or competition. How do organizations grow and change if it can't renew itself from the inside? Twelve years later, the Studio has finally created a school. They have just asked me to work with them. I hope that the training will have an organic structure. Actors want to learn technique when their learning is directly related to scene work. Organically analyzing plays to show actors exactly where and why one technique or another exists and is necessary to their art reduces their resistance; it involves them, not by demanding an act of faith or obedience, but out of an understanding of the nature of the creative process. Orson Bean founded the 15th Street School in New York, based on the orgonomic principles of Reich's work. Orson did this as a result of his therapy with Dr. Baker, which he wrote about in *Me and the Orgone*. To me, teaching is based not only on the knowledge one shares, but in sharing one's human experience, what one is.

Ellen Burstyn, who was the artistic director after the death of my father, phoned to ask me to testify in the court case that Anna had launched against the Studio over the rights to the audio tapes of the Studio sessions. I thought about it, and said that I thought those tapes belonged to no single entity. They were the common property of all the actors of the Studio, or the property of no one. I imagine Anna wanted them because she wanted to own anything that pertained to my father. She wanted the Studio, which she didn't get. She wanted her own acting career, which she didn't get. I didn't want to be dragged into an ugly, neurotic situation after having already walked away from it years earlier. I was making my own life.

Ghosts was the last of the four plays I directed during the Mirror's first full season. I envisaged a relatively conventional production, with all the indications in Ibsen's stage directions. Here, Gerry got stumped. It was the first time I saw her resist the pain of her character for as long as possible. I don't want to believe Gerry would run away from the character, no matter how much she resisted understanding her. She was avoiding the pain I knew she felt in life. She needed love and recognition as much as anyone I've ever known. It's so strange that she died just after winning both the Tony and the Oscar, the latter after having been nominated seven times. As for her personal life, Gerry said she felt beautiful, and desirable. We all need to. But I wondered, because of all the deep pain I saw "hidden from sight." I took a chance and cast a young actor, Christopher Batho, as Oswald, her son. He had studied with Gerry and me and gave a wonderful reading. It was a gamble I lost, because he didn't know enough. As rehearsals went on he got worse. What had been concentrated, sensitive, and explosive became chaotic and panicky. When the play began previews, I had to return to Europe. Sabra called to say that she was firing Christopher. Did I agree? If my approval were important, I thought she would have asked me before she decided.

Geraldine and the production got excellent notices. But I hadn't had time to reflect on the play. I agreed to do *Ghosts* again recently in Spain. I thought I understood it better this time. What has society done, and what is it still trying to do, to ourselves and to everyone we love, by hiding the truth? How long before we learn that it comes back to us? It's what the world is battling over today. There are repressive people, millions of them, who do not want anyone to be conscious of what life is. We see so many lost, confused people searching for love. We are still living under the influence of Victorian morality, which blames society's current confusions about understanding what love and sexuality is, about what constitutes greed as opposed to natural competition, about what an individual's responsibility is on attitudes of permissiveness, rather than on the repression that has led to the creation of those attitudes. They believe that the solution is to go back to living the lie that is the seed of the problem. They want to believe that life can be defined by tunnel vision and the ability to believe only what they want to believe.

Seven year later I redid *Ghosts* in Spain. I wanted to illuminate the truth that is revealed in the extraordinarily tortured web of personal relations in Ibsen's play. I wanted to strip the play to its essence, so I stripped away the set, and ignored the suffocating use of Realism that Ibsen originally used to revolutionize the theater. My focus was on the lies we tell about what love and duty should be, rather than what they really are. I wanted the audience to understand that the Pastor and Mrs. Alving had been, and in some way, were probably still, in love, and how fear, propriety, and correct thinking had not only destroyed their love and truth, but that of the generations that followed, and are still following. On the nights when the actors were involved, the production had a simple, human force I loved.

Vivat!

Vivat! Vivat! Regina! by Robert Bolt, about Mary Stuart and Queen Elizabeth, was the last play I did at the Mirror. It was originally done in London, and then in New York, in a very stylish production starring Eileen Atkins. This modern play would begin to challenge us to work on voice and speech, a simple way to approach classics. Some of the actors didn't want to work on their speech, and the union protected them. We couldn't have classes because it would prejudice us against those actors who didn't want to work hard.

I opened up the staging, using the theater aisles for entrances and exits. I visualized the play and the movement as an exciting action drama. It also made it move surprisingly fast. The reviews were very favorable. *The New York Times* concluded that the production's fast pace (it ran fifteen to twenty minutes faster than the original production) came from cuts. I hadn't cut a word. I just paced it without the historical costume drama approach of the English. To make the play modern I wanted to put the English in tuxedoes and the Scots in a basic outfit of corduroy pants, shirt, and tartans. Gerry and Sabra hated the idea of tuxedoes. They had been imagining the same luxurious, period costumes of the original production that most actresses adore wearing. The production worked, but I think my vision of the English in black and white, and the Scots in simplified tartans (with Mary Stuart in red and Gerry in white) would have been theatrical and more striking than the conventional choices that were imposed.

I felt artistically stifled in New York by a very conservative idea of reality. Working in Europe, where I was given the respect I thought I deserved, allowed me to relax because I wasn't fighting for recognition in order to do the work I am capable of. The increased contact with my own personal dream space in the total design of a production has given me a confidence and sense of freedom that enables me to be more articulate and decisive whenever these type of discussions take place. My openness and willingness to listen and discuss, because I always want whatever is the best idea for the production (whether it's mine or someone else's), has become a strength in my work rather than a weakness.

All my life, whenever I am asked how things are with me, I say, "Changing." I don't know what else to say. Our bodies change almost one hundred percent of all our cells within a year. Every time we breathe, we exchange millions of atoms, atoms that may have been used by anyone: Shakespeare, Euripedes, Moliere, Racine, Lope, Tennessee; someone you loved, hated, or wanted to know. Walt Whitman wrote,

> I dream in my dream all the dreams of the other dreamers,
> And I become the other dreamers.

Who are we, to have lived and thought that we are separate from the cosmos?

The first week of June 1985, an emotional earthquake shook the foundation of my life. Dr. Baker died while I was in Paris preparing a workshop production of Sartre's adaptation of *The Trojan Women*. At the same time, I had arranged to meet Sabra in London for a weekend in the hopes that some time together might save what felt like a dying marriage. I wasn't certain it was worth saving, but loyalty and obstinacy won out. I was actually surprised she showed up. It was rare for her to take any form of vacation. Two days before she arrived she told me that Dr. Baker had died. I've never registered his death. Even now, he's still alive within my secret dream space. I arrived after her, and we went to dinner in a restaurant near Covent Garden.

During dinner she confessed to me that she wasn't alone. I couldn't believe it. I was so shocked there was nothing I could think of to say. She was with Thomas MacAteer, an actor in the company whom I liked a great deal, and still do. It was clear he felt out of place, which revealed a sensitivity and respect I'll never forget. They are married now and have a child, so it all worked out in the end.

This was now the second wife who had confronted me with a lover. I guess something was wrong from everybody's point of view. My shock this time wasn't because she was having an affair, or even that she had arrived in London as part of her plan for a vacation with Thomas (which I ended up paying for, when she didn't pay her credit card charges). It was simply not being told beforehand. In the end, while I can forgive anything, that is unforgettable. I suppose my love had been worn down from being told I was brilliant one day but should feel grateful to her hiring me the next; from being told I was a lousy money manager when I went into debt trying to help her live in L.A. so she could pursue her dream while I worked in New York. This was definitely mismanagement. It was also love. Oh, well, the world is living on credit, including the banks and governments, and not on love. The planet is on the brink of Chapter 11. If, suddenly, we all had to pay as we go, the system would collapse.

I returned to Paris, holding back the tears until I got into the apartment near the Place Contrescarpe where I was staying. I was out of control as much from the shock and surprise as from the painful reality that a ten-year relationship was over. So strange, how things work out. Sabra asked me to help them rent a car to drive to Scotland, where Thomas is from, which I did, even lending him an expired driver's license of mine, as though I agreed to give him a part of my former identity, too.

Someone or something had died and I was alone. My life had been torn from its roots. I grew up in the theater, where everyone acts as though we are all intimate and personal friends. This is almost always based primarily on the fact that we live and work in a very small world; one must never forget that if one wants to keep a good grip on reality. I remember "friends" in Hollywood who wouldn't say hello when you weren't working.

I agreed to do a play in Madrid in the fall, and that summer I took my first vacation alone (aside from my dog, Star, who lived and traveled with me now, and whose unwavering love and loyalty set a standard for friendship, as most animals do). We spent two weeks in Nerja, in the south of Spain, in a beautiful, semi-abandoned house that had belonged to Federico Garcia Lorca, and was now owned by his three nieces. I felt as though I was a Chekhovian character: a man who never tried to make his dream come true.

Five years later, and somewhat the wiser, becoming the dreamer I dream I am, I was in Paris. A friend and former student took me to the apartment of a friend one day to have lunch. As we arrived, Anne was rushing out to go to the hospital, in agony from an attack of kidney stones. She smiled and laughed through the pain. We looked into each other's eyes and fell in love. She is French (divorced with two children, Juliette and Jean-Baptiste), a self-taught modern primitive (naive-folk-outsider art) painter, and a good one (she exhibits in France and the USA), who decorates apartments in the Venetian style, marbleizing walls and painting frescos, etc. I never thought I'd fall in love with a Frenchwoman, because so many seemed too involved in themselves. But Anne is different; a great example of the French culture's refinement, joie de vivre, and search for "le bonheur." She loves me, without confusing me with what I do.

Man, Beast, and Virtue

I met Anne after I had returned to Paris from Valencia, Spain, having directed a very successful production of Pirandello's wonderful, bitter farce, *Man, Beast, And Virtue*. A woman having an affair with a professor becomes pregnant. Her husband, a captain of a boat, is scheduled to come home for the one night a year he spends with her (rather than with his mistress). The professor convinces her that she must have intercourse with the husband, which doesn't normally happen. The professor's doctor friend gives him a drug that'll make the husband horny. He puts the drug in a cake that he brings to the house when he is invited to dine with the captain. During a raucous meal (in which the Captain breaks all of the dinner plates because the servant is slow to serve the spaghetti), the young son of the Captain and the woman eat most of the cake. There is enough left for him to eat, which he does to please the desperately upset professor. The Captain goes into his study and locks the door, seemingly to sleep alone, and the lovers agree that if she gets laid by the husband she will put plants on the balcony. In the morning, after some suspense, she puts five plants on the balcony. The production exemplified the maturity of my own evolution. The Spanish were amazed by my understanding of Mediterranean culture, and, after the next play I did there, declared that I was an expert on that culture. I just felt that I had some wonderful conversations with Pirandello as I rehearsed and delved deeper and deeper into the world of the play (which was helped by our using the brilliantly simple and clean, original Italian text as a source whenever we had some question about meaning). No matter how deep I went, or how much I thought I understood, the author was always waiting for me when I arrived at what I thought was a wonderful flash of insight. He would look at me with a twinkle in the sad, deep pools of his eyes and say, "Oh. You understood that, did you?" and laugh. "Wait till you realize what else is there." Not with any arrogance, but with the ongoing pleasure of souls sharing the knowledge that art and life can hold. The production had that same sharing of human experience, playing night after night. The theater was filled with my favorite sound, the pregnant silence of a group of people listening with their entire being attuned to the soul music of human life that great plays contain.

La Senorita de Treveles

A year later, in Valencia, I directed *The Senorita de Treveles*, by Carlos Arniches, a sad, wonderful comedy that I loved on the first reading. It is a story filled with longing, about an unmarried brother and sister who live in a provincial town in Spain. The author exposes the small-minded meanness of bored, middle-class society, people who love to gossip and laugh at the misery of others because it distracts them from their own unhappiness. Arniches was considered a minor writer and his characters were played as cartoons until the voice and music of life I heard deep inside the play was revived and brought to the surface, revealing a depth to his work that had been neglected and forgotten. I worked with Simone Suarez, who did the set, lights, and costumes. Our major design concept meeting took place over the telephone, when I called him in Madrid from a public phone in Yosemite. I said that I thought it should look realistic, but in the style of the period (1910-ish); beautiful and lush, and with three different design spaces for each act. He said, "Uh, huh."

Simone (who has just died of AIDS) was a small, fair-haired, intense man from Cordoba, who exuded an almost religious purity, and had a great nineteenth-century dream space in his work. It was perfect for the play. We worked very intuitively together, changing the design of the painted curtains that revealed different spaces from act to act during technical rehearsal. We also solved the problem of a costume change by not making it, which turned out to be a brilliant stroke: leaving the character Don Gonzalo onstage in the laundry room of the house, where we had placed his fencing class, in the simple white shirt and pants that were the underpart of his fencing costume. It gave him a Don Quixote look. That idea came out of desperation during the dress rehearsal the day before opening. The insight and intuition that marked my acting and teaching process was becoming a part of my directing work. The less I tried to be "right" and perfect, the more my own talent and humanity was able to express itself. Intellectualized, forced choices became a clear sign of a problem in the creative process.

Don Juan

Simone and I worked together again, on *Don Juan Tenorio* (a nineteenth-century Spanish version of the myth and the most popular play in Spain), and *Ghosts*. *Don Juan Tenorio* is mounted all over the country on November 1st, All Saints Day. It's a very flawed play, and cannot compare to either Moliere or Tirso de Molino in terms of dramatic poetry, but it allowed me to explore the Don Juan myth. No version of Don Juan addresses what to me is the central point—why do we all admire and want to emulate Don Juan? True, he is a man who appears to be free to do whatever he wants. He takes what he wants, makes love to any woman he cares to, and will cheerfully kill any man who angers him. In short, he seems to be the ultimate hero for men who feel that their lives are a celebration of smallness, a series of endless repressions and defeats: starting with mama and continuing on to papa, to school, to the boss, and so on, down through life. But it's not difficult to see that Don Juan can't be a happy man. He suffers desperately, believes in nothing, and has no love in his life. Why do we ignore the depth of his suffering? Do we all dream of pleasure based on revenge? I envisioned the production as a game of chess—everything in black and white, with people as pawns who childishly follow their culture heroes in order to share the illusions of power and success that are their rewards. I think the production shocked the audience, who were used to the play being treated superficially, as though it is a pagan celebration, a Spanish Halloween.

Long Day's Journey Into Night

My personal vision of life continued to express itself in my production of O'Neill's *Long Day's Journey Into Night*. I wanted the audience to perceive this family not as a great family in a great play (as I have normally seen it played), but as a family like most families, full of the same desires, pain, unsaid truths, compromises, and love hidden behind the walls we construct to protect our hearts and minds. The second night in Madrid I sat in the audience in front of a family who had seen *La Senorita* and thought O'Neill's play was also a comedy. As the family realized the play's true nature, in the middle of the first act when we become aware of Mary Tyrone's drug problem, they weren't sure they wanted to stay. But at one point the wife leaned over to the husband and said, "Oye, sabes algo? Son comos los vecinos." (Hey, you know something? They're like the neighbors.) It was the review I wanted.

Functional thinking helped me to discover the deepest human reality in each of these plays. In the productions of *Don Juan*, *Long Day's Journey Into Night*, and *Ghosts*, I stripped the plays down to their essence. I wanted my productions to be simple, pure, modern, and beautiful. I insisted that actors speak in human tones and eliminate the false tone that is often confused with theatricality. This tone also unified the diversity of the various acting styles the actors used, and made the characters lives totally accessible to the audience. Beneath cultural differences, we are all human beings, with the same perceptions, needs, and desires. All the playwrights I worked with seemed to agree with me.

I closed the New York branch of The Real Stage in 1985 and the Paris branch in 1989. I was tired of hearing people tell me they were working for me when it felt as though I was working for them. I always dreamed of an organization in which people shared, and took, responsibility for their work, working for themselves. I believe it is possible. I also realized that the only organization I would commit myself to would be a theater; it might have several realms of work, such as a learning center that would service professional actors, directors, and writers, but it would have to inculcate the freedom for the participating artists, including myself, to write, direct, produce, dream, and develop.

Three weeks after I closed the school in Paris, the Maire d'Asnieres called and asked if I wanted to create an International Studio Theater. I collaborated with the architect Philippe Robert and his team on the design of a lovely, two-hundred-seat theater in the former gymnasium of the Mairie. After three years of work, I moved on. When the Mayor and I began to discuss the contract, most of the conditions we had discussed were changed. I'd have the use of a space without being the artistic director programming its use. It seemed as though the building would quickly become a beautiful headache. The important part of the dream, however, called the Theater International de Recherche, is developing. When I began building the professional workshop, everyone I talked to in France told me how much they had always dreamed and longed for a place like TIR, a theater with a professional workshop where plays, actors, and directors could develop, and an organization that would create new works and realistic, humanized interpretations of classics. And I wondered why, if everyone wanted it, didn't it exist? So I set about making sure that the membership would be composed of professionals, people committed to the ongoing development of their creative processes. If I simply had people who waited for me to put on plays, I didn't need to develop an organization.

The years of travel have sharpened my longing to root myself in a place of my own, a home where I can write and teach and collaborate to develop projects for theater, film, and television. Whether I will succeed in this or not, or in what form it will exist, I can't say. I am laying the foundation for a theater center that could function internationally, between New York and Paris. I visualize an organization that creates a real cultural exchange, in a variety of ways, in more than one medium.

My own work has proven to me that my best work is not my fault. It is the result of the talent and life force that are channeled through me into my work. I can only take credit for nurturing what I was born with, and the will and determination I have employed. Are most people haunted by unexpressed feelings, broken dreams, unspoken truths, and the life they never dared to try to live? I was living with a crowd of unexpressed moments in my head. I have finally become more afraid of not trying to do what I dream than of doing something that no one I loved ever gave me permission to do.

Happy Days

My own evolution and my discovery of the natural laws of creativity brings me, in my own weird way, to Beckett. This intensely human writer, someone who Tennessee Williams and Harold Pinter said had made their work much easier because he opened up so many horizons, is still an outsider. He is thought of as too far out of the mainstream for the tastes of most audiences. I never expected to embrace Beckett in my dream space. I found him cold, intellectual, and almost impossible to read. I wondered if it was me or him, because I admitted to myself that I had trouble liking modern art. I often found myself admiring the fire exit signs, extinguishers, and naked walls of museums devoted to modern art. I didn't understand it viscerally, nor could I understand what most of the modern artists were trying to express in their paintings. I saw them destroying material form, breaking perception down into some subjective, chaotic, infantile configuration. I wanted to be able to feel what their world was and to understand how they got there. Living with a painter helps, especially one who also doesn't like spending too much time in the museum. We're lucky enough to share similar habits of enjoyment, and a humanistic idea of perfection. Before I met Anne, I had sworn never to live in a relationship where I had to compromise or hide my way of being.

I wandered through the Picasso museum in an old house in the old quarter of Barcelona. Because everything was laid out in a sequence, I could see the evolutionary process of this artist, who said, "I don't paint what I see. I paint what I think." It was strange, because from the beginning, when Picasso painted "normally," I saw that he always saw the two sides of people's faces. As he evolved, his manner of seeing life was more personally expressed. He passed through all the styles of his time—Cubism, Surrealism—until he arrived at his own. Of course, it was always there, but clothed in other people's thoughts, as he absorbed and experimented with other people's techniques.

I realized that modern art is like modern science. It broke from the materialistic attachment to objects, points and lines in space, and the practice of accepting only what we can see and touch. Modern art is a way of expressing a personal universe, a personal dream space, in which objects and space and the relationships of things to one another depend on what, how, and where the painter perceives what he wants to paint. The subject is determined by the observer, not some mechanical formalization of life. It is based on sensation and emotion. It was like my own personal dream space. It was beautiful. And so personal—not cold at all, not intellectualized, free of all the old rules of common sense, of recognizable, mechanical order, and three dimensional realities. Beautiful and confusing and terrifying.

Beckett suddenly became profoundly simple. His world was a natural evolution of my own perceptions. Beckett is just life expressed in minute detail. Reading the stage directions is exhausting. Seeing them in movement is illuminating. My consciousness opened, and I crossed into modern theater. One arts reporter kept insisting that I explain the theme of the play *Happy Days*. She kept asking, "Is it about life, or a couple? Is it a comedy or a tragedy? Is it real or is it abstract?" And I just kept saying, "Yes, that's right. It is like that."

What is our theater space becoming? We need new words to express our new perceptions of time and space. Past, present, future, real time, emotional time, normal space, dream space; our words are of "the old style," as Beckett says. We must escape the trap of old concepts, in which the cosmos is a perfect machine and human beings are an expression of that mechanical perfection. I needed to apprehend this intentionally in my dream space, not just to intuitively see it or feel it or hear it. And so, the fingers of my imagination reached out, like invisible webs of energy, and made contact with the dreamers who live in their own emotional time, and are always new.

Man, Beast, and Virtue by Luigi Pirandello
directed by John Strasberg at Centre Dramatic de Valencia 1988

CHAPTER SEVEN

THE NINE NATURAL LAWS OF CREATIVITY

Organic Script Analysis (OSA) places all techniques under nine fundamental natural laws of creativity.

These nine natural laws evolve from my own perceptions of the organic creative process, and, as they are used in Organic Script Analysis, they train you to become involved with the play in your personal dream space, so that you let the play tell you what to do. Some people feel that technique must be able to be rigidly controllable. Functional thinking proves that no technique will guarantee anyone's capacity to produce a work of art. But after years of learning and exploring a truly personal form of expression, an artist's work does show a personal perception of life and the knowledge and maturity which is thereby expressed. Their work will always be professional and have a standard of excellence that often garners applause for what they know is less than their best work. Sometimes their best work may even be incomprehensible to us, because we aren't capable of perceiving or understanding what they are expressing. In all art, the natural laws of creativity supersede all other forms of training. In the theater, they supersede classical representative training, the Method, Adler, Meisner, Michael Chekhov, and Grotowski. All techniques, methods, and systems try to reduce the creative process to what, in practice, becomes a mechanical series of rules and exercises. They limit, rather than expand, an actor's natural capacity for expression. All these techniques ignore, or mystify, the laws which are the basis of the creative process. The creators of these techniques have not investigated that which they couldn't see or touch, and the techniques are based on the supposition that conscious awareness and mechanical techniques are the only way to develop and train artists. Most actors who use them develop mannerisms which we call "styles of acting." They seem to imitate an original; something that mature artists would not do. However, within their limitations, they work, and an artist can use any number of techniques to help create a work of art. My work is not meant to eliminate or invalidate them, but to integrate these techniques into a more organic process.

OSA develops the individual's talent and creative process in two ways. One is through a long-term process that analyzes, defines, and trains the artist's perception, preparation and state of being (as Stanislavski proposed), and talent (which I have defined so that it can be consciously worked with), organic (functional) thinking, spontaneous inspiration, and intentional dreaming. The second is through a short-term process (what Stanislavski calls the work on the play), which trains the artist's organic analysis and understanding of plays. Together, they merge the actor's talent and knowledge of life with the form in which he is working. Some of these laws naturally carry over from the long-term work on the self into the short-term work on the play. Don't try to separate long and short term work from each other. They go together naturally, and training methods should teach this symbiosis. To separate them creates a discontinuity in how the actor thinks about what he is doing. The basis that OSA has in the essential laws of creativity is an important conceptual departure from other methods and systems.

The Law of Talent

Talent is an exceptional natural capacity to perceive and sense reality, coupled with an exceptional natural capacity to focus intentionally on specific realities and express them in a here-and-now form. It is an expression of our humanity, and has nothing of mechanical perfection to it.

Talent has to be defined or it cannot be consciously trained. Technique has always been judged on the basis of the talent of the artists who used it. But to judge a technique we must know how much of the result is due to the technique, and how much is due to the talent of the artist. We certainly cannot separate the two without first clearly defining "talent"; nor can we develop the individual artist's talent and ability to think organically.

It is impossible to describe exactly what an artist is doing that a technician is not. We have neither the language to express what we perceive nor certainty that what we perceive is true. If this weren't the case, we could teach anyone how to be an artist and predict when they will create works of art, since we would be able to define and develop the necessary techniques that would guarantee that result. (We can all learn to paint, but we cannot all become Picasso.) The creative process is not so objective and rational. Even an accomplished artist may not be able to explain exactly why one of his works has succeeded while another hasn't. He will know something is wrong, but will be only guessing as to what and why, otherwise he could fix any flaw in his art by exerting conscious will, technique, and the law of determined movement, as described below.

Perception and Consciousness

Perception is the most basic, observable, natural quality of talent. Very simply, perception is the conscious and intuitive awareness of what one senses and feels.

In Organic Script Analysis one believes and knows something because one feels it. Feeling has never been considered a reliable part of human experience; something that you can develop into a technique. You can't always reduce it to a normal, see-or-touch reality, because sometimes what you're perceiving may not be part of our ordinary world of common sense. (Using feeling as a technique is one of the strengths of sense memory exercises, because it is a means by which the actor can make what he imagines real. This is still not completely understood. Sense memory, however, reduces perception to recognizable emotions and sensations that is limited by the actor's real experience of life. The actor has to make a giant leap to create realities that he may imagine, but doesn't know.) Organically, perception and imagination are capable of creating new realities. In fact, perception and feeling is one of the qualities of animate life. All living matter senses and reacts to its environment. Read Stephen Jay Gould, Lyall Watson, Cousteau, *The Tao of Physics*, *The Dancing Wu Li Masters*, etc. The best survivors of any species are normally those animals that are the most perceptive, because they adapt and react more quickly. Perception is the basis for all real experience and empirical knowledge. When I help people make contact with their own talent, their perceptions become deeper, truer, more personal, and more interesting. There is no way to teach other than by sharing who you are and what you know. Otherwise, everyone teaching sense memory exercises, or any technique, would produce the same results in the actors they train.

Consciousness is different from perception. Organically it is a step beyond perception. This is not to say a better step, because consciousness is defined and expressed as a direct contact between perception and our thinking awareness. If that contact isn't maintained, consciousness will distort and inhibit perception. We often see this result in individuals who becomes narrow-minded, and ignore the feelings and sensations they don't understand or can't explain. They lose contact with the deepest part of themselves, where individual talent can perceive what is real and true. An observable fact of a good creative process is a contactful awareness of reality, in which the person can perceive what actually exists in his environment, and relate it to his own experience. The presence of a sense of truth, and an open mind that will not ignore what it doesn't understand or can't explain are also fundamental parts of a good creative process. All groundbreakers, in art and science, manifest these natural qualities. They see and do what was neither seen nor done before. Consciousness, apart from perception, is cold and rational, and may become distorted and more mechanical than functional. Organic thinking, which is how we recognize whether any process is valid and true, goes to the core of any situation. Its value is in its capacity to isolate the essence of whatever we are perceiving, the organic nature of what we are observing and analyzing. This is different from reductive thinking, which, by reducing the nature of life to one common denominator, ignores the differences, the intentions, and the organic nature of life. All life is interconnected, so that working from the deepest core will organically create movement and expression that is based on whatever reality one is considering. Reductive thinking tends to do the opposite, and makes us lose sight of the basic interactive nature of life. We are all plugged into, and running on, the same life energy.

The Law of Organic (Functional) Thinking

An actor's performance arises from his conception of acting. To change what they do, I have to change how they think. When actors express "real feeling" as the result of an exercise, the actor has not transformed or become completely involved in the world of the play. What they are doing may be wonderful, but it is at best only near-real, because the actor will be thinking as an actor rather than as a human being. I saw actors express "real feeling" and found myself unmoved. The separation between actor and human being decreed a divorce between "real" and "feeling." My mission has been to re-commit the actor's technique, whatever it may be, to the natural creativity of his humanity. The actor must live the experience of the play and really create life. If an actor wants to be real, there is only one way for him to achieve that transformation. He has to be able to think and act not like an actor but like the human being he imagines the character to be.

We can't use reductive reasoning to explain this act of creation, anymore than we can develop techniques that will guarantee the creation of a work of art. The implication that this sort of recipe/result approach can work was my father's main error. He hoped to devise a system that reduced acting to a Pavlovian habit of reactions to imaginary stimuli, a systematized mechanical process for creating and expressing emotion. His system works, like many training methods, because it is true as far as it goes. But Sense Memory (including Emotional Memory), like other systems and techniques, is always subordinate to the natural laws of creativity. Stanislavski intuited this truth in his later work, where my father parted company with his ideas. Stanislavski did not directly investigate the nature of talent or inspiration, but because he continued to explore the creative process he arrived closer and closer to a deeper understanding of it.

The better techniques treat the human being as an organic whole and not as a machine composed of separate parts which can be trained without any awareness as to how the whole functions organically. But up to now, none of these systems or techniques has been consciously based on the natural laws of creativity, because they couldn't examine or explain what happens when an artist is being creative.

This has led to the kind of analysis that trained the actor to stand outside a situation and judge it impersonally. How can an artist know what a character feels or how it behaves from this perspective? The artist is forced to rely on rationality and the conventional sense of why someone does something, without becoming involved and exploring the character's life from within. This analysis from the outside is what leads most actors to interpret a play by analyzing the superficial meaning of the lines. If they manage to get to the bottom of things by becoming involved it will be due to natural talent, which is functioning in spite of, and not because of, their techniques. In the same way, sense memory tends to reduce what an actor thinks reality is to an emotional basis. So if the actor who thinks of creation from a sensory point of view observes a ward full of people dying of AIDS, he tends to think that the most important thing is to create the reality of the disease. He may do this beautifully, but we don't really know who he is, or what the play is really about.

OSA uses organic thinking to get to the basic core of life in the play. It doesn't start with thinking what to do, or how to act the scene. Before this can happen, we have to become involved in the play's world, and explore it with all of our feelings and senses, in order to let the play tell us what to do. Only after we become involved, and begin to live and dream in the imaginary world of the play (like a human being, not an actor) can we begin to know how a character feels and why he does what he does. Our understanding is only limited by the knowledge and imagination of the artist.

Organic thinking is a term that stems from Reich's functional thinking, the systematic process of investigating one reality until it leads to the next, and so on; but as I interpret in my own way, I have changed the name. It is distinctly organic and open-minded. It does not teach that a good or correct analysis will prevent mistakes, as is the promise of most mechanical techniques, which are exercises in applying conventional ideas to any situation. Organic thinking takes into account the fact that exploration is both intuitive and conscious, based on personal knowledge and experience of life; one's knowledge and feeling of life merges with the play. Rehearsing will involve making mistakes and learning from them, because one focuses on a reality which may, or may not, lead one in the direction in which one needs to go. It might be real, and interesting, and all wrong for the play. The more mistakes, the more one will learn, because recognizing the allows for the exploration and discovery of a simpler, deeper, and truer reality that expresses your perception of life and the play. Eventually, and sometimes with surprising spontaneity, organic thinking will lead one to the core of the life of the play. This adventure in living is intuitive, pleasurable, and conscious. The Law of Organic Thinking recognizes that this is how art and artists function. The artist's creation will be unique and personal, not because he tries to be different but because he is different. Organic thinking explores from object to object, fact to fact, until it reaches the deepest possible truth that we are capable of perceiving.

The Law of Imagination

What is imagination, and why do some people have more of it? It seems to be intimately related to perception and talent, but it is not identical, because imagination can relate to truths that we can't see or touch, and alter that which we can. It is related to dreaming, but is different because it functions when our thoughts and feelings are focused on some object. What we imagine is an expression of our thoughts, feelings, and sensations about that object, even if we don't know if that object exists. We don't know whether what we imagine is real. Einstein once said, "Imagination is more important than knowledge, because with imagination you can change reality."

Imagination is the act or power of forming mental images of that which is absent. It is the ability to create new realities by synthesizing current or former realities into a new form. Imagination is an essential element of art and the creative process and one of the fundamental laws of creativity.

One can stimulate imagination in people who have it but haven't used it. But it is very difficult to do, because they must want to let go and not fear feeling ridiculous. One must practice using and directing imagination or it may function without any connection to talent and perception. I find it more difficult to stimulate in an actor than talent and perception, which are more easily connected to training the actor to intentionally dream. Certainly, this dreaming is important and does connect to imagination, but imagination is much more difficult to train. The actor must engage the observable realities and objects in the play until his imagination becomes engaged and can begin to take the leaps that lead us to create new realities or to reorganize the reality we perceive into a new form. A good imagination will discover realities and objects that aren't there yet but are gestating in the artist's personal dream space. Dreams can remain unattached to here-and-now realities. They can only come true if imagination also exists. Like the creative process, it is difficult to study because it's not part of the rational world. Scientists, other than those involved in quantum physics, are not noted for their desire to study that which they can't explain mechanically. This even includes most psychiatrists, psychologists, and those in related fields of study. One of the main difficulties to the study of nature that we can't see are the inadequate, antiquated maps and language for expressing what we are perceiving. We may need new words to express what time and space are. Language is how we express what we perceive and feel. Most people, if they pass through an emotional crisis, can't express themselves. They are trapped inside themselves, alone, without the means to reach out and communicate who they are and what they feel to the world. That is usually left to the imagination, and perception, of art and science.

The Law of Intentional Dreaming and the Personal Dream Space

The creative process is based in our capacity to direct talent, functional thinking, and imagination into what I call Intentional Dreaming. Learning how to dream intentionally about specific realities that make up the world the artist is observing will inspire him to believe and become involved in the dream space from which he will create.

Intentional dreaming isn't daydreaming about the success one hopes to achieve, or dreaming about a person you long to be with, or dreaming that you've seen someone who is dead, or having a powerful dream while you sleep that is full of events and disturbing, illuminating images, or dreams in which you resolve problems. In intentional dreaming, we project ourselves consciously into a world we want to explore, know, and understand. This is a world, at once real and imaginary, in which we involve ourselves in order to perceive it and ourselves in it, so that we can create its life. We may have a map of the territory that we have studied (like a script), but once we voyage to the territory itself we must focus on what we actually perceive there, and not what is on the map. Architects intentionally dream their bridges, cooks intentionally dream their dishes, athletes intentionally dream their actions in competition, actors intentionally dream their characters and the worlds in which they live.

The unpredictable quality of the creative process is the principle reason why an artist needs to develop an ongoing state of being, or preparation. He needs to remain centered and in contact with himself so that in a moment of inspiration in his personal dream space, he will be prepared to follow the object of his attention, and allow the impulse to express itself in form and action.

Each art form, because it exists in its own realm, has its own particular, observable realities from which all its techniques are developed. An actor begins to imagine the world of his character. I am talking here about an artist, not a technician, because a technician's attention is focused on what and how he is going to do that which seems evident to him once he has read the play. To an artist, what he imagines and chooses to do is not so evident. Normally he feels as though he is being pulled unconsciously into the world he imagines, like a child, or one about to dream. He begins to play, exploring the realities and objects in this world of his personal dream space as if it were real. If he is lucky he will become obsessed. If he is brilliant, he will become possessed. The imaginary world he perceives and then creates is at least as real as any reality we are aware of. We are aware of being in an altered state of reality, which is not on the maps of our normal, rational world. To those whose consciousness is open, the fact that we can't see or touch a reality in the sense of seeing and touching a material object is not an obstacle to knowing it exists. The war of our age is between those who want our consciousness to open and be raised, and those who want to shut it down. Perhaps it has always been like that.

For an actor, the world in which he focuses and intentionally dreams is the play. (I use the word play to include any text or improvised world.) The actor's work begins when the fingers of perception reach out and touch some particular reality that he observes in his personal dream space. His concentration is pulled towards and focused on it, and he begins to explore and question, consciously or not, by turning this specific reality over and over in his PDS, examining it as a sculptor examines a stone he is going to sculpt. The actor begins to ask himself, "What do I perceive?

What reality can help me to involve myself in my PDS, so I can believe I am living in the play?" Organic thinking always searches for the simplest and deepest reality. In OSA, there is no effort to make the right or correct choice. Organic thinking is not based on "correct analysis." It seeks to grasp the basic facts and truths of the given reality. There is a period of waiting, in which observer and observed begin to merge, something like falling in love. This stirring and simmering of life is in all creative processes before a recognition of some reality, old or new, stimulates a deep desire for involvement and creation.

The real artist waits until he knows what is real and true. Learning to concentrate and focus intentionally on objects in one's personal dream space is not easy. It's like Zen fishing, with invisible hook and invisible fish. We are both the rod and reel, using imperceptible threads of energy to find the fish that we hook, which then reels us in. Not exactly the same as normal fishing. It can't be forced, because if it is the actor loses contact with the object he is fishing for as well as with his center, which is where the reel of cosmic energy is poised. His work may seem accurate, but it will be dominated by rational thoughts and intellectualized, cerebral realities. It will be conscious, but not connected to talent and perception. And it won't help the actor become involved or transform. Learning to stay focused on one's PDS requires patience, will, and practice. The actor will learn that there is no way of knowing exactly how reality will affect and involve him until it has happened. Sometimes one isn't even sure when it is happening. But this awareness helps the actor train his concentration and presence to remain in contact and in the moment.

Sense memory, because it deals specifically with training an actor to create imaginary realities, helps most actors to anchor themselves in their PDS. It makes the irrational, the can't-see-or-touch, become a rational, see-and-touch, common sense reality. No amount of correct thinking or mechanical analysis will develop the actor's capacity to become involved, because it will not help him to believe. It will only give him a clear structure, like a painter who paints the subject accurately or the musician who plays the notes correctly. But that is not art, it is mechanical technique. Any profession needs technicians. But we do not live in a mechanical universe, and we aren't beautiful machines.

The Law of Spontaneous Inspiration

Achieving a state of being in which spontaneity is normal requires enormous practice. The artist's process requires conscious will and effort, no matter how much talent, intuition, and imagination the artist has. It also requires knowledge and intelligence, because without them it is difficult to perceive oneself and make one's work express personal and interesting choices. Without personal development, it is almost impossible to reach the level at which flashes of insight and intuition become an active part of one's personal dream space, where imagination and intentional dreaming can be consciously directed. Control becomes the capacity, if one is inspired, to consciously give in to the impulse and direct it into the art form. Mechanical control is just the opposite: the capacity to stop the flow of energy, whether it is being expressed in feeling, thought, or dreaming. Control in OSA is diametrically opposed to this mechanical idea.

Spontaneous inspiration happens consistently only to artists with extensive talent, experience, and the desire and willingness to work hard. The belief of some so-called artists that spontaneous inspiration can only result from not thinking about what one is going to do, and not developing the capacity to consciously become involved, is mistaken. It shows an incomplete understanding of the way artists develop their talent and the capacity to create a state of being in which the conditions for this "accident" of inspiration can be habitually established, accidentally on purpose. These "inspiration only" artists quickly fall into habits of imitating what they did when their talent was functioning, after it has stopped functioning because they didn't develop themselves or their craft.

Kandinsky, the painter, once awoke in the middle of the night in his atelier and beheld the most beautiful painting he had ever seen. He was unsure whether he was awake or dreaming, because the painting seemed familiar. He arose and moved towards it, only to discover that it was his own real painting that was lying upside down on his easel. His ability to recognize and trust his spontaneous perception of its beauty, in spite of the fact that it was a new form, an upside-down painting, led to the creation of the surrealistic movement.

Many people confuse the capacity to be spontaneous with not thinking or with being unaware of what they are doing. These people confuse intellectualized, mechanical thinking with organic thinking, and because they do they are trapped by their own fear and ignorance into believing that all conscious thought processes are rigid and inhibiting. OSA is based on organic, functional thinking, which is intensely personal and is based on being able to observe, listen, sense, and think about whatever environment one is focusing on. It does not assume that an actor or artist can be either too intelligent or too emotional. Any qualification of an individual's natural talent and capacity must be made on the basis of empirical fact, not on a theory of a mechanically perfect artist. All of the effort over hundreds of years to define perfection is useless in an irrational world. Perfection is simply being the most human that we are capable of being. There are techniques such as sense memory, types of voice training (relating to organic technique like those of Alexander, Mezieres, Feldenkrais, etc.), and movement work like yoga or tai chi which are useful because the techniques integrate, rather than mechanically split, our perception of who we are.

The Law of the Sense of Truth

Acting is not based on the capacity to express feeling but on the capacity to tell the truth. Art, and artists, express what they feel, but in a deeper sense than just expressing emotion. They express what they see and hear and think and understand about life. They do this not by being focused in some technique or mechanical acting process, nor in their desire to express emotion, but in their desire to truthfully express what they perceive about life; whether what they perceive is based in their own life experience, or the imaginary world of the play, or, most likely, in the merger of both. Sense memory work, technically, was training one's capacity to create imaginary reality, but when it was used as the fundamental basis of an actor's analytical creative process, it tended to lead the actor to think like an actor, and to concentrate on his personal feelings and emotions. Those personal feelings were often parallel and unconnected to the play, and unconnected to the reality in which art merges the artist's real perceptions about life and human beings. This over-emphasis on emotional results was something that we all learned to feel was fundamental to a good actor's work. Whether it was intentional or not was only really important to my father. The more I worked, the more I became aware that when actors expressed feeling, I was not moved by their emotion. I realized that it was because they hadn't involved me in the experience of the human being whose life they were living, so I neither understood nor cared about what they were feeling. They made me realize that they were actors expressing their own feelings for their own reasons. Their creative process involved neither the actors nor the audience in the character's life. Their obsession with feeling blinded them to the fact that the core of all creativity is in the artist's ability to transform his life into an art form, which for an actor means who the character is and what that character is living through. In fact, when they acted, they became less human. Their emotion seemed self-gratifying. They didn't need me, and weren't concerned with the character or the audience. They were concerned with themselves. Actors with less emotion and more personal involvement and truth involved both themselves and the audience, enough so that if they don't have the emotion, the audience will feel it for them. We see this empathetic reaction in really good actors, and especially in film acting, where if the actor is simple, present, and true we become much more involved in what is happening. Good actors make you believe that what is happening is real, and great actors make themselves believe that what is happening is real. I tell all actors, "When you don't know what to do, tell the truth."

Very few actors combine emotional expression with a sense of truth. It develops in the work process, as the actor becomes more aware of his own humanity, what he is doing, and what he really wants to do. The sense of truth grounds the work in an irrational world, making it more centered, because the sense of truth helps us perceive and clarify what is empirically real. It helps us get to the bottom of things. This getting to the essence of things is one of the observable realities of all the aspects of OSA, from functional thinking to working to develop talent and perception, to developing what real control is, to analyzing a play personally, from the inside out, rather than the outside in. Actors who have a strong sense of truth also seem to have the sudden flashes of illumination and understanding that mark an organic creative process. If people want to know, they will, because they feel compelled to discover the truth; and those who don't want to know will deny any reality, no matter how much proof is presented. In our time, witness the movement to deny that the holocaust took place.

The Law of Transformation

All art is transformative. The art of acting, in particular, involves the transformation of one's own human reality. There are two areas in which we can observe the reality of transformation. In one's outer circumstances of life (where one lives, where one works, one's acquaintances, etc.), and in who one is. The most obvious part of this transformation is of one's outer being, in look, facial appearance, hair, physical behavior, voice and speech, etc. This was marvelously exemplified by Laurence Olivier, who had more courage as an actor than anyone I've seen. He wasn't always real, but his observation of human behavior was admirable. He said he worked realistically when he was rehearsing, but that once he had created the character and the partition, he imitated what he had originally discovered organically. I saw Olivier several times, and remember him, especially in Beckett, playing both parts, Beckett to Peter O'Toole's King, and the King to Anthony Quinn's Beckett. When he played the King, Olivier played a temper tantrum as though he were having an epileptic fit, and rolled around on the stage for what seemed like a minute, which is a long time during a scene. What impressed me wasn't the reality of what he did but the courage he had in doing it. I've never seen another actor like that. In an interview in *The New York Times* several years before he died, he expressed the wish to have the courage one day to play a part without makeup. I found it sad, and very human, that this actor who was so known for characterization wanted to express the deepest part of himself as simply as possible. Another fine character actor is Dustin Hoffman, so memorable for his characters in *Midnight Cowboy*, *Tootsie*, and others. He makes a more conscious effort to be real than Olivier did and to consciously create and integrate his composition. If I have any criticism of Dustin it is that sometimes I can see him thinking not as the character but as the actor doing the character, what I call seeing the wheels turning. Other actors who seem to transform from the outside in, and who sometimes do it organically, are Paul Muni, Anthony Hopkins, Alec McCowen, and Meryl Streep.

The only actors that I have personally seen transform and be almost unrecognizable from one role to another are the English actors Michael Gambon and Daniel Day Lewis (in *My Left Foot*), and an American actor, Ed Flanders (when he played the father in a production of Eugene O'Neill's *Moon For the Misbegotten*). Gambon is completely different each time I have seen him in the theater in London, not only in his physical appearance but in how he appears to think and act. Fundamentally he is not himself but the person he has dreamt his character to be (or who his character has told him he is).

I never saw Eleanora Duse. Everyone who did, from all schools of acting, said that she was the greatest actor they had ever seen. Duse transformed without makeup—she transformed her inner being. Some other actors who I believe have this natural capacity to transform their inner beings are Marlon Brando (who has the talent to do it all), Robert De Niro, Bette Davis, Montgomery Clift, Geraldine Page, John Gielgud, Ralph Richardson, John Hurt, and Robert Duvall. I don't think any American actor in recent times has developed this talent to its fullest. No one has spent the time and effort working in the theater doing classical roles, which is the only way any actor is going to be able to fully expand and detail their work. Interestingly, some of the greatest film performances, such as the characters created by Chaplin and Buster Keaton, come from actors who performed on stage as children (Duse was also a child actress). Perhaps this contributed to their ability to maintain the spontaneity, flexibility, and childlike innocence to merge with a character organically and truthfully.

As films are made today, they demand short, concentrated and intense moments of truth. There isn't the time and space to be able to practice and develop talent and expression in conjunction with character transformation. The slightest falseness in thought, feeling or action is seen, and it destroys our belief. The best film performances, by actors like Tom Hanks, for one, seem to be very subtle essences of characterization. It is what works best under the conditions of film. It is why the environment of theater is so important to nurturing the art of acting. It is the fundamental reason for real national theaters, which nourish the art. I am not speaking here of those National Theaters that institutionalize reverence of art in the production of empty forms from the past, but of a theater, like the English theater, where the art is alive and growing, and where success is not measured only by power and money.

There is also the group of gifted actors who express themselves not only from their personalities but with a depth of reality that results from their ability to empathize with their characters. Peter O'Toole, Jack Lemmon, Anna Magnani, Jeanne Moreau, Simone Signoret, Romy Schneider, Gena Rowlands, and Vanessa Redgrave are examples of actors with this capacity. They do much more than movie stars do. Theater gets an actor past the point of holding onto his personality. It teaches humility, and gets even Americans past the "I don't care what you think, I'm working for myself" attitude that often seems to distance them and make them appear ungenerous. This narcissism lacks immediacy, and puts a veil over what they do.

All good actors transform to some degree. It is what differentiates them from movie stars, whose work is based on playing from their own personalities. Film actors project a humanity that is captivating, with a sense of truth that makes us believe whatever experience the character is undergoing. But there isn't a change in their behavior from film to film. They do not transform their characters. Seeing some of the films of actors like Spencer Tracy or Katherine Hepburn confirms this. They were not capable of character composition. This is not meant as a criticism, nor as a prejudice. It is a necessary analysis of what one artist is doing that others aren't so we can understand the creative process of acting.

The period of focused intentional dreaming, sketching, and physical and emotional involvement in the creative process cannot be replaced. I don't believe the process changes from theater to film, even though theater is based in verbal poetry and film is based in visual poetry. The art of acting is based in transformation and truth, regardless of the form. There are no shortcuts or substitutions for hard work in exploring personal dream space and emotional time. The biggest difference in theater and film is that the period of rehearsal in theater allows the actor the time to discover and develop his character, and it develops his capacity to use himself fully, in playing characters that demand enormous truths, not just little ones.

To live a life that is and isn't their own, artists need the time in their personal dream space. It is where all the love and pain and suffering that is part of life seems to become worthwhile, because it is necessary to the creative process. Pain and suffering seem to be part of what makes people aware of the depth of their own talent and humanity. It forces people to develop their talent, their humanity, and the inner strength and the sense of humility that seems necessary for merging oneself with the reality that the artist is dreaming in his PDS. Without those qualities, most artists won't be capable of real inner transformation: they couldn't give in to the impulses and intuitions and conscious awareness that develops out of their knowledge and desire to live the life that begins to exist in personal dream space. The falling in love which breaks down the walls and prejudices that separate most human beings from one another and most actors from their characters, and the marriage and birth of a life that is neither the artist's nor that of the character on the page but that of another human being is not a process any artist would dream of mechanizing. The creative process is neither rational nor mechanical.

Those who hope for some miracle of mechanized science for the creative process are simply not artists. Nothing, no amount of training, ever does anything more than develop what is already there. Artists also need a lot of time and experience to develop their own being and sense of truth. Without time and experience, their characterizations will be largely superficial and externalized. All organic creative processes help the artist become involved, and transform from within the life that is the subject of intentional dreaming. This is the same for artists who work from the outside in and those who work from the inside out.

The Law of Determined Movement

This law could be listed first or last. It is so important that without it no amount of talent, imagination, organic thinking, intentional dreaming, spontaneous inspiration, truth, or transformative capacity will suffice. If we cannot allow ourselves to move in a determined manner, trusting our intuition, acting on our real thoughts and feelings, following through on our ideas and impulses to see where they will take us, we will never recognize or know the truth. We will never express who we really are in our lives, or do what we are born to do. The law of determined movement rules the domain of what we call genius, intuition, will power, and determination. Most of us think of needing will power to do what we don't want to do. As a natural law of creativity, it means being able to help ourselves to do what we dream, imagine, or think we really want to do, no matter how hard we have to work for it. In reality, we enjoy working hard at what we love to do, being able to go as far as we need to in order to finish, and completely exploring and expressing whatever we are obsessed or possessed to do. The suffering and pain we experience is difficult, but surprising enjoyable at times; and in the long run, much more pleasurable than the pain and suffering that results from not trying to do what we want to do. We can see this law operating in all living things in their will to live, survive, grow, and change. Life is movement. When we say something is dead, it no longer moves. When we are stuck in a bad moment, this law is the one that will aid us the most. All artists who have been recognized because they have created a body of work with which we can observe and recognize their talent have been in harmony with this law. There are many other artists who have never been discovered because they didn't maintain enough determined movement. They gave up working, stopped trying, or perhaps they never began because they were unaware of this fundamental law of creativity.

The Law of Love

This law seems so obvious that it is often ignored. However, the best teachers and the greatest artists are driven by their love of what they do. If they are gifted enough, their love is expressed in the passion and desire to work until their talent and knowledge can be personally and truthfully communicated in the expression that they manifest in the depth and detail of their creations. Art is a spiritual endeavor. It is emotional, and reveals some truth we didn't perceive in that particular way. Art makes us accept that there will always be something new, and something which we don't know. It manifests the spirit of the artist and the culture which is the source material of the artist and his work. Looking at any work of art, no matter how painful its perception and truth, or how difficult it may have been for the artist to create it, always makes us feel a deep respect for life. This is no accident. Even the anger and pain that some art expresses is motivated by the artist's desire to reach out and express what he feels. This impulse is sometimes clothed in hate or rage, but in the depths of the artist the desire to create is, by definition, based on love and the desire (to paraphrase Aristotle) to bring life into being.

INTERACTIVE DIALOGUE

I create an interactive dialogue between myself and each actor with whom I work. This dialogue consists not only of an exchange before or after the scene, as is the case with many acting teachers, but during the scene itself. This is an important observable reality of OSA, because for an actor to think functionally, he must learn a part of the process while working, not just before and after. When I help the actor to perceive what realities existed in the play at that particular moment, an actor understands immediately and clearly the logic and sensation of real, organic thought. He sees the composition of the notes of life, something an actor has to become able to do consciously and with immediacy. All performing arts require this capacity to perceive oneself in the moment of work, just as an athlete does. This includes moments of spontaneous inspiration when imagination and involvement change one's perception and expression of the life you are focused on; a truth that is often manifest in a talented artist's creative process.

Inspiration and conscious perception can occur any time an artist is in his personal dream space (PDS). This may happen while reading a play for the first time, at the first rehearsal, before or after rehearsal, in the shower, walking down the street, or while asleep . . . in short, anytime, anywhere. So an actor must develop the habit of focusing intentionally on some reality when he perceives it, and actively relating to it. During this interactive dialogue the problem of intellectualization is eliminated. The habits of mechanical thought and contactless behavior are the most common problems. Contactless behavior means that people are not in contact with their environment and therefore don't know what's real. Mechanical thought means that many people are poorly centered, and tend to push energy upwards into their heads, thinking their way through life, and the thoughts are often separated form what they organically sense or feel. It is why we often rely on conventional interpretations and old maps. These habits have to be replaced by organic thoughts and feelings so that the actors become themselves, and are no longer actors who would be better actors if they could do what they talk about doing, and often think they are doing.

I've obviously witnessed scenes interrupted or stopped in the past, but not as part of an ongoing guiding and sharing of human contact and perception, intended to help the actor develop his own capacity to perceive what he is doing in the moment of doing it. At first I was afraid I was directing, imposing my own perceptions on the actors and interfering with their concentration. However, I realized two things. I could see realities and objects in the play that they needed to focus on so that they would be able to involve themselves in the play's world, but weren't seeing. More importantly, I saw that when I was actively contactful and present in the moment rather than being indirect in my critique as in the before-and-after method of teaching, the actors became more present and alive in each moment. And they improved. The spontaneity developed in this process is what improvisation, the Mirror exercise, and Song and Dance mean to teach.

OBSERVATION AND EXPRESSING EMOTION

OSA trains the artist's capacity to learn through observation, not only of life and his own work but of other artists' work. An artist's creative process is based on his capacity to perceive and express what he senses. The relaxed, detached state the artist is in when observing another artist at work is precisely the attitude to emulate when at work oneself. For theater artists in particular, functional thought during observation encourages the perception of realities in plays and in understanding the writer/artist's state of being. Artists who say they can't learn by watching have a problem in perception and concentration, especially since observation makes up at least half of anyone's learning process.

If an artist wants to be real, he has to think real. Organic script analysis relegates the importance of many techniques that people have used as the primary base of their work to secondary positions. Examples include sense memory, intellectualized text analysis (which is usually accompanied by mechanical line readings), improvisation, and other complementary techniques such as voice and speech. In a good creative process, the primary requirement is to establish natural and organic habits ruled by the artist's talent, knowledge of life, and need to express his knowledge and perception as specifically as possible. There is a heightened awareness of specific details of reality in the beginning of work, in terms of observing the realities in the PDS, and in the end, in the insistence on complete and thorough expression. All techniques begin, naturally, to subordinate themselves to the much more powerful organic process. And the artist begins to understand the importance of pleasure in working.

The actor's sense of truth becomes a real and active part of the creative process, and helps the artist recognize what is important to create so that he makes his personal dream space real in what we call normal reality. This also makes most actors behave more like human beings and less like actors; an example being whether they sound like actors or like human beings when they talk, or whether what they are doing reflects what they know about life. The sense of truth helps to perceive what your strengths or weaknesses are, and makes it easier to know what techniques in particular you may need to study.

Sarah Jane (Sabra's best friend, who became my friend and partner), an endless resource of life force, was shocked when I asked her one day if she had to cry to feel that she was doing good work. She realized the answer was yes, and I told her it was totally unnecessary. An actor can be very good without having a deep emotional capacity. If he is present, in contact with himself and his environment (real and imaginary), he will be spontaneous and responsive to what he imagines and what actually happens. In fact, if he does this, emotion may occur without any effort. Even if it doesn't, the actor behaves with simple truth, and his own humanity will draw him and us into the character's world. I helped her change her perception of what an actor had to do to be a good actor.

I believe you can be a better actor if you are not obsessed with expressing emotion. Most actors think if they are not concentrating on expressing emotion, they are not acting. As a point of fact, emotion is intensified sensation. For example, putting your hand near a fire gives one warm, pleasant sensation. Putting it too near the fire creates pain. Putting it into the fire creates intense pain, suffering, fear, anger, or some other emotional trauma. In life, we express emotion as the result of what we are living, and I believe actors should do the same. If they really live in the imaginary world of the play, they will feel and express emotion naturally. Expressing emotion, in the deepest sense, is for pleasure. It is not necessary to be emotional in order to be real and truthful. Deep emotional expression is only absolutely essential in major tragedies, where, if the actor doesn't have the capacity, the play will lack a fundamental level of reality, including its climax and catharsis. Even then, if the actor has to fake the emotion and does it badly, as many do, I'd rather have less emotion because if the acting is truthful and real, the play's reflection on life will be communicated to the public more clearly. The story won't be obscured by the actor forcing us to focus us on his generalized emotion. Live and let live. Let the play work.

A NOTE ON TRAINING AND PROCEDURE

Any training program must begin with the plays that the actor or director is going to tackle. The plays will determine which techniques (sense memories, voice and speech, body movement) the actor will need, and the actor will know why he must acquire the particular skill that the technique develops. Teachers may coordinate their knowledge to meet the needs of each individual student. Everyone works towards a clear, common goal.

Most programs today proceed from the opposite end, teaching technique independently so that the actor will, when done, be prepared to begin working on plays. This conditions the artist to approach art as a process in which the work on himself is separate from the work on the play. How is he going to think like a human being, transforming his life into another form, rather than like an actor, thinking about what exercises and techniques he should apply to a play, if the process doesn't inculcate organic reality from the beginning? Art is a natural, organic process. As the artist perceives the difficulty in imagining, creating, and expressing, he will want to learn technique, because he will understand its purpose from his own experience. It provides inherent incentive rather than relying on explanations or demands for obedience or acts of faith. An actor's work, as an artistic endeavor, involves an artistic concept. There are teachers, such as my father and some of his followers, who, consciously or not, have taught actors that understanding the play is not fundamental to their work. This has led to actors creating realities that may be truthful and interesting, but have no logical connection to the play. The actor never learns to think that it should. In production, if there is a disagreement, the actor has no clear way of understanding his mistake, or of convincing his director that his work succeeds. This estrangement between the play and emotional expression has done irreparable damage to the American theater and film community.

Where and when I direct a production will condition how I think about the set, light, costumes, who I think the audience is, and what I think the actors understand and are capable of doing. My Beckett took place on a beach and used vivid Daliesque colors because I did the play in Spain. People who know my work have also remarked on the fact that I seem to be able to synthesize what the actor knows about life and is capable of doing with what the play is about, to the extent that this particular actor becomes the only one who could play the part. All the elements that go into a production are synthesized, and the work of the artist seems effortless. The audience may barely notice it, because everything seems to make up such a simple and clear organic whole. This results from the fact that everything I do begins from my involvement with the play.

Meeting the Playwright and Going to Work

Intentionally dreaming about the play and the character takes up over half of the time in any actor's work. This interactive dialogue takes place mostly outside of rehearsal. The passionate, sometimes obsessive, need to know the world of the play demands that we imagine ourselves living in it as the actor-character. Directors and writers engage in the same dialogue with every character.

Changing any reality, no matter how small, can change the life of the play. Change the date, the time, the age of the character, or the place, and believe me, the life won't be the same. Try imagining what it would be like to be born in another city, or have a different name, or a different sex, or color of skin, or to speak a different language (which would make you think differently), and on and on. This adventure in living is not primarily concerned with how the actor is going to behave in the actual scenes of the play, but in finding out who, what, where, when, why, and how the character is. And you may have other questions. Believe me. You may have one years after you've played the part (as I did with *Ghosts*, years after I had directed it). If, in our own lives, we knew when we were young what we learn later, we might have chosen to behave very differently. In the theater, one can.

How much imagination one has, and how much conscious or intuitive contact comes with it, determines what kind of training and technique an actor needs, and what kind of parts the actor will be able to play well.

Exceptional education feels like a discovery, almost as if we didn't know who we were before. It's not easy to be who you really are. Strange to learn this in an art form that is based on transforming yourself into someone else. But it is essential to know who you are, or the fear of transformation and deep expression will paralyze or overwhelm you.

The first observable reality of organic script analysis is having good, simple questions that are personal and come out of the artist's desire to motivate himself and his need to get to the bottom of things. Functional thinking is not about academic, theoretical thoughts, correct thinking, or having the "right" ideas.

Long-Term Work

An artist must have something to reveal about life. Those who prefer mechanical perfection, and who do not want this personal involvement and human expression in art, are, from the point of view of OSA, choosing to be technicians. There is always some deeply personal, human expression in the work of any real artist, in contrast to the work of a wonderful technician. Long-term work is an ongoing process of developing a continually expanding awareness, and use, of oneself.

When the artist develops a state of being in which he can direct his talent to focus and intentionally dream about some specific reality, and respond spontaneously to its stimulus, there is almost always an accompanying sensation of intense, childlike pleasure. If you want to observe what a natural organic state of being is, watch a baby: the breathing, the open, direct look, the thoughtfulness, the physical pliability. The opposite is observed in most adult human beings. The free flow of energy through the body is an objective of OSA's long-term work. Everything that OSA does must be able to be verified in nature, and is based in our capacity to become aware of what is real and natural.

Sensitivity, innocence, and open-mindedness are observable realities of talent, accompanied by presence, contact, awareness, intelligence, and organic thinking.

Short-Term Work

The artist must acquire a knowledge of theater history and its evolution. Actors who don't read and work on a variety of plays will never develop their talent to its full potential. They will not be able to create their own interactive dialogues with plays; that process takes knowledge, practice, and the contact with (and development of) organic thought before their talent and imagination is capable of becoming deeply involved in the playwright's world. What marks a great theater artist is the personal nature of his understanding and interpretation of a play or character.

A play is an artist's reflection of life expressed in human behavior, condensed to its essence. Words are the music of human speech. When you see a play, it may seem so simple and real that you think that nothing special is happening. You are just involved in observing some crisis in the lives of other human beings. As their thoughts and actions are simply and profoundly revealed to us, the playwright's art, at the same time, reveals us to ourselves; perhaps to change us forever.

The writer is most alive in his work, and any fellow artist who works with him will learn to recognize that life. My father often recommended that actors work on scenes from novels and short stories (such as those by Hemingway, Dorothy Parker, Salinger, O'Henry, and de Maupassant) because their logic and reality and their descriptive, novelistic nature stimulated his imagination. It worked as far as the actor's involvement and expression went, but it didn't develop the actor's capacity to read a play! A play condenses what a novel would do in pages of description into one sentence that comes out of a character's mouth. The lack of organic, analytical training in how to involve his talent and imagination in the text forces the actor back on his own personal expression. Most people, when they think about analyzing a play, believe we are talking about a correct, perfect analysis. In the realm of OSA, there is no perfect analysis of a play. Everything is personal and relative to the artist who is doing the reading. Who he is, where he lives, what he feels about himself and about life, about human beings, will condition his experience and analysis of the text.

To read a play with the principle of functional thinking and organic analysis is the most difficult thing to do in the whole creative process of theater. This process ultimately leads you to compose what I call a partition (using the musical term) of the play's life. Most people are unconscious of the major and conventional assumptions they make when they are reading. Most don't read; they look for some recognizable element, so that they can put what they are reading into a familiar box, compartmentalizing it. In fact, they are in contact with neither their talent and imagination nor with the play. I don't like to tell actors what roles I think they should consider, because I want them to read the play with as open-minded an attitude as possible. Preconceptions and close-mindedness are the cancer of any creative process. We do not want any artist to prejudge a reality, thinking there is only one way to paint an apple, but we do want his consciousness to know what the apple is. There are many kinds of apples.

The intensely personal nature of OSA may seem dangerous or chaotic because it demands contact and communication both between the artist and the teacher and between the artist and the play; later, in production, it further demands contact and communication between the various collaborating artists and the play. It seems to be giving the artist license to think whatever he pleases. But real freedom requires intelligence, knowledge, and the responsibility to articulate the personal nature of his reality. The only way to become able to safely trust feelings is through one's personal development and evolution, one's intelligence and consciousness. In the end, this is what any artist does. He knows because he feels. (Real thoughts are felt, always based on observable realities.) He learns to recognize when he is thinking what he has been taught to think, as opposed to what he really thinks based on what he really perceives, once he practices enough.

A good director or teacher generally wants to work with good actors. He wants them for their talent, imagination, and originality. He isn't afraid of that talent. One of the most important capabilities and responsibilities of any director or teacher is the ability to create an open work environment. The individual artist is made to feel at home, so that each can concentrate on his personal dream space, in a collaborative spirit that ultimately supports the production's dream space.

PERSONAL REFLECTIONS

Art doesn't imitate life so much as it reflects life. All art reaches us and teaches us through its particular perspective. Dance and opera are simpler for us to accept as art forms than theater, because it is easier to see the artist's technique. Most people won't argue about whether playwriting is an art or not, though they're not so sure about acting.

The natural laws of creativity are not based on learning a way to avoid mistakes. It's being able to learn from what you do. Good actors make mistakes, and get better. Bad actors make the same mistake all the time. One can say this about living, too.

I don't make any claims that my work is good for everyone. It is very personal and demands serious commitment and a willingness to work hard and to search for truth. It is not a system or method that provides a very structured environment. The right method is whatever works for you. I tried for years to teach anyone who came to me, whether I liked them or not. I was trapped in mechanically thinking that I should be able to communicate with anyone. I wanted a system that didn't require intense personal contact and interactive dialogue.

I never claim to have taught anyone. I know I can only teach people what they want to learn. I've shared perceptions with them in our dialogues, but it's up to them to consciously deliver what we have discovered.

Some people still think the most difficult thing for an actor to do is memorize the text. If that would be true, acting would not be an art. Learning lines is a matter of memory and imitation, in which a machine-like human simulates human experience through a programmed sequence of behavior, actions, and feelings. I've known actors to waste enormous amounts of energy worrying about the text, exercises, methods, and the "right" way to work. It's both what they've been taught and their way of defending themselves from becoming involved. It anchors their anxiety, a feeling that has enormous, and disturbing energy in it. Once anchored in this way, it can't be directed into other realities.

Most actors can never be real because they are always focused on what they have to do or say next. My mother did an exercise with actors that I've never forgotten, because she did it with me once. You read a play once and then you lie down on the floor and relax. When you were ready, she would tell you to concentrate and say what you thought you had to say. She would sit with the text, and read the other parts. Most actors, after reading the play once, knew over half of their text and 100 percent of the punctuation. This made her tell actors to write or type their parts out without punctuation of any kind, so they would not have these literary judgments to overcome as they brought the play and the character to life off the page; a verbal reality, not a literary one.

When actors become involved in their PDS, the problems of anxiety and anticipation dissolve because the actors become focused on imaginary realities that are much more interesting than the feelings of fear holding them back. When we focus on resisting the law of spontaneous inspiration, we block the natural flow of life. Most of these negative habits of controlling are based on the fear of not knowing what's going to happen, fear of losing control, fear of life, fear of feeling—all the realities that make us anxious.

ACTING AND THERAPY

Does all this self awareness make OSA seem like it's a therapy? All art is therapeutic. What creative endeavor isn't? People who delve into knowing who they are, and what life is, are threatening to those who don't want to know. What are people who don't face themselves doing facing an audience? And why is knowing oneself so threatening? It will always amaze me that this bothered my father in his private life. The process of creation not only helps the artist know himself, it demands it.

Of course, there is a big difference between therapy and acting. Therapy has the goal of making a person happier and more fulfilled in life. Actor training has the goal of making a person the best actor they are capable of being. Someone can be emotionally healthy and a lousy actor, or a neurotic mess and a lousy actor. I know a lot of actors who went into therapy because they were aware of how they always betrayed themselves when they were working, rather than helping themselves to do what they dreamed and imagined they wanted to do. If I can teach actors anything, it is that they have two best friends when they work, themselves and the play.

La Señorita de Treveles by Carlos Arniches directed by John Strasberg
at Centre Dramatic de Valencia 1990

APPENDIX

The Tragedy of Hamlet, Prince of Denmark
IN MY OWN PERSONAL DREAM SPACE

I think this book would be incomplete without a personal example of Organic Script Analysis, despite the difficulty of expressing verbally one's vision of a work of art. I have chosen *Hamlet* because it is probably my favorite play. It is also the most analyzed play in history. Everyone will have an opinion of my analysis, but it is at least a means to demonstrate the personal, rather than correct, manner of organic script analysis, and I would consider active discussion, dissent, and/or surprise a sign that what I have to say was provoking people's involvement, which is what any good analysis does. And I must to mine own self be true. *Hamlet*, the play and the man, has been suspended in my personal dream space for years, ever since I worked on it all those years ago, and realized that I identified so completely with what I perceived his life to be; especially, at the time, his pain and suffering. Over the years, I have perceived and explored other facets of him and his world. No matter what I decide, or think I know, he and his world is so alive to me that it is constantly changing, as is my perspective on it. This personal involvement, and changing perception, is one of the basic qualities of organic script analysis, and any artist's work process. There is no perfect, rigid apple.

I asked Hamlet if he understood what causes the difficulty of explaining, and he said that often what one can't explain is the most important part of a work of art. (I was surprised that he was ready and willing to talk to me.) He also said that, if the truth be told, there is no perfect analysis of any work of art; there are only opinions. Some are based on knowledge, others on personal perceptions of life, some on both. But because we can only perceive life as we believe it to be, our senses are dulled, and our interpretations of what we feel is strictly personal. He said that this is what all art teaches, and humorously remarked that that included the play based loosely on the legends surrounding his life. I wanted to ask him what he meant by that. Had Shakespeare invented or interpreted realities of Hamlet's life? He interrupted my thought and said, "Doesn't everybody? Don't we all live illusions at we think are real until we discover they aren't? Those of us, at any rate, who want to know what's real." He went on to say that Shakespeare was expressing his own perceptions of life, sharing his subjective experience for our interpretation. He looked at me to see if I was still listening, and then added that the play was Shakespeare's perception of Hamlet's life. Being such a great artist, Shakespeare made illusion and reality interchangeable, depending on what he believed and wanted to express about life. Hamlet laughed and said that we once believed that the world was flat, that life could be measured in straight lines, and that some solid objects were impenetrable; and those thoughts were revolutionary in their time and opened our minds to perceive the world with deeper clarity and truth. Then he said that some people think that Shakespeare's idea of theater as holding, "as 'twere, the mirror up to nature" is old fashioned. Hamlet says it depends on what you perceive the reality of nature to be. What you believe to be true is true to you.

Hamlet read my mind, and reminded me that the Inuit word for the Arctic means "beautiful land." I asked him how he knew I was thinking about where the play takes place, and he smiled and said that just because he was physically dead didn't mean that his mind and spirit were. How he leapt from Denmark to the Arctic I don't know. But he said that most of us look at the enormous, desolate, pristine white expanse of ice and water and shiver with our feelings of bleakness and isolation, and the fear of freezing to death. Anyway, if I were to understand the Inuit, I would surely involve myself by trying to imagine the land of their choice from their perspective. Land tells us a lot about the people who choose to live there. No wonder Eskimos think that war is absurd. Hamlet said that if he had been an Eskimo, Shakespeare would never have written a play about him. He said that he often wished he had been one. Not that he would be alive today, but he might have lived happily ever after. And with Ophelia. There was a long silence in which everything was said, and then as an afterthought he said aloud that Arctic winters weren't much bleaker than Denmark's. I wasn't sure if he was being bitter, factual, or both.

Shakespeare often developed his ideas from someone else's stories. I wondered if this was because of the same Taurean laziness I felt, or the particular nature of Shakespeare's talent and imagination, or some other human trait. Hamlet didn't care, so I dropped the subject. I asked Hamlet if he knew why *Hamlet* is set in Denmark. He said that as far as he knew, in Shakespeare's time the English were still aware of how intimately their lives and history were entwined with that of the Danes, those Vikings of which he was one, and whom we all think of as being, in those days, men of action who sailed their ships all over the western world; and who fought, stole, raped, invaded, traded, married, and intermingled with many other tribes. Their language and blood are mingled in that of the English, along with the Celts, Normans (who were also Vikings), and the Anglo-Saxons. Warriors, voyagers, oarsmen, the Rus (men with oars) were the same Vikings who settled in early Russian communities, and became known as Russians. They are part of the foundation of western culture, which is a great reason for Shakespeare to have been interested in the legend of Hamlet to begin with.

Hamlet went on to say that he had been raised to think of himself as a warrior-prince, but that the role had never really interested him. He said that he had always felt different, relatively alone and out of place, thinking that he had been born into the wrong family. I asked him why he was telling me all this so easily, as we hardly knew one another. He looked at me and his lips curled into a look somewhere between a pout and a smirk, though lacking condescension, and asked me why I didn't want to admit right out that I'd been identifying with him for over thirty years, and that we had a lot in common, though he was far more aware of our differences than I was. Admitting to myself that what he was saying was true was a shock. It also made me wonder if he was talking about himself, or if I was imagining him as I wanted him to be.

We are very different. He was raised to think about the world in a different way than I was. He asked me how I could really understand what it feels like to be raised to believe that life was meant to be lived for taking what one wanted without any guilt whatsoever? In his time (and Shakespeare's), success and power were celebrated for what they were. There was no such thing as being too powerful. One might think about how one used one's power, but not about having it. The only serious question in the play for him was whether or not the ghost was a representative of good or evil. He said that I didn't even believe in ghosts, so how could I really know what it felt like to be him, particularly in relation to this dilemma. I had to agree, because until he said that, I had seen him as a prince who is so reflective he appears out of his time, while Claudius represented the traditional order and quest for success and power. Hamlet said that was ridiculous. A twentieth-century thought. If I wanted to make the play about that I could, artist's prerogative and all that, but that he wasn't at all out of his time. He just had to know whether the ghost was a representative of God or the Devil. Imagine if the ghost was evil and had said that Claudius, who after all is the younger brother of King Hamlet, had poisoned Hamlet's father simply to create some chaos in the world? He informed me that maybe it wasn't for power that Claudius married Gertrude. He didn't have to do that in order to be King, because the Danish succession was decided by vote. A King only had to be a member of the Royal family. He said that Claudius was a brave and forceful warrior-statesman, so his marrying Gertrude could have been due to other reasons. I thought he was implying that Claudius and Gertrude really loved one another, or at least had great sex. Hamlet ignored my unspoken probe and said that it would have been premature and childish to assume that Claudius was full of jealousy and hatred of his brother, and just wanted to possess everything. Even if it were, it wouldn't be the first time, or the last, that things like that happened between family members. Hamlet wondered how anyone ever thought that Claudius was weak. Even if he had manipulated and murdered his way to power, and then suffered from doubt and remorse, that wouldn't make him a weak man. Many men achieved power in that way. He said it still was going on in the "modern" world. (The quotation marks are mine.) It might even be possible to admire him for doing that, so long as it wasn't your father and mother he was doing it to. His actions were those of a successful politician who is fundamentally part of the world order. If Hamlet had succeeded in and survived killing him, he would have been thought of in the same way. He looked at me and said, "Death is the only thing that made my behavior noble." He was still bitter after all these years. He read my mind and said that no, it wasn't bitterness but a sad reflection on the state of human suffering. We still seemed unable to learn from studying other peoples' experiences. Even as far as his own life was concerned, we played the play, generation after generation, interpreting his life from our own perspective, but to serve what purpose? To learn what? Because, in our dialogue with him, most of us were only interested in hearing our own thoughts expressed through Shakespeare's words. And we call ourselves artists!

I found it difficult to understand how Hamlet's conflict about good and evil felt. It seemed a philosophical problem; an intellectualization of life. I wrestled with this reality in my mind until he finally told me that I had the same conflict. I was obsessed with knowing what the truth was, and I could only act freely when I believed I knew. He said that many men are like that, they see truth from their own perspective: it was a truth, even though it was often a small-minded one. That hit me where I live. He said that he wasn't the type who could just act impulsively in a matter as important as the life and death of another human being, regardless of who it was.

For some people, getting what they want is all that matters. Their desire was justification. He said that he was not a Greek prince, nor even one of his own time. He believed that he was a man for all seasons, humble enough or weak enough (as some people saw his behavior) that he needed to know what was real and true; so that when he acted he felt in harmony with the universe. He said that perhaps real kings could do whatever they liked, by divine right, but not most of the kings that we celebrate as great conquerors.

The thoughts seemed so like my own that I wondered who was thinking them, and even what thought is. Where do ideas come from? And why did I suddenly remember that when I was a child I wondered why 2 x 2 = 4? Those symbols and sounds are, after all, just symbols. Hamlet laughed and said that wondering about good and evil was much more practical.

He said that the only tragedy in the play was Ophelia's death, because she died having loved men who were unworthy of her pain and sacrifice. He said that, in his opinion, the play should be about that. A woman like Ophelia should have loved a real man who earned love and wealth by his own effort, in proof of his self-worth. I realized how deeply he still loved her. He looked at me and said, "Love is what gives life meaning." It made me think of Doctor Baker, in his book, *Man In The Trap*, when he named Abraham Lincoln, Mark Twain, and Hamlet as examples of chronic depressives. I am one as well, but I could never even mention that to Hamlet, because he would think I was a child trying to identify with the big boys. He laughed and patted me on the shoulder like an older brother might. Of course, I'd forgotten that he could read my mind. He said that a lot of actors who had played him had felt the same way. Some of them had begun rehearsals feeling that they would have to give him their strength, because they didn't know him, or understand what happens when an actor transforms and really creates life. But he said it was enjoyable sometimes, especially seeing the look on their faces when they realized that he was a person in his own right.

I asked Hamlet if he would rather have returned to university. After all, he reads books on stage. He said it was a twentieth-century thought, and that there seemed to be more and more young people who were being raised to be afraid of life. He thought that this was the result of people living in cities and being more and more removed from nature, including their own. He said that this was accerbated by the fact that young people always believe that they are more evolved than their ancestors. He added that if that were true, why have some civilizations regressed, or been replaced by ones that were, and are, less evolved? And why do people react with such surprise to the fact that life is hard? And feel, when thing don't go smoothly, that it's because they have done something wrong? Life is just hard, and one has to be strong and courageous to live through it, he continued, saying that he had never questioned the role to which his birth had assigned him. What people often interpret as fear and doubt in his behavior was simply his personal reflections and questioning of life. But he was young when Shakespeare first talked to him.

It was the first thing he said that I didn't believe. I was thinking that he had contemplated suicide. He looked so noble, and I wondered how I could have ever imagined that he was weak. He was incredibly strong—a man among men. Where does someone like that fit into life? He would have been a great king. I shivered, and wondered how I would ever maintain that presence if I had to bring him into being. He smiled and said that we got along well enough and that he'd help me.

I wanted to ask him if he'd made love to Ophelia, but probing him on that subject seemed...improper is the only word that comes to mind. Instead, I asked him what he thought about Fortinbras. He said that his name was perfect, and that he was OK to invite to parties or go to war with, but that his thoughts on life were not very original. It made me think again about how a man like Hamlet would fit into the world order in any epoch.

"Something's rotten in the state of Denmark." "Denmark," the world order, always seems full of people who are always pretending, acting roles. Denmark reminds me of growing up amidst all the beautiful people. The problem wasn't recognizing people who were acting in life, it was finding someone who wasn't. Hamlet said that people in the theater all think like that, including Shakespeare. I said that it's because we see people doing that. He shrugged and said that still, we all tend to exaggerate that point of view. He said that life is serious. God, he reminded me of a good looking, athletic Dr. Baker.

If Hamlet had become king, what would the world he ruled be like? I thought of my own time, and the assassinations of the Kennedys, Martin Luther King Jr., Anwar Sadat, and Rabin, leaders who were trying to help us evolve and change. I suddenly realized that Hamlet's death had not killed him. His spirit was alive in our conscience, forever. I thought I understood "To be, or not to be" in a new light, and wished that, if I ever saw the role played, or played it myself, it could have this quality of immediateness and spontaneity that allow for these flashes of insight, night after night. If actors acted on stage the way people act in life, no one would believe they were acting; they wouldn't believe it was real, either. It made me wonder how anyone could think that Hamlet is crazy. The world is sick and crazy. Half of Shakespeare's play is spent revealing the intrigue, deception, and gamesmanship that goes on in court, and how the different characters in the play react to living in that world. Hamlet laughed and asked me if I had thought that Shakespeare was dumb. I almost pretended not to understand what he meant, but realized that I was in the company of someone who had no need to pretend not to know anything, anymore. I fleetingly wondered if Hamlet felt like a lost child during his life, but it seemed impossible for anyone who had such a mature philosophy. Although, there are times that,

> Out of the mouths of babes
> Often times, come charms."

I asked Hamlet what book he was reading. He told me to ask Shakespeare, the actor playing him, or, nowadays, the director or dramaturg. As for himself, he read whatever was handy at the moment, and liked reading all kinds of things. He said that he thought that Shakespeare had him carry a book around and read it so that no one would talk to him, like people in subways today. I wondered if he liked the theater, but instead of asking that, I asked him what was the last book that he had read, and he said Paolo Coehlo's *The Alchemist*. As this was going nowhere, I tried to talk to Shakespeare, but he wasn't talking to me yet. I hoped that he would when I was in production. Anyway, the book I imagined for my production is Reich's *The Murder of Christ*. It is dedicated "To the children of the future." All the Hamlets, Ophelias, Laerteses, and Fortinbrases to come. I imagined that during my production four young children would enter, playing as children do, and stop a moment to watch the ongoing insanity and devastation of the life and world order that we consider to be normal. Hamlet thought it was a good idea for an audience of today, who are beginning to accept that children are human beings already full of life, and not empty vessels to be filled up with learning. I was pleased that he liked the idea, but it seemed small in comparison to who he is, and what he knows about life.

Maria Rosa by Angel Guimbra directed by John Strasberg
at Centro Dramatic de Catalunta (Barcelona) 1983

INDEX

THE COLLECTED WORKS OF HAROLD CLURMAN

Six Decades of Commentary on Theatre, Dance, Music, Film, Arts, Letters and Politics

edited by Marjorie Loggia and Glenn Young

"...RUSH OUT AND BUY *THE COLLECTED WORKS OF HAROLD CLURMAN*...Editors Marjorie Loggia and Glenn Young have assembled a monumental helping of his work...THIS IS A BOOK TO LIVE WITH; picking it up at random is like going to the theater with Clurman and then sitting down with him in a good bistro for some exhilarating talk. This is a very big book, but Clurman was a very big figure."

JACK KROLL, *Newsweek*

"THE BOOK SWEEPS ACROSS THE 20TH CENTURY, offering a panoply of theater in Clurman's time...IT RESONATES WITH PASSION."

MEL GUSSOW, *The New York Times*

CLOTH•$49.95
ISBN 1-55783-132-7

THE COLLECTED WORKS OF PADDY CHAYEFSKY

This four volume collection includes Chayefsky's finest work for the stage, screen and television. Available individually or as a boxed set.

THE STAGE PLAYS include:
GIDEON • MIDDLE OF THE NIGHT • THE LATENT HETEROSEXUAL • THE TENTH MAN • THE PASSION OF JOSEF D.
$12.95 • PAPER • ISBN 1-55783-192-0

THE TELEVISION PLAYS include:
MARTY • THE MOTHER • PRINTER'S MEASURE • HOLIDAY SONG • THE BIG DEAL • BACHELOR PARTY
$12.95 • PAPER • ISBN 1-55783-191-2

THE SCREEN PLAYS VOL I include:
NETWORK • THE AMERICANIZATION OF EMILY • THE GODDESS
$14.95 • PAPER • ISBN 1-55783-193-9

THE SCREEN PLAYS VOL II include:
MARTY • HOSPITAL • ALTERED STATES
$14.95 • PAPER • ISBN 1-55783-194-7

$59.80 The Deluxe Boxed Set • ISBN 1-55783-195-5

UNFINISHED BUSINESS

A Memoir: 1902–1988

by John Houseman

For over half a century, John Houseman played a commanding role on the American cultural scene. The *dramatis personae* of Houseman's chronicle represents an awesome roster of arts in twentieth century America. When he isn't conspiring with Orson Welles, Virgil Thomson, Archibald McLeish or a dozen others to launch one of five major new theatre organizations, we find him in Hollywood with David O. Selznick, Alfred Hitchcock or Herman Mankiewicz producing one of his eighteen feature films.

In *Unfinished Business,* the 1500 pages of his earlier memoirs, *Run-Through, Front and Center* and *Final Dress* have been distilled into one astonishing volume, with fresh revelations throughout and a riveting new final chapter which brings the Houseman saga to a close.

paper•ISBN 1-55783-024-X

CREATING A CHARACTER:
A Physical Approach to Acting
by Moni Yakim with Muriel Broadman

"Moni Yakim's techniques to attain characterization have been outstandingly successful in bringing out of his students emotional depth to enrich whatever they do on stage. [He] is an inspired teacher. His ideas and practices, which the book details, make it required reading for every serious student of the theatre."

—from the foreword by Stella Adler

"So often actors forget that there are bodies attached to their character's heads. Through Moni Yakim's technique I learned to develop the physical life of a character, lifting the character off the page and into reality."

—Patti Lupone

"Moni Yakim's teaching awakens the actor's senses and tunes the actor's physicality to a degree of self-expression beyond the merely naturalistic and into the larger realms of imagination and poetry."

—Kevin Kline

paper • ISBN: 1-55783-161-0

SLINGS AND ARROWS

THEATER IN MY LIFE

by Robert Lewis

"A decidedly good read. Breezy, intelligent, and chatty. A stylish, entertaining, and above all theatrical book."

—The New York Times Book Review

"He's a marvelous storyteller: gossipy, candid without being cruel, and very funny. This vivid, entertaining book is also one of the most penetrating works to be written about the theater."

—Publishers Weekly

"The most interesting book about the theater since Moss Hart's *Act One*."

—Clifton Fadiman

"A superior performance."

—The Los Angeles Times

paper•ISBN 1-55783-244-7